Music and Politics

For Marian

Music and Politics

JOHN STREET

polity

First published in 2012 by Polity Press
Reprinted in 2012, twice

Polity Press
65 Bridge Street
Cambridge CB2 1UR, UK

Polity Press
350 Main Street
Malden, MA 02148, USA

ISBN-13: 978-0-7456-3543-9 (hardback)
ISBN-13: 978-0-7456-3544-6 (paperback)

A catalogue record for this book is available from the British Library.

Typeset in 11.25 on 13 pt Dante
by Toppan Best-set Premedia Limited
Printed and bound in the United States by Edwards Brothers, Inc.

For further information on Polity, visit our website: www.politybooks.com

Contents

Acknowledgements

Those who still peer at CD covers, and there are not many of us left, will note a tendency for the list of credits to get ever longer, in ever smaller print. I would like to buck this trend, but I have incurred many debts in the course of writing this book. My first debt is to my publishers, Polity, and particularly to Andrea Drugan, Lauren Mulholland, Clare Ansell and Susan Beer, who have shepherded the book into print. I have sorely tested Andrea's faith and patience, and I am immensely grateful for her support. My second debt is to Seth Hague and Heather Savigny who worked with me on the Striking a Chord project, funded by the Economic and Social Research Council. An article we wrote together forms the basis of chapter 4, and interviews that Seth conducted have been used in chapter 5. Then there have been the many friends and colleagues, especially on the journal *Popular Music* and at the University of East Anglia, who have helped in a variety of ways, sometimes knowingly and sometimes in all innocence: Andy Bennett, Richard Bellamy, Mike Bowker, Barbara Bradby, Alex Brown, Valentina Cardo, Sara Cohen, Sara Connolly, John Corner, Debra Craine, Tim Dant, Nikki Dibben, Jan Fairley, Marion Forsyth, Steve Foster, Reebee Garofalo, Lucy Green, Chris Hanretty, Dave Hesmondhalgh, Sarah Hill, Jude Howell, Sanna Inthorn, Mark Jancovich, Mike Jones, Hussein Kassim, Dave Laing, George Lipsitz, David Loosely, Hazel Marsh, Lee Marshall, Allan Moore, George Musgrave, Ian Peddie, Michael Saward, David Sinclair, Steve Smith, Tim Snelson, Will Straw, Jason Toynbee, Matt Worley, Scott Wright, John Wulfsohn and Liesbet van Zoonen. There are four people whose friendship and whose work has been crucial to me over the long haul. They are Martin Cloonan, Simon Frith, Keith Negus and the late John Orman. Finally, I am, as always, indebted to my family – Marian, Alex, Jack and Tom – who continue to deride, albeit gently, my musical tastes and my obsessions, as only those closest to you can.

This book draws on ideas and arguments earlier versions of which appeared elsewhere. I am grateful to the editors and publishers of them:

(with Seth Hague and Heather Savigny) 'Playing to the crowd: the role of music and musicians in political participation', *British Journal of Politics and International Relations*, 10(2), 2008, 269–85;

'Breaking the silence: music's role in political thought and action', *Critical Review of International Social and Political Philosophy*, 10(3), 2007, 321–37;

'The pop star as politicians: from Belafonte to Bono, from creativity to conscience', in Ian Peddie (ed.) *The Resisting Music: Popular Music and Social Protest*, Aldershot: Ashgate, 2006, pp. 49–61;

'Showbusiness of a serious kind: a cultural politics of arts prizes', *Media, Culture and Society*, 27(6), 2005, 819–40;

' "This is your Woodstock": popular memories and political myths', in Andy Bennett (ed.) *Remembering Woodstock*, Aldershot: Ashgate, 2004, pp. 29–42;

'Celebrity politicians: popular culture and political representation', *British Journal of Politics and International Relations*, 6(4), 2004, 435–52.

Introduction: making connections

This book is about the politics of music, and about the music of politics. Its title makes this clear, but the connection between music and politics is less simple than it may appear. Confusion stems from the thought that music and politics are two discrete realms of human experience and endeavour. One is concerned with the organization of public life; the other with the creative use of sound and the appreciation of its beauties and meanings. And insofar as the two are linked, in, say, the protest song or in the censorship of music, one sees music intervening in politics, the other politics in music. The two realms remain recognizably distinct, and our interest or curiosity is how they respond to each other. We ask about how music can help to influence political thoughts and actions, and what censorship reveals about the powers and paranoias of states and political regimes. These are important questions, and much can be learnt from answering them. And indeed I address them in this book, but they do not go to the heart of its concerns.

What I want to argue is that they are not to be seen as separate entities whose worlds collide only occasionally, but rather are extensions of each other. I would like to persuade readers that music *embodies* political values and experiences, and *organizes* our response to society as political thought and action. Music does not just provide a vehicle of political expression, it *is* that expression. And, furthermore, states organize us through their management of music and sound more generally. The boundaries between the two realms of music and politics, I will try to suggest, are largely illusionary.

This is not an entirely new argument, but it is a neglected one. It was a common-place in Ancient Athens, and it could be detected in the eighteenth-century writings of Jean-Jacques Rousseau. More recently, it can be detected in the work of Theodor Adorno and Jacques Attali (1985: 3); the latter boldly announces: 'For twenty-five centuries, Western knowledge has tried to look upon the world. It has failed to understand that the world is not for beholding. It is for hearing. It is not legible, but audible.' Such claims, though, have been largely overlooked or dismissed by those who study politics, and some who study music. And even if the connections are recognized, and these old habits of thought not lost, their implications have not been fully realized. *Music and Politics* is my attempt to spell out these implications and the possibilities they represent for understanding the relationship between music and governance, between music and thought and action. Before delving further into this argument, I want to illustrate the thinking behind it with some examples.

The case of Simon Bikindi

In July 2006, I received a letter from someone called Wilfred Nderitu. Mr Nderitu, it turned out, was a lawyer. He wanted to know if I would act as an expert witness in a trial for which he was representing the defendant. His client was called Simon Bikindi and he was due to appear before the United Nations International Criminal Tribunal for Rwanda. Bikindi was charged with 'direct and public incitement to commit genocide'. The letter explained that Bikindi was a musician, and the UN prosecutors had indicted him because they believed that his songs had contributed directly to the slaughter of Tutsis. His songs were held to have been written with the deliberate intent of inflaming Hutu hatred of their Tutsi neighbours. The UN charged that specific songs composed by Simon Bikindi had a direct effect upon those who heard them.

Mr Nderitu rang me to discuss the case, but, to my considerable relief, nothing came of this conversation. It was not immediately obvious what kind of expertise (if any) I could possibly bring to such a trial, and I think Bikindi's lawyer shared this view.

The prosecution of those responsible for the mass murders in Rwanda was clearly right, but so too was it right that they have a fair trial. There was the question, a very real one in this case, about whether songs – melodies, rhythms and lyrics – could be the source of genocidal acts. My own immediate thought had been that this was, at best, unlikely. Although the history of music is littered with instances in which politicians and other guardians of public morality have decried the effects of music on people's behaviour, much conventional academic wisdom held that such effects were more imagined than real, a product of ideology, rather than reality. Research, insofar as there was any, suggested that there was no direct causal chain between songs and social action. Bikindi's trial did address this very issue. There were arguments about what his songs actually said, what messages they might be held to contain, about how often they were played on national radio in Rwanda, and what effects they might have had. Expert evidence was heard on both sides.

The UN International Criminal Tribunal for Rwanda sentenced Bikindi to prison for fifteen years for incitement to commit genocide. But significantly this decision was based on a speech he made to Hutus in June 1994 in which he demonized the Tutsis and called for their extermination. The Tribunal dismissed the charge that, through his songs, he instigated violence, in part because the songs were written before 1994 and in part because there was no direct evidence to support the claim that Bikindi had any part in their being played on the radio during the fighting. It might seem that the court took the view that songs were of no consequence. But that does not seem to be the right conclusion. Had Bikindi sung rather than spoken the sentiments he expressed at the meeting in June 1994, then he might well have been found equally guilty. And in any case, the court did not rule, as far as I can tell, that the songs on the radio had no effect, but rather that Bikindi was not to be held responsible for the fact that they were played and for whatever effect they might have had.

Although the Bikindi example is rare and exceptional, it is not unique, as Bruce Johnson and Martin Cloonan (2009) make abundantly clear in their book *Dark Side of the Tune: Popular Music and Violence*. They provide chilling documentation of music's involvement in torture and other forms of violence. The question of music's power, for good or ill, does not go away. Following the murder of the South African white supremacist Eugene Terre'Blanche in April 2010, attention focused on the song 'Ayesaba Amagwala' [The Cowards are Scared], which contained the line 'shoot the Boer (dubul' ibhunu)'. Earlier in the year, the Constitutional Court had ruled that the South African Broadcasting Corporation should not play it on the radio (*Mail and Guardian online*, 27 March 2010). Such songs, the judges ruled, when sung at ANC rallies, were an incitement to hatred and violence.

Our feelings about these examples are, I think, revealing of more general attitudes about the way music affects people. We may be wary of crude claims of cause and effect, but we are wary too of suggestions that the art we value leaves no mark – or that the art we hate is not in some way harmful.

The Taliban: silence and power

When the Taliban were driven from power in Afghanistan in 2002, the Western media represented the event with photographs of citizens

waving cassette players and radios. Journalists reported the liberation of
Kabul in terms of the noise now to be heard. Freedom was symbolized in
sound, in the opportunity to play the music that the Taliban had banned.
For the journalists and sub-editors, the power of the Taliban, and their
ruthlessness in exercising it, was captured in the silence imposed on the
Afghan people.

Of course, the true story is more complex than this. The Taliban were
by no means the first political leaders to regard music with suspicion.
Quakers and Trappists have long placed a great value on silence (Sim, 2007:
63ff). The Russian Orthodox Church, according to Tim Blanning (2008:
292), banned instrumental music in the eighteenth century 'because it
adopted an exclusive and literal interpretation of the last line of Psalm 150:
"Let everything that has breath praise the Lord" '. In her book *Dancing in
the Streets*, Barbara Ehrenreich (2007: 97–102) places the Russian church in
a tradition that saw the alliance of state and religion operating to deny all
kinds of public festivity, from singing to football.

The ban on music was one of the first edicts issued by the Taliban on
their accession to power in Afghanistan in September 1996. To ignore the
order was to risk imprisonment. If music was played at weddings, the head
of the family was liable to arrest and punishment (Baily, 2004; Majrooh,
1998; Yusufzai, 1998). Radio Kabul became Radio *Sharia*, and the output,
'once a comparatively urbane mix of international news, Asian pop, health
advice and topical soap operas, was immediately replaced with bulletins of
Taliban victories, religious homilies or fresh directives on how citizens
should comport themselves' (Griffin, 2001: 6). Not all forms of what might
be recognized as music were, in fact, banned. Forms of chanting remained
as part of religious practice. And importantly, the Taliban's strictures owed
more to their politics than to any widely sanctioned reading of Islamic
scripture. Nonetheless, the Taliban's behaviour, both in practice and in the
accompanying rhetoric, yoked music to power and to freedom.

The House of Lords and the value of music

Not all political interest in live music takes a malign form. In October 2004,
the House of Lords, the unelected second chamber of the UK parliament,
was earnestly debating the impact of the Licensing Act that had been
passed the previous year. The noble lords were exercised over the impact
the act had been having on live music. Defending the government and
dismissing any suggestion that it sought the demise of live music, Lord
Evans of Temple Guiting announced: 'the Government would like to see

more live music; they are doing everything they can to encourage this, and we are working to that end' (House of Lords, 13 October 2004). Within the rarefied setting of the Palace of Westminster, Her Majesty's Government appeared to be offering its unqualified support for the live performance of music. When the same issue returned to the Lords in 2011, the Peers once again voted for the need to protect live music. Lord Redesdale was moved to declare, 'I believe it is a human right to have unamplified music' (House of Lords, 7 March 2011). This thought, that music is connected to human rights, lies at the heart of this book.

From examples to arguments

It is easy enough, of course, to cherry pick examples and, as I did at the beginning, to make grand claims about the inseparability of politics and music. It is quite another thing to provide a sustained argument, and this is the task to which the rest of the book is devoted. The examples above are merely indicative of the kind of connections I have in mind.

In her book *Music in Everyday Life*, Tia DeNora makes a bold claim. Music, she contends, forges a relationship between 'the polis, the citizen and the configuration of consciousness'. 'Music', she goes on, 'is much more than a decorative art . . . It is a powerful medium of social order' (2000: 163). In illustrating this power she refers to the way muzak can be used to control an environment and the behaviour that takes place within it. But DeNora does not see music simply as a tool of control and oppression. It can also, she says, act to constitute identities and to articulate emotions that empower people. Frustratingly, as Simon Frith (2003: 45) has noted, DeNora's claims for music's political purpose appear on the final pages of her book. The reader is left to wonder about how such ideas might be grounded. What does it mean to say that music is a 'medium of social order'? All music? All social orders? How can a set of sounds – however dexterously composed and performed – 'order' human thought and action? My book is intended as a response to these questions. It is an attempt to show how and why music – as organized sound – can assume such an importance in people's lives.

In chapters 1 and 2, I address the familiar conjunctions of music and politics, the first being the censorship of music, and the second being music policy. Both entail examining the ways in which states actively engage with music. But while these aspects of the link between music and politics are marked by familiarity, I want to consider their less obvious features. By this I mean, how censorship and music policy explicitly and implicitly invest music with political principles and political ideals. The chapters ask what is meant when live music is claimed, as did Lord Redesdale, as a human right.

Chapters 3, 4 and 5 develop this thought further by looking, not at how the state sees music, but how music is used and seen by citizens in the demands they make upon that state. Here the question is how music contributes to the articulation of political ideas and to the organization of political action. Using examples such as Live 8 and Rock Against Racism, these chapters argue for music as more than a mere soundtrack to politics, but as the substance of politics. They look at how music comes to represent and articulate political ideas and identities, but also how music mobilizes movements in support of such notions.

The last part of the book is devoted to delving more deeply into the connections explored in the first part. Chapter 6 considers how music marks the sense of history that informs political ideals. It is, in a sense, about how music makes history. Chapter 7 traces the connection between musical taste and political values, mapping the interplay of aesthetics and ideology. This theme continues into chapter 8 where we chart music's place in a particular tradition of political thought. It is a tradition in which music is not merely a matter of taste or entertainment, but in which it is key to our understanding of social order. The last substantive chapter draws out the further implications of this tradition for our understanding of music as a form of political experience.

Politics

Before going any further, I want to make explicit what I mean by 'politics' in this context. I am conscious that there are those who argue that 'everything is political', or more modestly that 'all music is political'. There is, of course, something in both claims. Each seeks to challenge the view that there is a 'natural order' to human affairs or that 'there is no alternative'. Each highlights the thought that in all aspects of our lives choices are being made and values being articulated. But the danger of such a perspective is that it empties 'politics' of all meaning. It becomes a truism that is deprived of any insight or leverage. It does not distinguish those activities that can affect the exercise of public power from those that cannot.

Something similar can happen in talking of the politics of music. It may be true that, in one sense or another, Beethoven's *Fidelio*, Bob Dylan's 'Blowing in the Wind' and the Wombles' 'Wombling Song' ('Underground, overground, wombling free/the Wombles of Wimbledon Common are we') are all examples of 'political' music, but how much would be gained by an analysis that lumped them together? Equally, all concerts, all music industry decisions, and all consumer choices may be 'political' in some sense, but how much do we gain by saying so?

In trying to specify more precisely what 'politics' refers to, I follow Colin Hay (2007: 65) in adopting a 'differentiated yet inclusive' definition. Hay is not alone in taking this approach. It is shared by other writers, and particularly those who are concerned with the relationship between the political and the cultural. Their starting point is, typically, to denounce the traditional definition of politics, one that confines itself to the activities of parties and governments alone (Buckingham, 2000; Nash, 2000). It is not that such agents are irrelevant to any understanding of politics, but that they are not its sole actors. It would be a strange definition of politics that excluded the activities of social movements, such as those organized round sexuality or gender or ethnicity. It would be strange too to deny the force of the feminist slogan that the 'personal is political'. In this spirit, Stephen Coleman (2007: 15) argues for an 'expansive conception of the political' which contains 'the micro-relationships in which power is contested and negotiated within families and workplaces, amongst friends and strangers, on a daily basis'.

The danger here is that *all* aspects of the personal are treated as political, in the sense that all involve some aspect of power. David Buckingham (2000: 34) is wary of this move, arguing that such inclusivity 'is little more than a recipe for political quietism'. Buckingham contends that the personal should be treated as political only when this reconfiguration is recognized as such by the participants. In a similar vein, we need to be wary of conflating 'politics' and 'public life'. As Nick Couldry (2007) and his colleagues point out, they do not necessarily share the same contours. What is public may not automatically be political, just as what is private may not be either.

Colin Hay offers a synthesis of the elements that constitute our understanding of the political. He notes the multiple, and often contradictory, accounts of the 'political', accounts which distinguish between politics as a function, a process and an arena. His response is to identify four distinctive features of the political. To count as 'political', a situation must present people with a choice, and one which they can act upon; they must have agency. And in exercising agency, people must be able to deliberate publicly and with others and for the outcome to have an impact on others; it must be social, not personal (Hay, 2007: 65). Put simply, decisions that are taken alone and affect only the individual who takes them are not social and hence not political (Hay, 2007: 70).

What are the implications of these definitional points for the way I approach the relationship of music to politics? One answer would be that if musical pleasure and choice are purely private matters of personal consequence, they are not political. It is only when musical pleasure (or musical displeasure) spills over into the public realm and into the exercise of power within it that it becomes political. It is where music inspires forms of collective thought and action that it becomes part of politics. It is where music forms a site of public deliberation, rather than private reflection, that we talk of music as political.

Music

But while this book takes what, I hope, seems like a clear-eyed view of politics, and thereby allows for a more precise statement of how music and politics are connected, I do not thereby want to assume that 'music' is a self-evident category – far from it. Most of the examples I draw upon might be classed as 'popular music', but I hope that my argument is not dependent upon this particular categorization of music. The arguments advanced here can be applied to any form of music, whatever its genre.

This is not to deny the importance of music, but it is to open up the question of what sort of entity it is. This is not to invite wholesale scepticism. I do not want to deny the importance of music – and indeed all cultural forms – to the way we live. If *Music and Politics* was to have a guiding philosophy, it is provided by the novelist Carol Shields. In *Larry's Party*, she (1997: 58) writes of her eponymous hero: 'Larry listens. This is how he's learning about the world, exactly as everyone else does – from sideways comments over a lemon meringue pie, sudden bursts of comprehension or weird parallels that come curling out of the radio, out of a movie, off the pages of a newspaper, out of a joke – and his baffled self stands back and says: so this is how it works.' For Shields, Larry's world is constructed by what he *hears*, rather than what he sees. In some ways, this book is an extended footnote to this insight. What it tries to demonstrate is that how music works on us, and how we act upon music, are intimately connected to the way we think and act politically. This is not just a claim about individuals, but about the collectivities and institutions they form. It is true for governments, parties and social movements, and the power they wield or seek to wield. It is a claim, as I have said, about the music of politics, and the politics of music.

1

Sound barriers: censoring music

The urge to censor music for fear of its effects is as old as music itself.
Plato's concerns with the potential moral damage to be discerned in types
of music marks one of the earliest recorded examples. 'The overseers',
Plato (*Republic* 424b–c) is recorded as saying, 'must throughout be watchful
against innovations in music and gymnastics counter to the established
order, and to the best of their power guard against them.' In seventeenth-
century England the performance of unlicensed ballads could lead to fines
or imprisonment (Palmer, 1988: 245); in nineteenth-century Italy the libret-
tos of all operas were subject to the censors' scrutiny (Blanning, 2008: 268).
Throughout human history music has been the source of fear and the
object of repression. Every century on every continent has seen those in
authority – whether as church or as state – use their powers to silence
certain sounds or performers.

Here are two recent examples. Under the headline 'Islamist hardliners
force DJs to drop "evil" songs', *The Times* (14 April 2010) reports that: 'All
14 radio stations based in the Somali capital [Mogadishu] have complied
with an ultimatum by the hardline Hezb-e-Islami militia to stop broadcasting music, according to the National Union of Somali Journalists. Songs
– condemned as "evil" – were replaced with poems and jingles with random
animal or vehicle noises. "We abide by their rules," said Mohamed Haji
Bare, director-general of Danan radio. Those who flout the militia's brand
of Islamic law are flogged in public, have limbs amputated or are executed.'
Meanwhile, in the UK in early 2010 the grime artist Giggs saw all ten dates
of his tour cancelled, following advice from the Metropolitan Police, who
also, it was reported, rang various record companies to discourage them
from signing him to their label (Jonze, 2010). The police were worried by
the kind of fans Giggs would acquire. He had served a sentence for illegal
possession of a firearm. In an earlier century, music-hall and singing-
saloons were similarly targeted because of the bad behaviour they attracted
(Russell, 1987: 20).

Just as certainly as the censors have sought to impose their will, others have challenged their authority and their wisdom. In 1644 John Milton railed against would-be censors:

> If we think to regulate Printing, thereby to rectify manners, we must regulate all recreations and pastimes, all that is delightful to man. No musick must be heard, no song be set or sung, but what is grave and *Dorick*. . . . It will ask more than the work of twenty licencers to examine all the lutes, violins, and the guitars in every house. . . . And who shall silence all the airs and madrigals that whisper softness in chambers? (http://www.stlawrenceinstitute.org/vol14mit.html)

More than three centuries later, *Index on Censorship* (2010) devoted a special issue to the oppressive treatment of music and musicians across the world. However powerful or persistent the voices raised in protest at censorship, the censors continue to silence sound.

Stories of censorship tell a familiar tale. They speak of an authoritarian regime whose ruthlessness is exemplified by its treatment of music. So we read of the Chinese authorities imprisoning fourteen Tibetan nuns for singing songs in support of their country's independence (*Index on Censorship*, 1998); or of their refusal to allow Bob Dylan to play in China (*NME*, 4 April 2010), a ban that was lifted in 2011, on the condition that his set-list was approved by the Ministry of Culture (*Guardian*, 4 April 2011). We hear of a group of Turkish punk rockers who faced jail for a song 'criticizing the country's unpopular university entrance exam' (*Guardian*, 9 April 2007). These stories join those about the Taliban's blanket ban of all music in Afghanistan. Such reports reinforce the image of the states in question, but they do so by way of the value attributed to music as the object of the brutal regime's ire. In part, music stands as the epitome of freedom. Making music is regarded as a fundamental aspect of human freedom and a means by which we announce our liberty. At the same time, music stands for the trivial and inconsequential. The true terror of these censorious regimes, the stories seem to say, is embodied in the fact that their bullying extends to matters as mundane and trivial as music – as if music is not really that important, and yet it is censored.

This ambivalence offers, I think, an insight into the political complexities of the censorship of music. And in reflecting upon these, I want first to draw attention to some general patterns in the politics of censorship, before going on to consider the principles implicated in the targeting of music.

Background noise

Censorship is not the exclusive preserve of a particular system of government, regime or ideology. Keith Kahn-Harris (2007: 27) has documented the fate of metal music, which, in its various guises (from heavy to thrash to extreme), has been targeted by both left-wing and right-wing groups, united in their common assumption that the music 'cannot in and of itself be worthwhile'. During the 1990s, UK Customs officials tried to prevent the importing of Swedish metal music, while the authorities in Israel, Cuba, Egypt and Syria have all taken action against fans and performers of the genre (Kahn-Harris, 2007: 28). The stated reasons for these interventions have varied. It has been accused, for example, of promoting both Satanism and homosexuality. And it is not just state agencies who take on the guise of censor, as this story reveals:

> In a stunning last-minute move, Walt Disney Properties have pressured promoter Live Nation into canceling Machine Head's performance tomorrow night at the House of Blues venue in Anaheim (on their Disneyland property). Citing violent imagery, undesirable fans and inflammatory lyrics as the reason, the diversity-impaired corporation began pressuring the promoter on Saturday to cancel all upcoming heavy metal concerts. (http://www.roadrunnerrecords.com/BLABBERMOUTH.NET/news.aspx?mode=Article&newsitemID=80237)

These diverse attempts at censorship of heavy metal are political in the sense either that elements of state power instigate the action or because they represent the promotion of a particular political ideology. But they are not, it seems, directed at the explicitly political content of the music. This is not to say, though, that politics too may inspire censorship.

The communications corporation AT&T was accused of censoring a webcast version of the Lollapalooza tour because of the criticism made of George W. Bush. Pearl Jam's Eddie Vedder reportedly said 'George Bush, leave this world alone' and 'George Bush find yourself another home', but AT&T removed both comments from their Blue Room webcast (*LA Times* blog, 8 August 2007). The same year the band Death Cab for Cutie had their music seized by Homeland Security (*Harper's Magazine*, 19 October 2007). These instances of political censorship are not rare. Indeed, in a survey of music censorship over a twenty-year period, Vanessa Bastian and Dave Laing (2003) claim that 'politics' constitutes the main reason for censorship.

But while the political censorship of music is widespread, it remains associated with particular systems and ideologies. Both Stalin's regime and the Nazis took music very seriously, both as a form of propaganda and of oppression (Kater, 1997; Ross, 2007; Starr, 1983). Music that did not conform to the dominant ideology, or was to seen to threaten or subvert it, was denied a public hearing and the musicians subject to any number of threats to life and liberty. But there were complexities and subtleties to this brutal treatment. In Nazi Germany, Modernist music was mistrusted, but, notes Alex Ross (2007: 321), 'tolerated, provided the composer assumed the right ideological stance'.

Political censorship of music was also characteristic of post-war Eastern Europe, where the authorities were very wary of tours by Western musicians. The Polish authorities tolerated acts like the Hollies and the Rolling Stones, but were quick to shut the borders when their youthful communist fans expressed their enthusiasm rather more exuberantly than was thought decent (Doggett, 2007: 95). The Soviet Union also looked warily at the Beatles (ibid.: 197; Starr, 1983), while welcoming artists like Duke Ellington and Paul Robeson. Other parts of Europe have also seen similarly strict regimes. Under the dictatorship of the Greek Colonels (1967–74), the music of Mikis Theodorakis was banned by official decree, and he was both banished and imprisoned. Many musicians suffered a similar fate in apartheid South Africa. In the US, the McCarthy House Un-American Activities Committee brought a temporary end to the career of performers like Pete Seeger. The UK too has a history of music censorship, most blatantly in relation to Northern Ireland; songs showing sympathy for the Republican cause were routinely banned (Cloonan, 1996).

But despite these many instances of political censorship, it is not total or comprehensive. Much that might be deemed offensive is not censored; often what seems entirely inoffensive is banned. This suggests that whatever it is we are dealing with when we talk about censorship, it is not simply a matter of offensive and inoffensive objects. Rather it is about a process in which something comes to be deemed 'offensive'. The story of censorship is not, for the most part (if ever), the story of images or words that offended, but of the political interests that articulate and respond to the 'offence'. What is key is how music assumes an 'offensive' character to those with the power to respond.

Censorship in context

Consider the example of the Taliban's ban of music (to which I referred in the previous chapter). Why, in pursuit of their autocratic power, did the Taliban feel the need to outlaw music, and why, in celebrating their liberation, did people use music to symbolize their freedom? After all, the Taliban also forbade 'kite-flying, the possession of homing pigeons, . . . chess and marbles' (Griffin, 2001: 7), but it is notable that popular liberation was not accompanied by the clucking of pigeons or mass games of marbles. It seems, on the surface at least, that music had particular significance, although nothing in the Qu'ran or in the Taliban's public pronouncements established this case (Sardar and Davies, 2004). Furthermore, other Islamicist states have not banned music (Shammont, 1998; Verney, 1998). Indeed, the Taliban's rationale would appear to apply more to the particularities of their political circumstances than to any intrinsic features of music itself. The Taliban's policy was influenced by the fact that, following the Soviet invasion of Afghanistan, the conquering power had used music to help maintain its authority (Baily, 2001). To this extent, it was music's association with the Soviet oppressor that led to the Taliban's ban and to the difference between them and other Islamic regimes. It was not music as such; it was its political associations.

Seeing censorship in context does not just apply to authoritarian orders. Claude Chastagner (1999) documents the circumstances that led to the introduction of the 'Parental Advisory' sticker on records. For him, the key event was the foundation of the Parents' Music Resource Center (PMRC) in 1985. The PMRC was a lobby group designed to draw attention to, and end, 'the obscenity and violence of rock music' (Chastagner, 1999: 179). The PMRC was itself prompted into existence by a prior campaign by the National Parent/Teacher Association in the 1980s. But what was significant was that those behind the PMRC had close political connections to Washington. The women who led the PMRC were all married to leading politicians (Senators Baker and Gore). They were also well resourced, having secured financial support and office space from the owner of Coors beer.

The media attention that the PMRC attracted led to a Senate Committee hearing at which various musicians and the Recording Industry Association of America (RIAA) appeared. Although no legislation was being proposed by the PMRC, the RIAA pre-empted any recommendation by volunteering – before the Senate hearings had even finished – that they would introduce a warning sticker. Chastagner (1999: 184–5) argues that the RIAA made this offer for two reasons: first, to avoid legislative intervention in the regulation of content and to marginalize the PMRC's more draconian proposals; and secondly, to win political support for legislation to introduce a tax on blank tapes that would be of considerable financial benefit to the industry. Insofar as the sticker constituted a form of censorship (and we return to this question later), its story is not simply one of offensive music leading to a policy response, but of processes that, first, allowed concern to be expressed and then of political alliances and resources that enabled action to be taken.

Typically, even as we put censorship in context, we think of it as the business of 'state censors', but this is rarely the case even in the most authoritarian of regimes. Censorship is often routinized – usually becoming a form of self-censorship – and operated by a concatenation of functionaries in the security services, the broadcasting organizations and in the propaganda departments. In liberal regimes, the business of censorship can become part of the routines of pluralist, or quasi-pluralist, policy processes.

One such example of how context and contingencies shape what appears (or might appear) as censorship in liberal democratic regimes is provided by Bruce Johnson (2003). He tells of how the conservative Australian politician, Pauline Hanson, leader of the One Nation party, became the butt of a satirical song, 'I'm a Back Door Man', performed by drag artist Simon Hunt (in the guise of Pauline Pantsdown). According to Johnson (2003: 57–8), Hanson made extensive use of music in her campaign, deploying traditional songs to express her anti-immigration, anti-multiculturalism message. And it was partly in response to her reliance on music that 'I'm a Back Door Man' was conceived.

Hanson objected strongly to the song and secured an injunction to prevent it being broadcast (Johnson, 2003: 59). That injunction, initially for 28 days, remained in force for three years, after leave to appeal was refused to the Australian Broadcasting Corporation. Johnson (2003: 61) comments that this decision had 'very serious implications for satire and, more generally, for freedom of speech'. This case is an example of the complex network of relationships that are established in the enactment of censorship, and of the political dependencies created by it.

Michael Roberts (2010) has recently unearthed the story of how, in the early 1960s, the American musicians' union – the American Federation of Musicians (AFM) – attempted to ban the Beatles from performing in the US. For Roberts, this attempt represented the clash of two sets of interests. On the one side sat the union, desperate to preserve the jobs and skills of their members, and feeling threatened by rock'n'roll in general and the so-called British invasion in particular. On the other side were the fans (and the interests they represented), who were desperate to reap the pleasures and benefits of the new music. Roberts shows that what might be seen as an attempt to instigate censorship – to deny the right to perform to a group of musicians – was motivated by the very real anxieties of the AFM. This was not a simple case of an offence inspiring a kneejerk response. At the same time, Roberts points to the reluctance of the AFM to recognize rock musicians as professionals who deserved the protection of organized labour. The fans, responding to the threat of a ban, argued for the cultural value and importance of the Beatles and the culture they represented. It was this argument, as Roberts (2010: 14) notes, which won the day. The point is, however, that had the AFM won and the Beatles been banned, then we might have regarded this as an act of censorship. Whether we do or not, perhaps more important is recognizing that acts of censorship involve a complex chain of events in which interests conflict and coalesce to create the circumstances in which bans are implemented and in which music is, as a consequence, invested with particular meanings and forms of power.

These examples illustrate specific cases of a more general phenomenon: the regulation of media content. What they highlight are the multi-agency aspects of censorship and the political contingencies that affect them. These more general features resolve into differences between political and media systems, and routines by which media content is managed (Freedman, 2008; McGuigan, 1996). This system- and context-based approach helps to explain the patterns in censorship, and prevent us becoming distracted by the particular instances. It helps to account, for example, for the tendency of African American artists to feel the effects of censorship more often than other artists (Johnson and Cloonan, 2009). But in adopting a broader perspective on censorship, we need to think carefully about what actually counts as censorship, and how it might be distinguished from the other routine and legitimate practices of media management.

A matter of definition?

Martin Cloonan, an international authority on music censorship, has argued for a broadened account of censorship. He (2003: 17) usefully also distinguishes between levels or stages of censorship, separating out prior restraint from restriction and suppression, and identifying what is involved in censorship in each case. In calling for 'a better understanding of the term', Cloonan (2004: 3) asks whether there is not more to the idea than 'some person or body' preventing 'a musician or group of musicians from performing a musical work'? He asks whether we can also talk of censorship when a musical work is not published because it is deemed 'uncommercial' or if a radio station refuses to play something because it deems that its audience will not like it? He does not offer a direct answer, but rather seeks to 'problematize' conventional wisdom. Does censorship require deliberation and intentionality? Does it have to be systematic? Can it result from acts of omission as well as commission? Can we talk of self-censorship? Cloonan invites the thought that, in a world of privately-owned media, there might be 'market censorship' (Cloonan, 2004: 4). Cloonan has in mind the case of the 'Parental Advisory' sticker, but imagines it applying more widely.

Cloonan does not offer detailed answers to these important questions, but it is evident where his inclinations lie. He wants to see commercial practices as representing potential sites of censorship. While choosing not to release or play a song because there was no market for it might not be deemed censorship, refusing to do so because of the content of the lyrics would count (Cloonan, 2004: 5). Equally, his definition does not include instances where a radio station refuses to play a song because it will not appeal to their listeners. Nonetheless, Cloonan wants to be able to claim that censorship can occur even where there is no deliberate intention to do so, and thus 'the daily, market-informed, operations of the music industry' may contain examples of censorship.

Cloonan's broadened account of censorship has an intuitive appeal to it. Censorship should not be attributed only to the deliberate intent of identifiable censors. But at the same time, such a definition presents problems of its own. How do we distinguish and investigate decisions made about what is released or broadcast? How should we distinguish a judgement about what an audience wants or expects from a prejudice that is disguised as a judgement about popular taste?

These sorts of questions emerge if we are to claim that censorship takes place within the 'normal' operation of the market. It is, of course, possible that the capitalist industry acts as a censoring machine, dedicated to promoting only that music which accords to its lights or is acceptable to it. But such a definition would be so broad as to be meaningless. Equally, there is a tempting alternative in which the industry is itself portrayed as an immensely complex interplay of networks and conflicting interests. Under such circumstances, it might be argued, that what happens owes as much to luck or chance as to any other cause. In which case, it would be hard to ascribe 'censorship' to any given outcome.

In his discussion of the PMRC and the introduction of the 'Parental Advisory' sticker, Chastagner argues that censorship is involved, even though the music remains available and is not in the formal sense 'banned', and even though the PMRC explicitly renounced the idea that they were advocating censorship. Chastagner's (1999: 186ff) claim is that the information provided by the stickers *instigates a process that leads to censorship*. He suggests that the sticker legitimated, or at least gave a pretext for, the targeting of certain artists, and for local authorities to initiate bans, for State authorities to regulate sales and for record companies to intervene in new ways in the content of the music they released. Chastagner (1999: 188) documents examples of each of these, and describes the appearance of a 'chill factor', in response to which artists, producers and distributors became ever more cautious.

Fascinating – and important – questions are raised by Chastagner's argument. His suggestion is that the 'information' provided by the sticker led to censorship, even where its originators did not intend this. The first question raised by this is whether indeed the PMRC can be seen to be *responsible* for censorship even where this is not their intention. Chastagner certainly believes that the PMRC, despite their protestations of innocence, were party to the acts of censorship taken by others. He is, I think, making the counterfactual claim that had the PMRC not drawn people's attention to the content of records by the Dead Kennedys and others, the authorities would not have acted as they did. This may be true, but to make the PMRC *responsible* for the acts of others is clearly debatable. The second, and perhaps more pressing, question raised by Chastagner is whether, in any case, the decisions of the various actors – local and state authorities, and record companies – constituted censorship. This is the question also raised by Cloonan in his attempt to broaden the definition of censorship. The point is that, in extending and enriching the account of censorship, we link culture – in this case, music – ever more closely to the routine management of everyday life. The regulation of music is co-extensive with the regulation of human interaction more generally.

This argument is well made by Jim McGuigan (1996) in his attack on conventional accounts of censorship. He has two targets. The first are those people who might be labelled 'libertarian utopians'; those who, in taking up an anti-censorship position, imagine or advocate a world without censorship. The second target is the so-called 'free' market, the rhetoric of which seems to indicate an absence of censorship. McGuigan's aim is to establish the ubiquity and inescapability of censorship, but not to endorse a position of fatalist resignation.

McGuigan's argument begins from the observation that there are two forms of censorship – regulative and constitutive. The former identifies the conventionally recognized understanding: explicit and deliberate attempts to prevent the publication or dissemination of media content. The latter refers to the censorship that occurs in the name of the civilizing process. It is this latter form of censorship that leads to McGuigan's general assertion that censorship is a fact of social life. In adopting this position, McGuigan aims to shift the debate away from a crude either/or position in which one is either for or against censorship. Instead, the issue becomes concerned with what kind of censorship is acceptable. Here he makes two moves. One is to suggest that the market is implicated in the 'civilizing process' (or an uncivil version of it), and to that extent acts as a censor in the way that it allows or excludes certain kinds of cultural experience. The second move is to assert that, drawing on George Gerbner's work with Larry Gross (1976), it is evident that media content has a 'cultivation effect'. Both moves serve to challenge the indifference, in the first case, of those who view the market as truly 'free'; and in the second, of those who claim that 'media effects' are to be treated with deep scepticism. In other words, McGuigan's argument adds support to Cloonan's view that market mechanisms can act as a form of censorship. Such claims also form part of Nick Couldry's (2010) more recent critique of neoliberalism and its capacity to suppress the popular 'voice'.

But in extending the concept of censorship to include the practices of the market and of those ideologies that promote it, we are still left with a problem: how to distinguish between those forms of regulation that promote civilization (the banning of homophobic songs, for example) and those bans that have no such rationale (for instance, Clear Channel's decision to ban the Dixie Chicks from their radio stations after the group made critical comments about President George W. Bush from a London stage). There is more to the argument about censorship than defining it and revealing the processes that constitute it. We need also to be conscious of the political principles that are invoked in the business of regulation. If, as Cloonan, Couldry and McGuigan suggest, censorship is built into the routine practices of cultural economy, then the question becomes one of how we discriminate between the exercise of these practices. While it is easy to see censorship at work when we are privy to the kind of world that George Orwell describes in *Nineteen Eighty-Four*, and when acts of overt suppression and self-denial are reported; it is much less easy to see their equivalent in the frenetic activity of the modern music industry.

Music and free expression/speech

In this final section, I want to argue for an approach to censorship of music in which the focus is on the political principles entailed – most notably, those of 'free speech'. My thought is that music, far from being merely a source of entertainment or distraction, is important to the realization of such principles. In this sense, the censors are onto something, even if they are not always aware of it.

The injunction secured by Pauline Hanson against the song which parodied her, argued Johnson (2003), represented a denial of free speech. Chastagner (1999) too linked the actions of the PMRC to the same principle. What is entailed when this link is made, when a song is treated as a form of speech? An answer to this question is to be found in the story Paul Chevigny (1991) tells of his fight with New York City over their cabaret laws.

The First Amendment of the US Constitution famously states: 'Congress shall make no law respecting an establishment of religion, or prohibiting the free exercise thereof; or abridging the freedom of speech, or of the press; or the right of the people peaceably to assemble, and to petition the Government for a redress of grievances.' The wording makes no attempt to define 'speech', nor to suggest any exceptions to the general principle. But of course there is a considerable step from principle to practice. For much of the period of the Amendment's existence, the Supreme Court has tended to operate with a two-tiered account of speech, so as to distinguish that which is worth protecting from that which is not (Sandel, 1996). For Michael Sandel, such a distinction is important to ensuring that hate speech ('fighting words') and pornography are denied the same protection as forms of expression that are deemed more valuable. Chastagner (1999: 182–3) also makes this point, noting how successive court rulings have come to identify obscenity as 'speech without redeeming social importance' and hence not deserving of special treatment as free speech. But while a two-level theory of free speech has value, much turns on how the distinction is drawn. Kahn-Harris (2007: 27) complains, for instance, that metal music is not protected from censorship precisely because it is deemed not worthwhile.

The temptation, in such circumstances, might be to take the line – one that appears increasingly to be that of the Supreme Court – that there are no such distinctions between types of speech, and that all speech be protected, irrespective of content. But as Sandel and others have pointed out this is neither possible nor desirable. Freedom of speech necessarily conflicts with other principles – the right to privacy, the protection of reputation, and so on. Or as Onora O'Neill (1990) points out, there is always a conflict between the rights of the speaker and the rights of the listener. Furthermore, as McGuigan and Sandel recognize, words can hurt. Hence, there are grounds for denying protection to hate speech, whatever form it takes.

If it is accepted that distinctions must be made, then questions remain as to how music might fit into this? To put it more precisely, what aspects of music constitute speech? What is said on stage or sung on a recording? What about sounds without words? Chevigny's battle with the New York authorities provides an answer. Chevigny was involved as a lawyer in representing the musicians' union in their fight against the cabaret laws that restricted the number of instruments on stage to three and barred percussion and horns. These laws had a long history and had been an attempt to manage the granting of licences and the regulation of city zones.

Chevigny's strategy was to make the case by reference to the First Amendment. His prospects for success had been enhanced a few years before when a 1981 Supreme Court ruling (Schad vs Borough of Mt Ephraim) established that there was no principled way of distinguishing between 'entertainment' and other forms of expression (Chevigny, 1991: 107). While the 'entertainment' involved in the Mount Ephraim case was a bookshop that charged customers to watch a 'live nude dancer', the Supreme Court ruling ranged more widely, and included the following statement: 'Entertainment, as well as political and ideological speech, is protected; motion pictures, programs broadcast by radio and television, and live entertainment, such as musical and dramatic works, fall within the First Amendment' (quoted in Chevigny, 1991: 108). This ruling brought music clearly within the remit of free speech. (Although, as it happens, it did not protect 'social dancing', which in a subsequent case, failed to get First Amendment protection (Chevigny, 1991: 115).) But this was not the end of the argument.

The right to play a tune in public might be protected, but would there be protection for the mode of performance? Would the First Amendment protect the principle that the tune should be played on five instruments rather than three? With drums, rather than without? Certainly there are music critics and musicians who would insist that the instrumentation is an intrinsic aspect of the performance and should therefore benefit from protection, but these claims might not automatically secure the support of the courts. The New York authorities had not outlawed all music, just certain forms of its performance.

For Chevigny to succeed, it was necessary to show that particular musical sounds, not just the notes, were worthy of protection. The argument he advanced was this. The First Amendment requires that authorities not discriminate in respect of the content of speech. Typically, this has been understood as points of view or opinions. Music as sound (as opposed to words or lyrics), he conceded, could not be seen as expressing opinions in the traditional sense. Instead, he insisted that musicians were expressing ideas whose form was tied directly to the 'style and instrumentation' (Chevigny, 1991: 112). As Chevigny (1991: 114) notes, establishing this connection depended not just on matters of law, but also of taste: 'If the judge did not care for jazz or some other sort of music that is played in clubs, he was not likely to care whether the ordinance was "content-neutral" or not, or even to grasp how the content issues applied in our case.' Nonetheless, they set about building a case which established that the three-instruments rule discriminated 'against the content of most vernacular music'; that Dixieland jazz required at least five or six instruments 'to get adequate point and counterpoint'; that without a drummer Latin and African styles become impossible (Chevigny, 1991: 119–20). The three-instrument rule, they contended, discriminated against horn players and against the type of music that used them. The case addressed a number of issues, as it was required to, but the aspect that concerns me here is that which connects forms of musical performance to rights of free speech. And importantly the court's decision supported the connection. The numerical restrictions were deemed to affect content and therefore to be in breach of the Constitution's protection of free speech (Chevigny, 1991: 128). This was the ruling: '[I]t is the plaintiffs' main contention that the numerical limitation imposed by the ordinance restricts the cultural expression of musical composers and is therefore "content" based. In this regard, they argue that most music cannot be rearranged to be played by only three musicians without losing the essence of the composer's idea. I find that such a three-musician limitation restricts the plaintiffs' freedom of expression' (Justice Saxe, quoted in Chevigny, 1991: 128).

It is important to see how music comes to be protected by the highest political principles. Such examples give credence to Lord Redesdale's insistence that listening to live music is a human right. But there is another element to be considered, one that drives the urge to censor. This is that music has power. It is this that underpins the argument for its free expression and for its suppression. Music, it is assumed, can make a difference; it can do things to the world and those who inhabit it. Consider music's power to shock.

Music as a source of fear

While we have relatively little trouble in comprehending the shock effect of videogame violence or sexual explicitness on television, it is less easy to see what it is that might be inherently shocking in different forms of music.

Music can frighten people (Johnson and Cloonan, 2009). We know the scary effect of a sudden burst of noise, or of the artful devices used by soundtrack composers to create a sensation of fear (which is not the same as fear itself). But I am concerned with a different kind of fear. This is a fear of music's power to harm the sensibilities, and even the moralities of its audience. In *An Intelligent Person's Guide to Modern Culture*, the philosopher Roger Scruton devotes a chapter to the threat he identifies in popular music. Against the backdrop of popular music's rise to global dominance, he turns attention to its banality. 'The music', he writes, 'is assembled with machine-like motion, with repetition as the principal device.' It makes use of the 'mesmeric sound-effect or cheesy crooning'. Its melodies are 'made up from curt modal or diatonic phrases, with no internal variation or prolongation'. 'It is not that such music is tuneless', he grudgingly concedes, 'rather that the tunes come from elsewhere, like food from the supermarket shelf, to be heated in the microwave' (1998: 90). And so he continues, drawing attention to the 'paltry tunes', the lack of any conclusion, the absence of skilful musicianship, and so on (1998: 90–3).

For Scruton, of course, the problem with popular music is not its aesthetic inadequacies, but its effects. In part, this is to be measured in what the audience misses – the lack of fully realized melodies and song structures (1998: 94), but also it is measured by the absence of genuine and meaningful experiences (1998: 96). Modern popular music offers fantasy instead of imagination, isolation rather than community, and 'an unreal ecstasy which also penetrates and pollutes what is real' (1998: 99). Scruton's final condemnation of modern popular music is that: 'it has destroyed the old forms of music harmonic and rhythmic textures sound all about us, replacing the dialect of the tribe with the grammarless murmur of the species, and drowning out the unconfident murmurs of the fathers as they trudge away towards extinction' (1998: 104). These are dramatic claims, and ones that many may find risible, but what they do is suggest that music has the power to disrupt the social and political order. It does not just shock and scare; it changes hearts and minds. It is this thought, together with the link between music and political principle, that makes censorship of music more than the misguided response of tyrants or bureaucracies. It places music at the heart of political life.

Conclusion

The language and terms in which Scruton identifies the dangers of music represent the mirror image of Paul Chevigny's defence of music as speech or expression, and deserving of the protection of the US Constitution. Both writers are, in their very different ways, placing music at the centre of their concerns for the good society. Music in neither case is regarded as 'mere entertainment', but rather as the embodiment of fundamental values and principles. If music is to be seen like this, and to be weighed in the balance with other important and defining political values, then the relationship between music and politics is deeper than might otherwise be recognized. Or to put it another way, if we reject the claims of Chevigny and Scruton, then we are consigning music to the category of mere entertainment and denying it any wider significance. At the same time, it is not to be supposed that censors are reliable guides to the meaning and power of music. They are, though, symptoms of its potential and possibilities. The behaviour of censors may be, in part, explicable by reference to their political interests and circumstances, but they are not reducible to them. We need to take seriously the sounds themselves and the arguments and principles that they evoke.

2

Falling on deaf ears? Music policy

Echoing the wording of the US Declaration of Independence, *A Music Manifesto for Scotland* boldly declares: 'We hold these truths to be self-evident: Humans make music and music makes us human' (Cloonan and Frith, 2011). The document then goes on to list a series of policy commitments that it urges the Scottish government to adopt. These include maximizing the opportunity for people to learn musical skills, to perform music and to play it. From a proclamation of the fundamental importance of music, the *Manifesto* sets out a policy agenda.

In the last days of the New Labour government, parliament debated the Digital Economy Bill. One of its many aims was to curb the illegal downloading of copyrighted material, including music. It required Internet Service Providers to report those who were doing this, and for the offenders (or rather those deemed responsible for the broadband connection) to be cut off. Critics of the act argued that, in fact, such measures represent a gross infringement of civil liberties and human rights, while its defenders insist that it is essential to the protection of musical creativity (UK Music, 2010). Like the Scottish *Manifesto*, the bill is representative of another example of the state's role in managing music, and the political values attaching to it.

If the last chapter was about what states and their agents do *to* music, this is about what they do *with* it. My argument is that states are, in their distinct way, the composers and creators of music. They are important for understanding the differences in the sound of music across the world, why it serves different functions and conveys different meanings. Insofar as it makes sense to talk of the sound of Britpop, or of the sound of New York or of any other centre of music-making (or indeed their absence – why there was a Liverpool sound, but not a Birmingham one), then part of the explanation is political, in the most conventional sense of that word. But in doing so, I want, as in the last chapter, to show how political principles, as well as political practices, are implicated in the way in which the state engages with music.

For some analysts, of course, the state is a well-nigh irrelevant actor, if by 'state' we mean the nation state (Castells, 2009). From this perspective, music policy, or indeed almost all other forms of public policy, are the product of global processes and interests. While I do not deny the importance of the transnational realm (especially the European Union), I am wary of announcing the death of the nation state as a core actor, as are others (see Cloonan, 1999, 2007; Frith, 1993; Frith and Marshall, 2004). And like David Hesmondhalgh (2007), I am also conscious that many of the claims made for the effect of globalization are often speculative extensions of theoretical possibilities, rather than the grounded results of detailed empirical research. The story told here, therefore, focuses on what we have learnt about the role of the state in the making of music, and how this has varied according to time and place, and according to ideology and interest. The chapter's narrative is, though, not just marked by the place of institutional politics in music's fortune and fate, but also in the values – the notion of 'excellence', for example – that are deployed in public policy, because embedded in such ideas are important assumptions about the political role and worth of music.

Propaganda

Apart from its role as censor, the state is most typically linked to music through the idea of propaganda. States announce themselves in musical form. The national anthem is the typical example. No international sporting event is complete without the sound of national anthems, whether to accompany the host or the winners. There is, of course, a danger in eliding state and nation, but nevertheless, it is important to recognize the complex political stories that recount the emergence of national anthems. Tim Blanning (2008: 257–8) tells of how the 'Marseillaise' was sung both by republicans and their enemies during the French Revolution, and subsequently was crucial to 'the sacralization of the nation' and the acquisition of cultural form for the collective entity (Blanning, 2008: 260). During the 2011 popular uprising in Syria, President Assad attempted to quell the rebels by insisting that nationalist songs be played in all public spaces (*The Times*, 31 March 2011).

In the more mundane world of the modern democratic election, those who seek the popular vote use music (and musicians) to brand their political promises. In 1997, New Labour adopted the cheerful optimism of D:Ream's 'Things Can Only Get Better'; four years later, they chose the smoother, more satisfied, aspirational sound of the Lighthouse Family's

'Lifted'. In 2010, the Conservative Party launched its manifesto to the accompaniment of David Bowie's 'Changes' and Keane's 'Everybody's Changing', and the Liberal Democrats set their Party Election Broadcast (PEB) to the sound of Brian Eno's 'An Ending (Ascent)'. Meanwhile, Barack Obama's 2008 presidential campaign seemed to resound to a beat composed by the greats of US popular music, crossing genres and eras. Whether with the Will.i.am video streamed by millions or the array of stars that adorned his inaugural concert, Obama glowed in the cool, reflected glory of his new-won friends. Like many presidents and presidential hopefuls before him, music and musicians were key to political communication (Street, 1986).

Examples such as the national anthem and the electoral soundtrack seem benign when set against the use of music as propaganda by the Nazis and Nazism. The Nazis were acutely aware of the political potential contained within a national anthem. Michael Meyer (1991: 105) reports that Hitler 'decided that the German national anthem was to be played in a solemn manner, giving specific instruction as to tempo, while the Horst-Wessel song was to have a faster beat in the manner of a revolutionary fighting song'. But even as Nazism sought to create its own distinctive music, other sounds were retained despite their 'alien' character. Jazz, for instance, was not outlawed because it 'served certain propaganda functions' (Kater, 1997: 21–2). Music was not just used to communicate particular messages to Germans; it also formed part of foreign policy. The Nazi regime sponsored performances of (carefully vetted) music in embassies and concert halls around the world (Meyer, 1991: 142ff).

In the same way that the Nazi regime actively censored music and musicians for nationalist purposes, it also used it in an attempt to promote its racial politics. One of the Nazis' core aims was to create a type of music that was 'untainted' by what they regarded as 'alien' influences (Negus, 1996: 201–4). Music was seen as one key element in establishing 'Germanness'. Or to put it another way, particular musical forms were deemed inconsistent with ideas of racial purity: 'atonality contradicts the rhythm of the blood' (Meyer, 1991: 21; Kater, 1997: 178). Asked many years later as to what kind of music the Nazis wanted, an Austrian composer replied: 'The opposite of Schoenberg – music in C major' (Kater, 1997: 177). This was not just an aesthetic preference; it was a political statement, grounded in the notion that musical style conveyed political values. Music, writes Michael Kater (1997: 11), was to be 'put to the service of an idea'.

The Soviet Union, especially under Joseph Stalin, was similarly committed to realizing the propaganda potential in music. Here the focus was not, of course, on racial purity, but rather on communism's triumph over capitalism and the heroism of the Soviet people. However, the language that defined this role echoed that of the Nazis. Shostakovich's *Lady Macbeth* was condemned for 'the deliberately dissonant, muddled stream of sounds' that it contained (quoted by Ross, 2007: 216). The propagandist uses of music, therefore, was not simply a matter of appropriating sounds to the cause, but of investing those sounds with specific political meaning. This investment was itself dependent upon the state's capacity to manage the production of music in the first place.

Managing music in authoritarian regimes

How did authoritarian states manage the ideological use of music? It is not simply a matter of insisting that certain values or identities be inscribed in music. Not only do the values have to be identified and communicated, but they have to be embodied and implemented as policy. The process of implementation entails the translation of ideas into forms of action. As Keith Negus (1996: 203) notes, music policy combined 'economic imperatives and cultural values'. And the business of policy making is not simply technocratic. Politics is also involved – there were, for example, arguments between Hitler and Goebbels as to what exactly their music policy required (Kater, 1997). The complexities of politics and policy were themselves overlaid, as Meyer (1991: 20) suggests, by the fact that, in the case of the Nazis, ideology and culture were seen to be intimately connected. As an authoritarian regime dedicated to controlling all aspects of citizens' lives, the Nazi state was bound to involve itself in those aspects of life that other systems might leave to the private individual and the market. Its fascist and racist beliefs were to be expressed and realized both culturally and politically. The result was a process of 'cultural centralization' (Meyer, 1991: 97), combined with what Kater (1997: 33) describes as the 'nazification of music', a process expedited by the creation of the National Socialist Reich Orchestra and by the Bayreuth Festival. Although they were very different in their ideological commitments, the Soviet and Nazi regimes evolved similar basic structures for the management of their officially sanctioned music. They also seemed to share a conviction about the political importance of music and about the value to be derived from it. In other words, their music policy was not simply a product of their ambitions to control every aspect of their peoples' lives. It was also driven by a belief, however distorted, of the power of music. This begs the question as to whether non-authoritarian states take a different view of music's role.

Managing music in liberal capitalist regimes

Within liberal capitalist regimes, music policy involves a number of different sectors of society – from education to trade, from immigration to intellectual property law. In his survey of state policy on music, Martin Cloonan (1999) identifies five such areas: censorship, broadcasting, law and copyright, cultural policy, and identity. The key to his argument is that these various policy arenas have identifiable material effects upon music, some as part of a deliberate intention (e.g. broadcasting quotas), and others as unintended consequences (e.g. trade tariffs or immigration policy). Within these different arenas there are further effects. Broadcasting policy, for example, has multiple aspects, all of which have an influence on music-making. States differ in the general regulation of the broadcasting spectrum, and in the role allocated to the market. Market-based and public service broadcasting differ in the opportunities they allow to performers to experiment and in the relationship these performers have to their audience (as consumers or as citizens). In a commercial broadcasting system, musicians provide a means of linking audiences to advertisers. In public service broadcasting, music forms part of a different remit – in the case of the BBC 'to inform, educate and entertain'. Simon Frith (1988), for example, argues that the Beatles were a product of the creative space engendered by the BBC, one that was not available in US broadcasting. Similarly, government decisions to apply quotas to broadcasters in order to limit the quantity of foreign music played are designed to promote the domestic music industry (Mason, 2003).

Equally important to the character of music in a country are the laws governing copyright and intellectual property (Frith and Marshall, 2004). The possibilities created by new media have radically altered the conditions under which music is produced and distributed, and hence the music industry has been lobbying for government support in the attempt to curb piracy (IFPI, 2010; Music UK, 2010). Education policy too impacts upon the making and appreciation of music, just as immigration policy affects the opportunity for musicians to travel and perform outside their own country. Taxation policy alters the incentive structure for musicians (and other artists). Licensing policy, perhaps most vividly, affects the opportunities to perform and the audiences who can attend those performances (Chevigny, 1991; Homan, 2003).

But while there are common issues or common areas of policy in relation to music, there is wide variation in the way in which these policies operate and what institutions are assigned to operate them. As Roger

Wallis and Krister Malm (1984) pointed out many years ago, it matters whether or not you are small or a large nation. It also matters whether music is seen as 'culture' or as 'business', or how the balance between the two is struck. In Barbados, for example, music was viewed as 'culture' when it was incorporated within the general framework established in 1984 by the National Cultural Foundation, whose main responsibility – initially at least – was to support the venues created by the government (Harewood, 2008). In time, Cultural Officers were appointed to oversee particular cultural forms, including music. 'Music' became closely associated with calypso and with the festivals and competitions designed to promote it. But as Susan Harewood (2008: 213–5) shows, music became not just a matter of culture, but also of commerce. This shift in policy served a number of interests and goals. It helped to promote tourism; it developed national identity; and it helped to 'discipline' the product (calypso). And when Barbados experienced a sharp economic downturn in the 1990s, music policy shifted even further away from treating music as culture towards exploiting its commercial potential (Harewood, 2008: 216).

In Finland, which has a history of actively promoting music and which also regards it as a business, the government has in recent years increased substantially the subsidies it provides to the music industry in order to boost the export of Finnish music (Mäkelä, 2008). The state has contributed to the cost of marketing, recording and touring. Much of this has focused on exporting Finnish music, and thereby has sought to expedite the commercial process, flying in foreign journalists to report on Finnish music festivals (Mäkelä, 2008: 257–8). Similar export-driven concerns are evident in New Zealand's music policy, which emerged from a gradual recognition of the commercial potential of the music industry, and thence to proactively promoting it (Shuker, 2008: 271–3). According to Roy Shuker (2008: 273–7), the policy agenda evolved first as a debate about radio quotas, and then as a deliberate strategy of support for New Zealand's artists. With the election of the Labour Government in 1999, the policy was extended beyond broadcasting to the creation of a Music Industry Commission, 'charged with "growing the industry"' (Shuker, 2008: 277). Initially directed at the domestic performance of the industry, New Zealand's policy increasingly looked to promoting the export market (Shuker, 2008: 279–80).

In Australia, as in Barbados, music policy has focused (albeit not exclusively) on live music venues. This policy has been delivered and devised at the local/city level, and has been tied to a mixture of concerns, ranging from tourism to law and order. It entailed laws on building regulations as

well as those on public assembly and noise abatement, and it was often
enacted through the mechanism of the licence (Homan, 2003 and 2008).
In Germany, one aspect of music policy involved the promotion of German
music through Radio Goethe, funded by the German federal government
and broadcast to colleges in the US (Krause, 2008: 226).

The point of this whirlwind survey of national music policies is not,
however, just to establish that policy matters and that the various levers
available to government do indeed change the opportunities to perform,
hear, and make money from music. What is also important is that these
policies address questions about whether music is a culture or an industry
(or both), about whether it can and should be used to promote certain collective identities and values. The answers embodied in the policy represent
views on whether music matters in politically significant ways. This was
explicit in the policies of authoritarian regimes, it is less explicit in western
liberal capitalist societies, but it is there nonetheless. Music policy gives
an answer to the question of how importantly we should value music.

Justifying and explaining music policy

What, though, are the 'answers' contained in these various music policies?
Much of the evidence described in the previous section derived from a
recent collection on music policy in a number of different liberal regimes
(Cloonan and Frith, 2008). It revealed variations of many kinds, but perhaps
the most telling are those to be found in the ends to which music policy
is put. These range from the need 'to reflect audience tastes and interests
. . . [and to] support citizen welfare in the production and consumption of
local popular music' (Breen, 2008: 206), through to 'nation-building both
at the national and international level' (Harewood, 2008: 220). And while
others also identify national identity as the key purpose of music policy
(Krause, 2008: 226), there are those who offer a very different goal: 'diversity of both venues and music genres and performers' (Homan, 2008: 252).
Finally, music policy is represented as delivering economic security to the
nation's music industry (Mäkelä, 2008: 268; Shuker, 2008: 282). In short,
nation states imagine entirely different ends for their music policy, and even
when they share an aim, there is no guarantee that it will be either understood or implemented in the same way.

This points us to Michael Sandel's (1996) idea of policy as lived theory,
as the practical expression of political philosophies and values. This is as
true for cultural policy as it is for economic or health policy. Or as Shane
Homan (2008: 243) observes, the regulation and promotion of live music

is revealing of 'attitudes to commercial entertainment, and the place of popular music in relation to other forms of cultural entertainment'. It is also implicated in views of how urban life should be ordered and what interests deserve to be protected, issues that emerged in Chevigny's story of music regulation in New York. Homan (2008: 252) charts the shifting agenda of state and city regulators as they move between music venues as sites of public order problems to community resources.

These values and ideas – the lived theories – are, though, couched in many different languages and exist in many different fields. Music policy is directed, as we have seen, towards economic well-being and to sustaining the commercial life of countries and regions. It is also directed towards the labour market, to the need to provide training for the workforce, which in turn is linked to education policy, although that too may be directed towards equipping children to appreciate musical culture as much as to perform it. Material matters are overlaid by cultural, political and social concerns. Music policy is, for instance, intended to promote social and cultural diversity. Or it may be directed, and this is importantly different, to realizing ideas of freedom and choice. Finally, music policy may be designed to enhance democracy – the promotion of calypso in Barbados was intimately linked to a rhetoric of the 'voice of the people' (Harewood, 2008: 215).

In short, music policy is invested with a wide variety of political purposes and powers, and to an extent can be explained in these terms. But other factors are involved, extending from the geo-political (the relative size of nations in the global economy) to the political and ideological (the value placed on music and the distinctions made between forms of music). There are also policy-specific factors: the part played by institutions in shaping policy and in allocating resources to it, and to the political networks that set agendas and allocate priorities. Music policy, like all policy, is a product of structural processes and the interests organized in (and out of) them. By way of illustration of these intersecting factors, it pays to look at one specific instance of music policy.

A national agenda?

In 2004, the UK's Music Manifesto was launched. It was a joint initiative of the Department for Children, Schools and Families (previously the Department for Education and Skills) and the Department for Culture, Media and Sport. Its primary stated aim was to 'ensure that all children and young people have access to high quality music'. Although this was a

New Labour government policy, responsibility for its implementation was delegated to 'a voluntary, apolitical' group, chaired by the managing director of Classic FM. In 2007, the DCSF contributed £332m for three years funding, which was allocated to, among other things, 'Sing Up' and 'In Harmony'. The first of these cost £40m and was designed to 'put singing at the heart of every primary school'. 'In Harmony', by contrast, took its model from Venezuela's *El Sistema* programme, which was meant to connect the teaching and learning of musical skills to social change more generally. Partnerships were formed across the country to promote music in schools. Success was measured in terms of increased levels of 'self esteem' (Staffordshire Music Partnership 2008–9).

Among the Music Manifesto's declared aims was that of harnessing 'the power of music'; another was to engage in 'workforce development'. Between them these two aims reveal much that is most fascinating about music policy: the belief that music can *do* things; that it can bring about social and economic change for individuals and communities.

The Music Manifesto was but one thread in the weave that has constituted the UK's music policy. This point is amply made by Martin Cloonan (2007), whose book, *Popular Music and the State in the UK*, has as its subtitle, 'Culture, Trade or Industry?' This question captures Cloonan's argument: that music policy incorporates a number of areas, and that in doing so it sets up tensions which cannot be resolved easily, and that any attempt to find a compromise has consequences for the character of British music and the various interests tied to it. It is a zero-sum game.

Cloonan argues that music policy in the UK has operated with two assumptions. The first is that music policy should not challenge the relations of ownership that operate within the music industry. This is not just a matter of the balance of power between small and large UK companies; it is also a matter of the ownership of British music and the claims of multinational corporations upon it. The second assumption is that those responsible for devising and implementing music policy should take a narrow view of the constitution of that industry, seeing it as a single entity confined to the production, distribution and retail of (recorded) music. Cloonan is critical of these two assumptions, and points to the political and aesthetic consequences of the government's failure to move beyond them.

Robert Cluely (2009) offers a similarly critical perspective on music policy. He argues that the UK government works with a particular set of assumptions about how the creation of music occurs. One of the central of these is that the natural arc of music production is from small enterprises to large ones, and that music policy should aim to support and develop this relationship. 'The DCMS assumes,' argues Cluely (2009: 219), 'that small producers are essential to the strength of the music sector and that small producers need government support.' But this assumption, he suggests, is not warranted. Large producers can be as capable – if not more so – of nurturing talent or genres that will flourish in the market place.

But while critics like Cloonan and Cluely are sceptical of the assumptions which typically inspire UK music policy, they do not paint an entirely bleak picture. Cloonan (2007: 19), for example, applauds the attempts made by the Greater London Council to reinvigorate the music industry in the 1980s. The GLC's efforts were part of a broader set of initiatives to promote the city's cultural economy. What these represented was a recognition that popular music was not to be seen simply as 'entertainment', and as such to be contrasted with classical music (which was designated as 'art' and as such as deserving of public subsidy). The GLC treated music as both economically and culturally important, as being at the core of the local economy.

For Cloonan, the emergence of (popular) music policy is a feature of changing perceptions of what kind of entity was being dealt with. For as long as it was 'entertainment' it could be assigned to the market. When, in the late 1960s, it became 'culture', it began to attract the support and protection that was granted culture more generally, and when it was seen as a global product it could be exploited for tourism and national promotion (cf. Cool Britannia). Gradually, following assiduous lobbying by the music industry, the government came to recognize the economic importance of music. It was at this point that music came within the purview of the department responsible for trade and industry. The results of this could be discerned in New Labour's various initiatives. These extended from the expansion of the budget for arts subsidies, via Lottery funding, to initiatives for youth music education and training (including the New Deal for Musicians initiative), through to the Music Industry Forum, designed to ensure the fuller recognition of the music industry within government policy making, and the Licensing Act (2003), which was designed to modernize the regulations that applied to the live performance of music (Cloonan: 2007: 40–58). These initiatives were not uncontroversial – the Licensing Act has, as we have seen, attracted the wrath of the House of Lords, not to mention many musicians and their representatives. The same was true when, in 2010, the competition authorities approved the merger of two giants of the live music business, Live Nation and Ticketmaster (Competition Commission, 2010). What, however, these debates do is that they highlight the interplay of political and cultural values, of aesthetics and economics.

This brief case study of UK music policy serves only to illustrate the political dimensions of the state's involvement and its impact. My concern has not just been with the intentions and implementation of music policy, but also with the political value attributed to music in the process (and how that value informs policy). The nation state, though, is not the only actor involved in making music policy.

A transnational agenda?

The European Union was relatively late in incorporating music into its policy agenda (Laing, 1999: 33). The EU had tended to see music, and other forms of culture, as something best left to individual states – in the spirit of the principle of subsidiarity. This was in part because music was linked primarily to heritage and national identity; and in part because the EU acknowledged the right of states to break the rules of the union in respect of culture – hence the tolerance, say, of France's protection of its film industry (ibid.: 53). However, in the mid-1990s, this perception changed, driven by increasing awareness of the importance of music to the larger economy (EMO, 1996). Subsequently, the EU introduced some measure of standardization in respect of copyright laws and other aspects of the commercial life of music, including the free movement of artists within the EU. It has also, through the culture budget, provided an important source of subsidy. The recognition of the economic value of the cultural and creative industries has led over time to calls for greater strategic investment in this sector (KEA, 2006/9). Although the EU continues to express support for general principles of cultural diversity, it is apparent that the main driving force behind music policy is a particular view of its commercial value.

The EU, though, is not the only transnational body involved in music policy. UNESCO (United Nations Educational, Scientific and Cultural Organization) has also promoted the interests of performers through a system of grants and competitions. UNESCO's Music Education and Career Prospects World Directory has tried to enhance the employment prospects of musicians. Its International Music Council is charged with promoting musical diversity and cultural rights – 'the basic right for all people to express themselves and communicate through music'.

Statements like this recall the discussion that ended the last chapter on censorship, when we saw how the right to perform music was linked to fundamental political rights. A similar move is apparent, as I've suggested, in national and international music policy. Implicitly or explicitly states and transnational organizations place a value on music, a value that brings together the political and the cultural. But reconciling the two is no easy matter.

Auditing culture

Where dictatorships may value culture in propagandist terms, measuring it according to some notion of ideological consistency, liberal democratic regimes have to find a different rationale. One of these is 'excellence'. It provides an apparently neutral criterion by which to legitimate the spending of public funds or the imposition of regulation. 'Excellence' represents, suggests Brian Barry (2001: 199), a value to which all liberals can show allegiance. Why would any government commit funds – taxpayers' money – to anything that was mediocre? Except, of course, that it is not this simple. Not only does the notion of 'excellence' carry with it many possible meanings, but also there may be rival values to which music policy is committed – revenue, diversity, inclusiveness, and so on. In what follows, I look at how politicians have used the idea of 'excellence' to rationalize their policy towards culture, and how in doing so they have tried to reconcile competing political and cultural values.

In 2004, Tessa Jowell, the Secretary of State at the UK's Department of Culture, Media and Sport, published an essay entitled *Government and the Value of Culture*. In speaking of her commitment to supporting excellence in art, Jowell also linked this to her political agenda. 'Engagement with culture', she said, 'can help to alleviate the poverty of aspiration' (paras. 1 and 29). Excellence in art, it seemed, was to be valued for the social benefits it generated. But Jowell was quick to insist that this was not an argument for treating art as a form of social engineering (a view she attributed to J. S. Mill), but to value *art for its own sake* (a view she attributed to John Ruskin) (paras. 12–15). Her argument was that the social value of art was realized through the effects that it had as art, a point she made by distinguishing between mere 'entertainment' and 'cultural engagement'. The latter was to be distinguished by the demands it makes of audiences (para. 3); entertainment, we are left to assume, made no such demands. Her argument, therefore, entailed a number of different moves – first, attaching art to social value, and second, distinguishing art from entertainment. How were such distinctions to be made in practice?

This question poses a problem for a democratic politician because it threatens to set her against the revealed preferences of the market. While

Jowell acknowledged that 'mass public demand' was not a sufficient guide to cultural value (para. 4), she could not, as a democrat, turn to her purely 'subjective' judgement to decide what qualified as valuable art (para. 5). Instead, she identified formal criteria for making distinctions, one of which was 'complexity' – demanding art reveals itself in its attempt to reflect the world's complexity (para. 7). 'Complex cultural activity', she said, was key to human development (para. 9). Such cultural complexity, she added, was not the exclusive province of high art (as traditionally defined), it could be found anywhere – in any genre or cultural form (para. 10). Nonetheless, it was cultural complexity that identified excellence in art and justified state action.

This attempt to balance value distinctions with a notion of democratic equality became more explicit when her attention turned to 'access'. There should be, she said, no barriers – either economic or physical – to accessing the excellent (paras. 17 and 31). She offered an analogy with sport, where increasing access, she claimed, increased quality (paras. 17–18). She seemed to suggest that access *creates* the conditions for excellence in the way that competition racks up quality or performance. Whether this comparison is valid, Jowell's argument was that government should fund excellence in creativity and performance, and increase access to it.

Jowell's attempt to define government cultural policy in respect of excellence was not the last word on the topic. Indeed, her successor at the DCMS, James Purnell, commissioned a report on how to apply the notion of excellence. The result was Sir Brian McMaster's (2008) *Supporting Excellence in the Arts: From Measurement to Judgement*. The McMaster's report echoed the distinctions and ideas spoken of by Jowell. McMaster also linked cultural value to social relevance, and attached this to the idea of complexity and to art's transformative powers: 'Excellent culture takes and combines complex meanings, gives us new meanings and understandings of the world around us.' It gave us, argued McMaster, new experiences and sensibilities (2008: 9). Without making the formal distinction between entertainment and cultural engagement, he echoed Jowell in welcoming art that involves 'experimentation and pushing boundaries', art that was able to 'question, to provoke, to aggravate and, at times, to anger' (ibid.: 10–11). But where Jowell eschewed an association between excellence and any particular art form or genre, McMaster made special reference to 'orchestral or operatic work' in discussion of the excellent (ibid.: 10). But beyond these general statements of what qualified as 'excellent', McMaster said little. Instead his concern was with the conditions that produce excellence.

The answer lay with the individual: 'the arts are driven by individuals, be they a great creative artist or a brave and imaginative curator or producer', and these individuals must engage in risk taking and enjoy 'freedom of expression' (ibid.: 5 and 7). Although this seems to evoke a classically libertarian portrait of the artist, McMaster did not advocate market-style, commercial risk-taking. Quite the contrary, he required 'financial security', because, he argued, the market is liable to compromise integrity (ibid.: 7 and 16). Excellence came through 'freedom', where that was measured in the autonomy of artists and funding bodies, staffed by those with 'appropriate expertise' (which means, among other things, the inclusion of at least two artists or practitioners, together with peer review) (ibid.: 12). So while McMaster identified 'excellence' in conventional ways, his proposals for realizing it were unusual in that they did not advocate market mechanisms.

The reason for dwelling upon these attempts to define excellence, and to promote it, is to reveal the ways in which political and cultural value are aligned in policy making in an attempt to reconcile aesthetic judgements with democratic accountability. The process of reconciliation goes to the heart of my argument as to how politics and music are intimately connected.

Markets and states

At their most basic level, Jowell and McMaster want to rationalize and legitimize state intervention in the arts. In a liberal state, as Ronald Dworkin (1985) and others have pointed out, there are powerful reasons for leaving art to the market. People should have the art they want, and the only adequate test of this is what they are prepared to pay for. Any other arrangement is paternalist and unfair. State subsidies tend to be used to fund art that the rich enjoy. On the other hand, insofar as art is a public good, it may be the victim of market failure. But what would justify intervention in the market? It might be claimed that society as a whole benefits from the presence of the art, from, for example, the tourism that it generates. But, suggests Dworkin (1985: 224–5), this trickle down effect is unlikely to be sufficient to justify state funding of art, since it remains the case that it is the privileged few who benefit most. Instead, says Dworkin, an alternative rationale for justifying state funding might be the effect that high culture has on culture generally. Here the suggestion is that culture is viewed as 'a seamless web', and that 'high culture and popular culture are not distinct but influence one another reciprocally'. In such circumstances, the funding of high culture could be justified because it 'provides popular culture with form: musical comedy and television thrillers alike exploit genres first developed in opera and novel'. Funding culture has a 'spillover effect'. But this too Dworkin dismisses, not least because of the difficulty of identifying and measuring such an effect.

Culture is too important to be risked in this way, suggests Dworkin (1985: 228); it is 'too fundamental, too basic to our scheme of values'. He argues instead that 'it is better for people to have complexity and depth in the form of lives open to them', and this claim justifies intervention to protect and promote culture for such goods, even where individuals may not see the benefit. This larger goal of preserving the culture is achieved through a focus on artistic excellence (Dworkin, 1985: 233). This argument for state subsidy, one that appears to underpin the policy documents produced by Jowell and McMaster, may seem to have benign political consequences. But this is not necessarily so.

If 'excellence' is the only criterion for state subsidy, then other goals, such as diversity, are unable to provide sufficient reason. This, at least, is the argument of the political philosopher Brian Barry. In his book, *Culture and Equality*, Barry (2001) – like Dworkin – argues that excellence is the only coherent ground for state intervention in the arts. In making this case he sets himself against those who argue that state support should derive from a commitment to multiculturalism (Parekh, 2000).

Barry is no philistine. His account of the value of art echoes those used by Dworkin, Jowell and McMaster. 'The chief beneficiaries of the world's literature', he writes (Barry, 2001: 31), 'are those whom it enables to break out of the limited range of ideas in which they have been brought up.' And art is to be protected by principles of free speech so that it might be deployed, among other things, 'to mock, ridicule and lampoon' (ibid.). However, the arts subsidy is justified only by reference to its quality. There is no argument, Barry contends, for subsidizing art made by professionals for a market (or there is no special reason that applies to art to distinguish it from other goods produced for a market to satisfy consumer demand). The same goes for amateur art – there is no more reason to subsidize it than there is subsidizing 'any other hobby' (Barry, 2001: 198). Quality alone provides the rationale.

Quality is not reducible to subjective judgement: 'If it is merely a matter of opinion that Beethoven is better than banjo-playing, then it is a mere matter of opinion that either is better than the monetary equivalent in groceries. And in that case there is no case for earmarking funds at all: let people spend the money on Beethoven, banjo-playing or groceries as they choose' (Barry, 2001: 199). For Barry, there can be no defence of the public funding of art other than its excellence, where this is an objective not subjective judgement. Any particular or parochial defence of a subsidy fails because it does not generate reasons as to why art alone should be treated in this specific way.

The consequence of Barry's argument, like Dworkin's, is that subsidizing art in the name of multiculturalism, or any other political goal, is not justified. Only excellence suffices since this alone generates a special claim. Barry's argument is subject to a number of criticisms, which might be bracketed under two headings (see Kelly, 2002). The first includes those who challenge the notion of 'excellence' as meaningful in discourses about art. For them, all judgements are necessarily the product of interests and ideology (Bennett, 1990). The problem with this is that it leads to relativism, unless some other criterion is substituted for 'excellence', which changes the language but not the structure of the argument. Alternatively, the notion of excellence might be retained, and Barry's argument challenged instead on the way 'excellence' might be discerned. This approach would allow for the claims mounted by multiculturalism, in that identity is factored into the measure of excellence. The point is, however, that whatever line of argument is adopted, state policy on art and culture is inextricably implicated in it. States, in this sense, live an answer to the dilemmas posed by intervention in the arts.

Conclusion: music policy re-visited

This might seem like a long detour in a chapter on music policy, but I hope it serves to make an important point about the inextricably political character of that policy. It is not political only in the sense that state agents are involved in its design and implementation, but also in the judgements and values which it contains. Music policy is about the value of music and about the criteria by which this is assessed. What I have tried to show is that music policy is, by its very nature, engaged with profound and important political questions. At their heart lie arguments about the value of culture and how this value serves to provide a rationale for policy, for the spending of public money and the allocation of scarce resources. Such issues sit at the heart of music policy, even that of authoritarian states. For while these latter are not occupied with the same demands for legitimacy, their policy still derives from some account of what music can do and how the state should act in relation to it.

It is because of the conflicting arguments that underlie the politics of culture that music policy takes many forms, why it varies between countries and within (and across) countries. These differences find expression in, and are shaped by, the corporate and institutional interests organized around music. The various political instruments used to make and implement music policy are products of political constitutions and political cultures, among many other factors. Hence the extent to which policy is located in broadcasting, trade and industry, education, law and order, and so on. But as I argued in the previous chapter, state involvement in music entails investing it with political value and associating it with particular political principles. This is not to suggest that there is a neat and permanent association of principle and practice. As Keith Negus (1996: 208) remarks, 'even a state with as much apparent political power as Nazi Germany could not control the production and consumption of music in a straightforward or effective manner'. The agencies for making and implementing policy, and the individuals who staff them, also articulate and embody particular interpretations of the political value to be ascribed to music. These differences, though, constitute variations on a theme, a theme that continues as we turn to the way in which music is made to convey political ideas and represent political interests.

3

Striking a chord: from political communication to political representation

In 1766, according to Tim Blanning (2002: 88), Joseph Haydn wrote to Prince Esterhazy of Hungary:

> The most joyous occasion of your name-day (may YOUR HIGHNESS celebrate it in divine Grace and enjoy it in complete well-being and felicity!) obliges me not only to deliver to you in profound submission six new Divertimenti, but also to say that we were delighted to receive, a few days ago, our new winter clothes – and to submissively kiss the hem of your robe. . . .

The relationship between composer and royalty indicated by this letter is clear enough. The musician pays obsequious homage to the prince. Contrast this with the relationship of another musician and politician, as described by Alastair Campbell (2007: 406–7; 592), Tony Blair's Director of Communications: 'Monday 17 December 2001: He [the Prime Minister] wanted to get out of a dinner on Africa with ministers . . . He agreed reluctantly but when it came to it, it was Bono and Bob Geldof who got the invitation up to the flat.' This time the relationship between artist and power is reversed. It is the musician who commands the respect of the ruler.

While Bob Geldof and Bono may be unusual in their ability to secure the time and attention of political leaders, they are typical to the extent that they, like many other musicians, have used music to communicate political ideas and values, and, perhaps more importantly, to claim representation of causes and peoples. One of the sources of music's perceived power – the power that states seek to repress and to harness – lies in its ability to convey ideas and embody communities. It was power not lost on Tony Blair (2010: 91), who writes in his autobiography of the need for his party 'to reach the people listening to Duran Duran and Madonna'.

This chapter is about music both as a form of political communication and as a mode of political representation. My argument is that the former is possible only because of the latter. It is not enough to be able to speak up; you must be able also to speak *for* a people or cause; you must represent them. But this idea of 'representation', where there are no elections or formal mechanisms of accountability, is all too rarely analysed. It raises not only intriguing issues of how music and musicians might claim to represent a cause or community, but also under what conditions such a relationship becomes possible and credible.

What is also rarely considered is the way sound itself communicates politically. There is a tendency to reduce the politics of music to words and lyrics. These are important, but their importance can be exaggerated at the cost of the other elements of the musical experience. This is a large topic, to which I return later. Here I want simply to ask questions about what we mean by 'political' music, and where the politics may be located (how voices, rhythms and melodies, as well as lyrics, might convey political ideas). Such questions are important to any understanding of music as a form of political communication and representation. Why do musicians get taken seriously as commentators and representatives? What is it about someone, whose skills lie in hitting a note or composing a tune or holding an audience, that allows them to think, not only that they have something significant to say about the state of the world, but that what they say should be taken seriously? How and when do a musician's politics secure them invitations to exclusive chats at 10 Downing Street? And in the case of Bono, not just there. In 2002, a *Time* cover asked, 'Can Bono save the world?' The answer to this question was not a dismissive 'no'. Instead Bono was treated with reverence, as a potential saviour of a world in which conventional forms of political leadership and public policy had failed. After all it wasn't just *Time* and Tony Blair that regarded the lead singer of U2 in this way; so did a host of world leaders. Bono was pictured at the White House with George W. Bush, at the Elysee Palace with President Jacques Chirac, and in the Vatican with Pope John-Paul. At the moment he is best friends with Barack Obama.

Sounding off: music as a political platform

Although Bono's political involvement may be unusual, at least in terms of the status and prominence of those he has button-holed, but in other respects it is almost common place. Music has been a site of political expression for centuries, whether as part of the folk tradition or of the classical canon.

Roy Palmer (1988) recounts the history of the popular ballad, in which the plight of the poor and the iniquities of taxation have long been documented. Historians such as E. P. Thompson (1963) and political scientists such as James C. Scott (1990) have placed song prominently within the stories they tell of class struggle, just as other writers have located music at the heart of the fight for civil rights in the US (Saul, 2003; Ward, 1998; Denisoff, 1972). Certain genres of popular music, it seems, are viewed almost exclusively as political: the blues, gospel, soul and hip hop. The deliberate and intentional use of music to express political ideas is not confined to popular genres. Classical music has a similar record (Arblaster, 1992; Blanning, 2008; Ross, 2007). This is typically associated with the operatic form: Beethoven's *Fidelio*, Verdi's *Nabucco*, John Adams' *Nixon in China*, and so on. Politics is present too, albeit in veiled form, in hymns and national anthems.

Explicitly political music is not the preserve of the fringes of musical culture. It is there in the mainstream. Protests at the war in Iraq provide just one recent example of pop stars assuming the guise of political activists. In the UK, George Michael sang Don McLean's 'The Grave' on *Top of the Pops*; Chris Martin of Coldplay used his appearance at the Brits Awards to protest at the war; Elton John and Damon Albarn and countless others signed public petitions against the war; Ms Dynamite rapped with the Reverend Jesse Jackson at a Hyde Park rally; and the Dixie Chicks disassociated themselves from their fellow Texan, George W. Bush, from the stage of their concert in Shepherds Bush. These public displays of protest were echoed on the web, where a plethora of anti-war songs could be heard, from the likes of Nanci Griffith, REM, the Beastie Boys, Lenny Kravitz and John Mellencamp.

Nor is the political song an exclusively Western phenomenon. On the continent of Africa, or in Latin America, political music abounds, and has done so for as long as it has in other parts of the world. Many of the struggles for independence from imperial rule or other forms of oppressive control have been accompanied musically (Mattern, 1998; Slobin, 1996). The names of Thomas Mapfumo (Zimbabwe), Victor Jara (Chile), Fela Kuti (Nigeria), Miriam Makeba and Hugh Masekela (South Africa), or Mikis Theodorakis (Greece), are but a few of those who represent this tradition.

But in chronicling the global spread and historical scope of political music, there is a danger of seeing it as a universal and ubiquitous phenomenon. It may be true that political music has always been with us, but it has not been everywhere and it has not always taken the same guise. Indeed, the most interesting questions lie in asking how and when political songs come to be written or performed. While it is important to recognize their longevity, it is also important to see how they have emerged in particular places and times, and to ask why only some political songs have succeeded and survived. Roy Palmer (1988: 240) refers, for example, to songs that have been in circulation for over a century: what accounts for their resilience? Is this a function of musical skill or political context? This is an impossible question to answer, or one in which the response is as much a matter of speculation as anything else. There are, though, aspects of this question that can be addressed. We can, I think, say something about the conditions under which musicians feel able (or compelled) to comment on politics. In identifying these, I focus primarily upon Western popular music and musicians, and on songs and statements or gestures that are explicitly 'political'. While all songs are ideological in the sense that they contain a perspective on the world and relationships within it, a political song, I shall assume, is one that self-consciously recognizes the ideological content and seeks to draw the listener's attention to it.

Narrowing the focus by concentrating on the explicitly political still leaves much to consider, and requires us to make at least one distinction between types of political music. This is the contrast that Dave Laing (2003: 345) draws between 'protest music' and 'music of resistance'. The former he describes as 'explicit statements of opposition' and the latter as 'coded or opaque'. Both derive from the deliberate intentions of the performer, but each is mediated differently by the political circumstances (or the perceptions of those circumstances). A protest song identifies a specific issue or enemy. A song of resistance may have no such focus or narrative. Its politics may lie in the mere act of singing. During the so-called Jasmine revolution that gripped the Middle-East and North Africa in early 2011, many of the demonstrators sang as they protested. Their singing gave voice to their defiance and helped to constitute their identity as a people, but the songs they sang were not, formally at least, 'protest songs'. They were, though, songs of resistance.

The distinction recognizes the importance of context to music's political role. But Laing's contrast itself needs to be distinguished from two other ways in which contexts and circumstances may play a part in making music political. The first of these was discussed in chapter 1, and has to do with how the action of states – as censors – invest music with political significance, even where none is intended by the performer. In other words, the explanation for the music's politics lies with the actions of the state and the capacity of all music to bear political weight. Equally, and often in such circumstances, fans may use music to express political ideas that the performer never imagined – as happened with the children in Soweto who, protesting at Apartheid in schools, reportedly sang Pink Floyd's 'We don't need no education'. Here the explanation for the politics of the music lies with the particular intentions of the school pupils. Something similar can be seen in Robert Cushman's (1995) portrait of dissident youth within Soviet Russia. The music of T. Rex, seen in the West as 'glam rock', became symbolic of the dissatisfaction felt by Russian youth. The explanation for such political associations would seem to owe almost nothing to Marc Bolan and T. Rex, and everything to the context. Finally, music can become 'political' through the interpretations put upon it, again irrespective of the performers' intentions or the apparent content of that music. This is characteristic of the way music may be used by historians and others to express the sentiments or spirit of a time. The music's significance, its politics, is a product of the interpretation of the commentator, not of the intentions of the performers. In its crudest form, this is evident in the soundtrack chosen to accompany documentaries about the past. In its more subtle form, it is there in the way that historians capture the sentiments of a given period.

My point is not that these other ways of linking music to politics are unimportant or invalid. Far from it. They feature prominently in later discussion. My concern here is just narrower. It is about how and when music that *is intended to be political* gets written and performed.

Becoming political

Why and when do pop stars come to see themselves as political commentators or political activists? While we can list many examples of the songs that are explicitly and intentionally about politics, they will always be in a minority. Most performers, most of the time, are not making political statements or gestures. And even if they were, we might still be curious about why professional entertainers, who make their living from selling records or playing live, feel able or obliged to pronounce on the serious business of politics.

Musicians can become involved with politics in one of two ways. These can be captured, albeit crudely, in the contrast between political activism and political argument (or polemic). The first describes the case of people who happen to be musicians, and as such have acquired a public presence or status, which they use to support causes or candidates. The second captures the case of those who use their music to give expression to their political views. The two may be linked – Sting and Bruce Springsteen, for example, perform both roles – but they are not necessarily so. Elton John is not noted for his repertoire of political songs, but he became actively involved in the campaign against the Iraq war. While, by contrast, Morrissey writes songs with explicitly political messages, but does not actively engage with politics. The point of making this distinction is that the explanation for each may be quite different – why musicians stand on platforms may differ from the reasons they deliver polemics. Coldplay's Chris Martin commented: 'My songs have nothing to do with war, they're all about the sad insecurities of a balding rock star' (*Guardian*, 17 March 2003), and part of the reason for this, he contends, is that a topic like export tariffs for developing countries does not easily translate into the subject for a song (*Today*, BBC Radio 4, 2 November 2005). Put another way, the explanation we give for why musicians write political songs need not be the same as the explanation that we give for their political participation; and equally, the fact that they write political songs does not tell us whether they will be interpreted politically.

What follows are a series of suggestions and ideas about how we might account for the political engagement of pop stars. They try to capture the different arguments that might help explain political involvement. My uncontroversial contention is that we need a multi-faceted account, one that is sensitive to both musical and political dimensions. To begin, though, it is important to re-iterate and develop a point already made: that pop's political engagement is less common than can sometimes appear.

Mapping political songs

There is a danger of exaggerating the degree of political engagement. The reaction to the Iraq war was, in many ways the exception, rather than rule (Weinstein, 2006). Nonetheless, Dorian Lynskey (2011) identifies over one thousand protest songs in the period since 1939. Even so, most pop stars are *not* engaged in politics. The same is true of the musical content that they produce. The period when punk was at its height (1976–8) might have been assumed to generate a wealth of political music. However, a survey conducted by Laing (1985: 27) of the debut albums of the top five punk groups released in 1976–7, found that a mere 25 per cent of the songs had any direct social and political comment. This is the same proportion that were about 'first person feelings', and only slightly more than those that were about 'romantic and sexual relationships' (21 per cent). While such statistics compared favourably with the content of the Top 50 at the same time (60 per cent were about sex and romance; 18 per cent about music and dancing), we might conclude that (a) punk was not as politically obsessed as it is sometimes portrayed; and (b) that mainstream pop is not typically about politics.

Looking through a list of UK Number 1 records from 1952–2001 (see www.britishhitsingles.com), it is striking to see how few had any explicit political content. Were charity records (such as Band Aid's 'Do they know it's Christmas?') to be included as political songs, then the number would increase marginally. Typically, the politics comes in the form of social comment – songs like the Specials' 'Ghost Town' (1981). Protest is largely confined to Pink Floyd's 'Another Brick in the Wall' (1979). The year of Woodstock (1969) is an exception. It echoed to the sound of several explicitly political hits: 'The Ballad of John and Yoko', 'Something in the Air' (Thunderclap Newman), 'Bad Mood Rising' (Creedence Clearwater Revival). Two 1983 hits voiced anti-war sentiments: Frankie Goes to Hollywood's 'Two Tribes' and Nena's '99 Red Balloons'. Bands with a reputation for being 'political' have had number one records (e.g. The Jam, the Specials, Manic Street Preachers and U2), but it has been rare, though, for their hits to have been their most political songs. A crude generalization might be that the more explicitly political the song, the lower the chart placing. This was the case for Public Enemy, the Clash and Bob Marley. The simple truth seems to be that, for the period until 2001, explicit political content was rare in mainstream pop, a point Dave Harker (1992) made when he noted that the soundtrack of *The Sound of Music* dominated the album charts in the era of political radicalism, the 1960s. In a similar vein, Richard Cole (1971: 390) noted that his laborious exercises in content analysis had found that 'love' was the predominant theme in popular song, and that the only variation was to be found in the form and character of courtship and love. Other topics hardly got a look in.

It might be that the period since 2001 has seen a glorious flourishing of political pop. Certainly, there has been much discussion of how, after 9/11 (Ritter and Daughtry, 2007), music has changed. And of course, the use of sites like MySpace to distribute music has increased the possibility of making political pop. But if our focus is on political music that finds an audience, then relatively little has changed.

In mentioning events like 9/11, we touch upon the most familiar explanation for why political music is made: that it is a response to 'reality', and to the way the world is (or should be) changing. Reflecting on John

Lennon's alliance with the far left in the late 1960s, Tariq Ali (1987: 252) wrote: 'It was the period that politicized John Lennon.'

The tunes they are a'changing

There is, after all, a particular plausibility to this claim which has to do with the relatively low costs of entry to music, at least when compared to film and television. This makes it conceivable, at least, that music is well adapted to reflecting or responding to reality, and that certain styles of music-making are disposed to take advantage of this potential. Gordon Friesen, one of the founders of *Broadside*, the publisher of the early protest songs of Bob Dylan and Phil Ochs, makes just such an argument: 'The question was frequently asked as to why so many *Broadside* writers concerned themselves with topics like wars; why didn't they write more often about love, flowers, winds upon the hills? Well, the magazine did print such songs. But topical-song writers, as distinct from other creators of music (which is often commercialized escapism), have always tended to deal with reality' (quoted in Cohen, 2000: 15). Friesen's suggestion is a straightforward one: music, especially folk music, chronicles contemporary reality. It is a form of news reporting, and folk musicians are a form of journalist or political commentator.

This same thought is reflected in histories of rock music, in which the assumption is that music reflects its times: 'Because popular music always interacts with its social environment,' writes Reebee Garofalo (1997: 14–15), 'it often serves as a lightning rod for the political controversies that invariably accompany change. . . . popular music has been connected quite explicitly with social change and political controversy'. The music becomes a filter through which change is mapped and expressed, and its politics is a product of that change. Here is Garofalo (1997: 184) again, this time writing about the rise of the civil rights movement in the 1960s: 'it is possible to analyse the impact of the movement on national consciousness by charting the trajectory of popular music during the period'. In a similar vein, Paul Friedlander (1996: 14) argues that rock's turn to humanitarian causes (Live Aid etc.) was a product of 'a Western political environment dominated by Thatcher-Reagan conservatism'. Explaining the Stones' adoption of a political stance in an earlier era, Friedlander (1996: 113) writes: 'Students took to the streets on the continent, and Mick and Keith spent time in America, enveloped as it was by the political and cultural maelstrom . . . These experiences seeped into their new material.' Punk's engagement with anti-racism is seen as a direct product of the rise of racist politics (Friedlander, 1996: 257). Mark Anthony Neal (1999: 28) applies this argument to an entire musical tradition: 'As the political terrain for blacks began to change after the Brown vs the Board of Education of Topeka, Kansas trial in 1954, so did the style and content of the dominant forms of black popular music.' In short, the argument is that music's politics is primarily a product of its political context, that in some way or another political change produces songs that reflect, and reflect upon, their times. Lynskey's (2011) vast chronicle of the protest song draws heavily on this idea. 'Before Motown came around to reflecting the rage of black America,' he writes (2011: 183), 'the rage of black America came to Motown.'

The problem with such accounts is that coincidence may be mistaken for causation. According to Lynskey (2011: 493), Jerry Dammers was not aware of who Nelson Mandela was as he [Dammers] began to write his most famous political song, 'Free Nelson Mandela'. While it is possible to correlate the rise and fall of political pop with social and political change, this connection depends on, first, highlighting the political pop, at the expense of other types of pop. It ignores all those songs that are not 'political' or not 'political' in an explicit way. In other words, it takes a very partial view of the available data. It then supposes some kind of causal connection between the times and the sounds. There is little attempt to provide the theoretical or empirical base for the connection. But what would such a connection look like? Is it possible to link social and political change to the emergence of specific sets of sounds?

My scepticism stems in part from a fascinating study by Stanley Lieberson (2000), who investigates patterns in the choices that parents make in naming their children. We might suppose that fashions in names reflect change in the wider world, just as others suppose that the production of political songs reflects changes in the political realm. It is this assumption that Lieberson tests. He (2000: 273) asks whether the changing taste in names can indeed be explained extrinsically – do 'cultural events reflect the social order'? He looks for patterns in the choice of names that might coincide with equivalent changes in the world outside. Put simply, does the naming of children follow the fame of film or sports stars? Are there more Marilyns after Marilyn Monroe, or Jennifers after Jennifer Lopez? Lieberson's conclusion is that such patterns are much rarer than might be supposed. 'Although broad social developments do affect fashion and taste,' he writes (2000: 273), 'their influence is neither as common nor as overwhelming as . . . commentators would have us believe'. His conclusion is that the extrinsic account rests upon very weak evidence (2000: 274). Instead, Lieberson contends that 'internal mechanisms' are more often the source of change. Changes in the fashion for names are part of an intrinsic, rather than extrinsic, process.

And although naming babies and writing songs are obviously very different phenomena, it may be that we can learn something from Lieberson. It might be that political music emerges, not because of changes in the wider world, but because of the internal dynamic of the music industry. An example of this can be found in Michael Haralambos's (1974) account of the decline of the blues. In direct contrast to the claim that the blues was a product of material conditions – decline, depression and unemployment – Haralambos argues that, in fact, economic circumstances do not provide an explanation. The blues *declined* even as unemployment among African-Americans *increased*. What we might conclude from this is that, whatever the connection between social conditions and musical form, it is much more complex than has traditionally been allowed for.

Becoming political: a biographical approach

An alternative approach is to focus less on the general patterns of cultural and social change, and to concentrate instead upon the individuals. This, at least, has the advantage of not assuming grand cultural-political shifts. Biographies of the politically active musician tell the story of their engagement in terms of personal values and commitments. Music is a product of what the performer sees and thinks. Lynskey (2011: 205) relates how Neil Young wrote 'Ohio' immediately after seeing the shootings at Kent State University on television. Jon Wiener (1984: 52–3) describes how John Lennon's 'political interests continued to develop' during the time he was meditating with the Maharishi; how his awareness of sexual politics was learned from Yoko. The writing of 'Revolution' for the 'White Album', according to Wiener (1984: 61), 'marked John's decision that he had political responsibilities, and that he ought to fulfill them in his music'. Lennon's observation of, and involvement in, political change, the argument runs, transformed his music. Lennon's political music was an extension of his personal history. In a similar way, Dave Marsh (1987) maps Bruce Springsteen's political engagement by tracing the star's involvement with community initiatives. Marsh (1987: 271) explains it in terms of the information Springsteen received from the workers he met: these encounters were 'integrated into the bedrock of his performances'. Joan Jara (1983) echoes this narrative of personal enlightenment and awareness in the biography of her husband, the radical Chilean singer Victor Jara, who was murdered in 1973 by the Pinochet regime. She writes of his growing political consciousness, of family traditions and encounters with different forms of musical expression (much of Jara's formative years were spent in the theatre). All of these combined to account for his emergence as a singer of, what he chose to call 'revolutionary songs'. In a similar vein, Robert Cantwell (1996: 342–3) explains Joan Baez's political commitments by reference to her family background.

Such explanations do not just apply to those in the folk tradition. Colin Chambers (2006) locates Paul Robeson's politics in his personal experiences. Gerald Meyer (2002: 312) explains Frank Sinatra's politics by reference to his family background and life experiences: 'The political part of Sinatra's life – activities, associations and avowed beliefs – grew out of his early experiences and reverberated throughout his life, in ways large and small.' Sinatra himself attributed his politics to his mother's own political commitments (Meyer, 2002: 314). And so on. The artists' politics are a consequence of their personal experiences.

There is obviously an intuitive appeal to connecting the personal and the political to the content and character of the music. How else would we account for Neil Young's 'Ohio' or Steve Earle's 'John Walker's Blues', about the US citizen who joined the Taliban? The danger, though, lies in generalizing from such examples. Not every political event generates its own songs, and not every musician feels obliged to respond to the ways of the world. 'Regardless of his commitment to human rights and racial equality,' writes Keith Negus (2008: 34), 'Dylan had no desire to be part of a left political agenda and no wish to be treated as a public spokesman, even less a prophet.' Dylan's behaviour warns against neat and simple stories of cause and effect. We need to distinguish between the politics of the individual and their persona *as a musician*. Biographical narrative accounts look back from the knowledge of the politicized artists, and find elements in their lives that 'explain' that politicization. But such explanations fail to account for those who eschewed politics, while still encountering the same or similar life experiences, or why some political events inspired no one. Biography may be revealing, but there is no guarantee that it holds the key to political music.

The limits of the biographical approach are highlighted by Robin Kelley (1997) in his general critique of accounts of cultural history that rely too heavily upon social change for their narrative. African-American cultural history, he argues, too often treats music (and other cultural forms) as a direct response to ghetto conditions, and in doing so eliminates the creativity and pleasure that are inextricably bound up with cultural experience, indeed without which that experience would not exist. Kelley (1997: 19) contends that culture is not a 'set of coping mechanisms that grew out of the struggle for material and psychic survival', and hence it is not appropriate to 'reduce expressive culture to a political text to be read like a less sophisticated version of *The Nation* or *Radical America*' (Kelley, 1997: 37). His claim is not that the music is autonomous, untouched by its context, but that in placing it in its surroundings – and accounting for its politics – we need to acknowledge its specific characteristics *as music*, as a cultural form designed to entertain and move, not simply to document a changing world or to manage its cruelties.

Becoming political: an institutional approach

The corollary of this argument is that politics too needs to be treated, not as a form of general abstraction ('the winds of change'), but as constituted by a range of specific factors and forces, which have a particular impact on music and musicians. It is not just a matter of political events *inspiring* songs, but of political processes creating the conditions in which music can resonate with political thought and action. It is the latter aspect, the creation of the opportunity to engage politically, that underpins Michael Haralambos's (1974) history of the blues and soul. In a sense, Jim Crow laws were as much a part of the story as was the imaginative energy of the musicians. In the same way, Peter Wicke's (1992) account of the role played by musicians in the collapse of the Berlin Wall is as much about how the German Democratic Republic politicized music and created a platform from which the musicians could assume the guise of political leaders. Similar stories can be told of the way in which musicians engaged with politics in the Soviet Union and Eastern Europe more generally (Cushman, 1995; Sheeran, 2001; Szemere, 2001). The organization of the regime established the possibilities for political music. The fact that this was explicit, or at least more obvious, in authoritarian regimes does not mean that it was absent in liberal ones.

Just as the state is a key actor in authoritarian political structures, so political parties and social movements can be important agencies in connecting music to politics within liberal democratic regimes. Take, for example, the rise and revival of political folk music in the 1950s and 1960s. Rather than seeing this as a straightforward consequence of global political change (the Cold War, nuclear deterrence, etc.) or personal biography, writers such as Robert Cantwell (1996) and Michael Denning (1997) focus on the impact of specific entities like the Popular Front alliance of the centre and left in the US (and Europe) in the 1930s. The Progressive Party was intimately linked with People's Songs (Cantwell, 1996: 165), just as the Popular Front was instrumental in the framing of Sinatra's politics (Meyer, 2002). In the UK, Topic Records (2009) were intimately connected with the Communist Party of Great Britain. The political movements and parties acted, in the language of political science, to frame politics and to act as 'political entrepreneurs' – equivalent to rock entrepreneurs like Bill Graham or Harvey Goldsmith – in the way they created a bridge between cultural and political activism. Each fed off the other. The Campaign for Nuclear Disarmament (CND) and traditional jazz were linked like this in the UK in the 1950s (McKay, 2003); something similar occurred between the Socialist Workers Party and Rock Against Racism in the 1970s (Goodyer, 2009). These organizations and movements mediated the politicization of music, and the politicized music mediated the activism.

Ron Eyerman and Andrew Jamison (1998) make the most systematic case for this view. They argue that social movements create a context within which music can assume a political role. Musicians become political as a result of a political process that creates a particular opportunity structure. The musicians' political commitments are, as it were, called into being by the movements that need what the performers have to offer. In other words, while personal biography and history may have something to do with the politicization of musicians, so too do other political processes.

Becoming political: a political communications approach

The fact that musicians can perform as politicians is also a product of the way in which politics has been transformed. Think of the case of Bruce Springsteen, or the many other musicians who supported Barack Obama, in his bid for the US Presidency. The particular role of the artist as champion or advocate of political cause, their endorsement of candidates and campaigns, has much to do with the ways in which politics has been 'personalized'. Elections are increasingly about 'personality', and elections are organized around displays of personal style. At one level this explains why a politician like Tony Blair chooses to pose with a Fender Stratocaster or Bill Clinton with a saxophone; at another, it explains why musicians, as experts in style, can easily transmute into politicians who represent political ideas and constituencies. Bono, Bob Geldof, Annie Lennox, Chris Martin and Michael Stipe are just a small sample of the set.

They are the product of the generic and technological conditions of mass media, especially television (Meyrowitz, 1985), and the larger changes in the form of political communication in the modern era (Mancini and Swanson, 1996). Individuals become the focus of politics. John Keane (2002) describes the contemporary order as one of 'communicative abundance' in which celebrities and stars assume the decisive function in representing contemporary identities and sensibilities (British tabloid newspapers regularly feature front pages whose sole concern is the activities of a soap-star or sportsperson). Colin Crouch (2004) describes the modern era as one of 'post-democracy', in which rituals of democracy, now devoid of any real substance, are turned into spectacles (like leadership debates), in which the performance conventions of showbusiness hold sway. Thomas Meyer (2002: 65) attributes this trend to the dominance of a 'media logic' that leads to 'politainment', and to a world in which figures like Bono and Bob Geldof speak for 'us'. Meyer (2002: 79), who is no fan of this process, writes: 'If democracy is nothing but legitimation by the most successful form of communication, then the communication artist is the best democrat, with no effort whatsoever. And if the authentic play of body politics is the most efficacious form of entertaining communication, then "brief-case politics" with its institutionalized procedures and long-winded arguments might as well bow out now.' In other words, the phenomenon of the politically engaged musician owes as much to transformations in the forms of communication as it does to the conscience and commitment of the stars. Musicians are not simply attracted to causes like moths to a flame.

Becoming political: a musical approach

But the story of how music and musicians engage with politics cannot end with these political conditions and narratives, even if these are where much of the political communications and social movement literature ends. We still need to explain what it is that music offers to political movements and organizations, and indeed how it is that music communicates political ideas. This thought is present – albeit in rather banal form – in the way in which parties and politicians select the music to accompany their rallies or their advertisements, but also in the fears that inspire acts of censorship. Music is not simply the end product of political processes. It too takes institutional form, bringing with it practical and generic features.

The entrepreneurial role played by a party or a social movement is itself dependent on the organizational form taken by music and networks which connect musicians and sustain their art form. One way to think of this is to consider the 'capital' that is traded in the alliance of music and politics.

We owe this perspective to Christian Lahusen (1996) who has documented in meticulous detail the ways in which pop musicians come to promote causes like Amnesty's Human Rights Now! tour of 1988. Lahusen identifies the many forms of 'capital' that make such moments possible. These extend from the basic economic capital necessary to put on concerts, through to the social capital that forges the links between cultural performers and political organizers (a matter of knowing Peter Gabriel's phone number or that of his manager). The argument here, as elsewhere, is that the political engagement of musicians is not simply a product of their personal commitments or their biographies, or indeed of their times, but of the networks that organize them into (or exclude them from) political activity. The elaborate negotiations between Tony Blair's Labour Party and the Britpop musicians who supported him (initially, at least) is another example of this phenomenon. John Harris (2003) recounts how the two factions circled each other, acting out a nervous courtship, tentatively testing the water and holding secret meetings, before announcing their engagement to the public.

A key player in this elaborate ritual was the music industry. Typically, the music industry is seen as the enemy of the politically engaged musician, like a protective parent doing their best to thwart what they see as an unsuitable marriage. We are familiar with stories of how the political content of popular music has been ruthlessly policed by commercial 'imperatives' (see Denisoff, 1975; Harker, 1980). We know that Paul Robeson, Frank Sinatra and Harry Belafonte suffered commercially because of their association with left-wing causes (Chambers, 2006: 26–35; Meyer, 2002: 324; Ward, 1998: 323). Although such processes are sometimes portrayed as crude forms of 'gate-keeping', others have argued that they are more the product of the complex interactions of large organizations (Negus, 1999). The outcome, it might be said, is the same: the 'right' to be political can be granted and taken away by the institutions which produce and regulate popular music. The treatment of the Dixie Chicks by Clear Channel in the US, and Madonna's decision to withdraw her video for 'American Life' because of its politically contentious, (anti-)war images, might suggest that insofar as the industry plays a significant part in creating the opportunity structure for political engagement, it does so to prevent such engagement (Hollywood.com, accessed 1 April 2010).

It is important, though, not just to see the industry as simply acting negatively to prevent political participation. Motown, for example, came to promote the political activism of performers like Marvin Gaye (Smith, 1999). Initially, the company had confined its support for black power politics to a subsidiary, and only gradually allowed its mainstream artists to make explicit their political concerns. There were sound business reasons for this move, just as there have been for rap's political content (Negus, 1999: 84). Rap's claim to be on (and about) 'the street' is a discursive device that enables the record industry to manage its forms of production. Rap's politics is partly conditional upon its production through independent labels, at one remove from the corporations that subsequently license or distribute the music, and partly a product of a marketing strategy built around the rhetoric of 'telling it like it is'. And as we shall see in the next chapter, Bono's involvement in a variety of political causes has been expedited and managed through the industry.

Becoming political: a genre approach

Contained in the industry's role as a mediator of political activism is the part played by genre, and the mechanisms that police it. Genre sets the conventions within which music operates, opening up or closing down its political possibilities. When the boy band Blue announced it was to set up a 'Live Aid 2' to support victims of the Iraq war, they were derided. Much the same happened to George Michael when he released a single, 'Shoot the Dog' (2002), that satirized the Bush-Blair relationship, or when Geri Halliwell, the ex-Spice Girl, became one of the UN's Goodwill ambassadors (*The Times*, 24 October 2000; Sinclair, 2004: 189). Their claim to political authority was threatened by their perceived lack of artistic credibility. While the response may have been a product of crude sexism (in the case of Halliwell) and other media prejudices (in the case of Michael), it also highlighted a disjunction between the genre in which these musicians worked and the role they assumed or the topics they addressed. To this extent, genre mediated the possibility of political engagement, or at least its credibility and effectiveness.

There is a danger of turning genre into an iron cage that allows no leeway. In her analysis of rhythm and blues, Mary Ellison (1989: 1), for example, seems to suggest that a law of nature is at work: 'The coupling of black music with protest is a natural alliance.' But generic conventions help to explain the politics in music; they cannot, though, determine it. They establish norms that apply to lyrical content and other elements of musical expression. They rule out certain topics and modes, and rule in others. Thus it is that political content may be organized into or out of musical forms. Folk provides a home for political sentiments in ways that dance music does not; and those genres that accommodate politics may differ in the type of politics they sustain (Redhead and Street, 1989).

Nonetheless, genres are not absolute arbiters. The historian Brian Ward (1998: 303), for example, writes about the musicians who supported the civil rights movement in the 1960s: 'While it may appear heresy to some, the fact remains that in certain respects Joan Baez was more important and conspicuously committed to the early Movement than James Brown, while Harry Belafonte did more to assist the struggle for black freedom in practical terms than all the soul icons of the 1960s combined.' Not only does genre not determine political engagement, but the political form of a genre is itself a product of other factors – as we have seen with the mediating role played by entities like the Popular Front.

Being political

Until now, our focus has been upon how musicians become political, how their circumstances, biographies and genres, combined with the contribution of other actors, create the possibilities and incentives for political engagement. Little has been said so far, however, about what it means – as a musician – to be political. This is as much a matter of style as it is of principle and commitment. While we may know something about the hypocrisies of musicians – the environmentalist who flies by private jet, the socialist who exploits their household staff, the campaigner against poverty who becomes a tax exile – we are rarely in a position to be sure what exactly their principles are and what they do in pursuit of them. What we can do is to see and feel the way they enact their politics as performers.

Key to this is being taken seriously. While this 'seriousness' is constituted by media representations, and by the management of those representations, it can coalesce in the form of what John Kane (2001) calls 'moral capital'. He uses the term to identify a feature of certain individuals who, as a result, are able to command respect and authority. It is a form of charisma. Nelson Mandela is the paradigm case. In a questionnaire to leading British politicians, Mandela was the default answer to the question: 'which living person do you most admire?' (*Guardian Magazine*, 24 April 2010). Although Kane does not talk specifically about musicians, the idea of moral capital is useful in identifying a potential resource for performers who ally themselves with political causes. But if it helps to see artists as possessing moral capital, the question that is begged is how this moral capital is created. While part of the answer lies in the strategic media management of their image, another part lies in the way they perform the role of political activist in their creative life. This is a matter of style.

Style is key to performed politics. The study of popular music has paid woefully little attention to the business of creativity (for an exception, see Negus and Pickering, 2004), but it has spent even less time on the way it connects to political expression, to the link between creativity and conscience. Jason Toynbee (2000: 41–2), though, invokes the image of a 'radius of creativity' within which various creative possibilities exist, mediating between 'subjective experience and objective social relations.' Political music, by this account, emerges as a product of a particular combination of possibilities within the 'radius of creativity'. While it may be that only certain performers follow this route, for all the reasons we have discussed above, their pursuit of it makes them less exceptional than might at first appear. This is because, I want to suggest, they are engaged in the business of 'representation', and that this is necessarily both political and aesthetic in nature.

Traditional notions of political representation present it simply as a mechanism whereby the representative stands or acts for a community or interest (Birch, 1964; Pitkin, 1967). And the political musician might well describe themselves in these terms. But, of course, they are not subject to the same systems of scrutiny and accountability that apply to the conventional political representative. But even within the theory of political representation, there are those who argue that to confine it only within these formal mechanisms is to do a disservice to the idea. Political representation depends as much on the symbolic gestures as it does on institutions of accountability. Michael Saward (2006), for example, argues that the 'representative claim' can derive from many different bases and be legitimated in a variety of ways. It is conceivable, therefore, that a musician can also be a political representative.

This possibility emerges most strongly in Frank Ankersmit's (2002) account of the aesthetics of political representation. His argument is rooted in the observation, first, that political representation pre-dates democracy and, second, that it borrows its meaning from aesthetics, from the way works of art stand in relation to some notion of reality. Ankersmit (2002) starts with the two familiar, competing accounts of representation. The first is representation as resemblance; the second is representation as substitution. Ankersmit dismisses the 'resemblance' version on the grounds that it is incoherent to claim that marks on a canvas or words on a page 'resemble' the things to which they refer. They are 'substitutes'; they liter-

ally re-present objects or ideas. Furthermore, the suggestion that reality
can only exist within representational form is used to underpin Ankersmit's
claim that politics too can only exist in representational form. 'Without
political representation,' he (2002: 115) writes, 'we are without a conception of what reality – the represented – is like; without it, political reality
has neither face nor contours. Without representation there is no
represented . . .'

One of the implications of this argument, according to Ankersmit (2002:
116–7, his emphasis), is that 'the politician must possess the essentially
aesthetic talent of being able to represent political reality in new and original ways.' And this in turn leads to a discussion of the character and
importance of 'political style' (Ankersmit, 2002: 132ff). Style is the way in
which politicians and parties communicate their relationship to the electorate and to their future public goals. As Dick Pels (2003: 50) puts it: 'Political
style . . . enables citizens to regain their grip on a complex political reality
by restoring mundane political experience to the centre of democratic
practice.'

Ankersmit suggests that the question of whether a state or any other
agency represents its people is a matter of 'taste'. Representation, whatever
the principles or ethical values informing it, does not reflect the world so
much as organize knowledge about it. Just as art creates a version of reality,
making present what is otherwise absent, Ankersmit contends that political
power comes into existence via the act of representation. It is a product
of style and creativity: 'When asking him or herself how best to represent
the represented, the representative should ask what political style would
best suit the electorate. And this question really requires an essentially
creative answer on the part of the representative, in the sense that there
exists no style in the electorate that is quietly waiting to be copied'
(Ankersmit, 1996: 54). Although such arguments have typically been
applied to fascism, especially that of Mussolini's Italy (see Falasca-Zamponi,
1997), it can also be applied to liberal democracies (see Corner and Pels,
2003; Cheles and Sponza, 2001; and Meyer, 2002).

Ankersmit allows us to see the relationship of performer and audience
in explicitly political terms, but without the sacrifice of its aesthetic dimension. The 'radius of creativity' within which the musician works involves
both political and aesthetics possibilities. They perform 'representative-
ness'. It does not follow that all attempts are successful or that the politics
is coherent or consistent with any given set of principles. What it does
suggest is that in linking music and politics we need to focus, not just
on the mediating political processes, but also on the aesthetic ones. It is

the combination of these two that allows us to understand what is implicated in music's engagement with politics, and crucially how, in making this connection, it also involves the audience.

Fans and citizens

The representative claim is that the musicians are, in some sense, 'in touch' with both those who follow them and the world that they inhabit. This is what lies behind Blair's desire to reach the fans of Duran Duran and Madonna. It is a claim about fandom. John Thompson (1995: 220–5) has argued that being a 'fan' is an important, even defining, characteristic of modernity; it entails formation of relations of 'intimacy with distant others'. As one of Bruce Springsteen's fans once said: 'I think it's good that, say, someone in his position, or anyone in that position, when they write a line on a piece of paper, millions of people get to hear it, as opposed to when I write something only I get to hear it' (quoted in Cavicchi, 1998: 118). But to claim representation involves more than the creation of a community; it implies action too. This is evoked in Nick Hornby's portrait of his life as a fan of Arsenal football club. Writing of a championship victory, he says (2000: 179):

> The joy we feel on occasions like this is not a celebration of others' good fortune, but our own . . . The players are merely our representatives, chosen by the manager rather than elected by us, but our representatives nonetheless, and sometimes if you look hard you can see the little poles that join them together, and the handles at the side that enable us to move them.

This representational relationship is established by the affective capacity of the cultural performance. Indeed, Lawrence Grossberg (1992: 86) suggests that this very capacity is intrinsically political in that it can generate a sense of 'empowerment' that makes possible 'the optimism, invigoration and passion which are necessary for any struggle to change the world'. Liesbet van Zoonen (2004: 49) too draws this affective connection between fandom and politics when she argues that 'fan communities and political constituencies bear crucial similarities'. But 'fandom' or cultural consumption do not of themselves establish a claim to represent politically. Research conducted by David Jackson (2005 and 2007) has revealed that young people can change their political sympathies in accordance with the views of musicians, but that this effect is not evenly distributed. It turns out that, for Canadian youth, Avril Lavigne is more persuasive than Alanis Morissette.

Conclusion

This chapter began with questions about how and when musicians engage with politics. It has encountered a variety of perspectives and arguments, and it has suggested that any adequate account needs to move beyond a concern with personal conscience and political circumstance. It has to look at the political and musical institutions that mediate the link, the genres that articulate it, and the distribution of capital that makes it possible. The capacity to 'represent' is, as this chapter has tried to show, the product of a complex chain and set of contingencies. Many factors shape the affective bond that underpins representative claims, including the aesthetics of the performance and the organized commercial interests. In certain contexts and under particular conditions, performers can lay claim to represent those who admire them. They give political voice to those who follow them, both by virtue of the political conditions and by means of their art. And as Ankersmit claims for traditional forms of representation, this is not a matter of mimetics but of aesthetics, of creatively constituting a political community and representing it. It begins with the political sentiments and political sounds, but the route is a long and winding one. Representation is only the start. To represent is one thing, to engage quite another. The next two chapters explore in detail the implications of these arguments by considering the cases of Live 8 and Rock Against Racism.

4

All together now: music as political participation

On 2 July 2005, several hundred thousand people took part in mass political action. In the era of the new social movement, there was nothing unusual in this. Except that the instigators of this event were many of the western world's most famous pop musicians (including Bono, Bob Geldof, Alicia Keys, Jay-Z, Madonna, Pink Floyd, Paul McCartney, Stevie Wonder and Elton John) and the political participation involved little more than watching a series of performances. The occasion was Live 8, the culmination of the campaign to 'Make Poverty History', and an event that Bob Geldof said marked the moment 'when the boys and girls with guitars finally get to tilt the world on its axis' (quoted in the *Daily Telegraph*, 4 June 2005).

Political action of this kind hardly bears comparison with drudging through city streets, carrying a banner, chanting slogans, and listening to speeches. It certainly is not equivalent to confronting water cannons or strapping yourself to a tree as the bulldozers move in. Nonetheless, Live 8 was represented and reported as an example of mass political participation, directed at changing the minds and actions of the G8 leaders. The front page of the London *Times* read: 'Rock stars' plea to G8 – don't fail world poor' (*The Times*, 2 July 2005). It was a headline that suggested that the rock stars should be taken seriously, and that the G8 leaders should take note.

A few days after the concerts and after the meeting of the G8 leaders, Bob Geldof announced, 'A great justice has been done. . . . Mission accomplished frankly' (quoted in *Guardian*, 12 September 2005). According to Geldof, Live 8 had succeeded in its aim; it had prompted a major political change on the part of the world's most powerful nations. Nothing, of course, is this simple, but Live 8 does raise interesting and important questions about how and whether music can organize a form of political participation. This involves more than musicians acting as 'representatives', speaking about the world and its peoples; it entails the thought that the combination of musician and music can mobilize a movement and cause change. The immediate task is to ask what it would mean for music and musicians to create the conditions for political participation.

From participation to partying?

Traditionally, political participation has been taken to involve writing to elected representatives, 'working in a group to raise a local problem, going on a protest march or canvassing for a political party' (Parry et al., 1992: 3). It requires more than voting, but not a great deal more, and is 'directed towards persons who are in authority, and able to influence decisions' (ibid.: 7). This relatively narrow definition is intended to incorporate 'the more regular day to day patterns of citizen political activity' (ibid.: 3). Politics is distinguished from other areas of life – family, leisure and work (ibid.: 8). It is a definition that would seem to exclude Live 8, at least insofar as it is portrayed as providing entertainment, but from another perspective it could be seen as a protest 'directed towards persons who are in author- ity', if, that is, we regard Live 8 as a 'protest' by those who gathered to watch the performers. Would it be right to describe those who watched it on television at home as 'protestors'?

But while Live 8 can be shoe-horned into a conventional definition of participation, it falls at the next stage when attention turns to the 'impulse' to participate. Geraint Parry and his colleagues, who produced one of the major surveys of political participation in the UK, distinguish between three modes of participation: instrumentalist, communitarian and expres- sive. Where the first two are linked directly to the perceived interests of the participants and their 'community', the last is defined as participation intended to 'express' the participants' 'feelings or display their stance about a matter' (ibid.: 15). Such a definition would also appear to allow for events like Live 8, since it would seem to constitute a prime example of public expression of feelings about debt relief and global justice. However, while such expressive activity may constitute a form of political participation, Parry and his team exclude 'the most symbolic of activities' because they broaden the definition of participation 'too widely' (ibid.: 16). They justify this exclusion on the grounds that, first, their adopted survey method does not allow them to capture expressive participation, and that, secondly, such participation is 'less relevant to policy formation' (ibid.). Parry and his col- leagues see participation more narrowly as 'taking part in the processes of formulation, passage and implementation of public policies'. They insist that participation must entail 'a form of action', and so it is not enough 'to show an interest in politics or to talk about it to members of the family' (ibid.). Such a move would seem to push Live 8 to the very margins of political participation.

One response might simply be to redraw the definition of participation to include the expressive and the passive dimensions, and thereby to bring Live 8 and its audience back in. This is tempting, but such a move may raise as many problems as it solves. If we treat Live 8 as an instance of political participation, should we also regard Live Aid as one? The difference is, of course, that Live Aid was about raising money for a humanitarian cause (the famine in Ethiopia), while Live 8 announced itself as being about 'justice, not charity'. Live Aid was not directed at government or global policy; Live 8 was. And if we concede that Live 8 had an explicitly political agenda, we have to return to the question as to who were its participants – the performers? Does it include just the fans at the concerts or the ones who sat at home watching it on television? Does it include the 27 million people who 'signed up' to Make Poverty History by sending a text message or those who wore the white bands? To take another tack: if we are going to recognize the possibility that leisure activities – listening to music at home – can constitute a form of political participation, then does it matter if the music is by Bono, Billy Bragg or Joan Baez, or by James Blunt or the cast of *Glee*?

Such questions are not as trivial as they may first appear. They raise the very real issue of how and when we identify an act of political participation, and whether the performance of music might be included. What is evident is that traditional definitions of political participation, and the research methods associated with them, will tend to neglect or under-represent participation of the Live 8 kind.

Music as talk (and as participation)

Conventional definitions of participation, as we have seen, view it as a form of *physical action*, as taking part in activities that have as their direct intention (if not consequence) the changing of public policy. There is, though, an alternative approach. This involves a broader definition of participation, in which both formal and non-formal governmental realms are included, and in which 'political non-participation', like the boycotting of certain consumer goods, counts (Hay, 2007: 74). This definition includes in its understanding of political participation ordinary, everyday 'conversations' – the ones that take place 'in a bar, pub, coffee shop or whilst loading the dishwasher', but which express 'exasperation, frustration, irritation or, indeed, approval directed at formal political processes' (Hay, 2007: 75). Including such areas and acts might seem to broaden the definition too far, but as Colin Hay argues (2007: 77), this is not necessarily so: it shifts the definition of politics to its 'content', rather than its arena, and that content has to include 'genuine collective or social choice'. It is not just any 'conversation' that becomes political, only those 'directed at formal political processes'.

Hay opens up the possibility that participation in Live 8, in a variety of guises (as performer, concert goer, or television viewer), can qualify as political participation. He does not insist that it must be seen like this. And indeed if it is, we need first to consider how music belongs with the other kinds of conversation he imagines. Among the many conversations that Live 8 provoked, some were clearly not political (the ones about the presenter Jonathan Ross's dress sense), but others were (the ones about the absence of African musicians on the stage in Hyde Park). By introducing conversation into the category of political participation, Hay is expanding the form the latter takes, while retaining a sense of politics as public and collective. The question we face is whether this revised version of political participation allows a place for music.

In fact, Jürgen Habermas, who is often seen as the architect of this deliberative approach to politics, gives more prominence to the place of music in the public sphere than is often acknowledged. Many are familiar with Habermas's claim – echoed by Hay – that the public sphere represents that space in which 'private people come together as a public' and as such challenge 'the general rules governing relations in the basically privatized but publicly relevant sphere of commodity exchange and social labor' (Habermas, 1992: 27). We are also familiar with the conditions that are necessary to the maintenance of such talk (Habermas, 1992: 32ff), conditions in which, in her discussion of counterpublics, Nancy Fraser (1992: 123) includes 'journals, bookstores, publishing companies, film and video distribution networks, lecture series, research centers, academic programs, conferences, conventions, festivals, and local meeting places.' But not, apparently, music.

Habermas does, however, find a special place for music. The public sphere is not constituted simply by literary debate and deliberation about politics, but by engagement with fine art and music. For Habermas (1992: 39), a condition of the public sphere is the separation – via the cash nexus – of art and culture from dominant religious and political structures: 'Admission for payment turned the musical performance into a commodity . . . For the first time an audience gathered to listen to music as such

– a public of music lovers, to which anyone who was propertied and educated was invited.' As art and culture circulate within a market economy, they assume meanings that are not confined to their place in some pre-designated order. Accompanying this separation is the emergence of the cultural critic (and the associated media) to give voice to these meanings, and to a public authorized to make judgements – public taste – in its own right (Habermas, 1992: 40–3). Music was implicated in this process of democratization through the space it created and the discussion it provoked. Until the end of the eighteenth century, music had 'served to enhance the sanctity and dignity of worship, the glamor of the festivities at court, and the overall splendor of ceremony' (Habermas, 1992: 39). Musicians worked to commission and served their patrons. This changed with the emergence of public concert societies. Accompanying this change was the enhancement of the status of musicians, and hence their place in public discourse (Blanning, 2008).

In summary, Habermas makes music part of a system of political participation in which talk is key, and which allows us to see the possibility at least that Live 8 might constitute a version of that participation. But how do we give substance to such thoughts?

Music and movement

The literature on the role of music and musicians in public action has grown greatly in recent years. Some of it has been inspired by the experience of the former Soviet bloc, where music and musicians were involved in expressing opposition to the regime and even in organizing resistance to it (Cushman, 1995; Ramet, 1994; Sheeran, 2001; Steinberg, 2004; Szemere, 2001; Urban, 2004; Wicke, 1992). Music was not just (or even) a source of information or of polemic; it formed the infrastructure of political action. Playing and listening to music took on the guise of 'political resistance' (Peddie, 2006). More than this: the cultures formed around music constituted a kind of political participation. Having music perform these roles is not exclusive to authoritarian states. It is apparent in histories of the civil rights movement and the post-war popular left in the US (Denning, 1997; Denisoff, 1971; Saul, 2003; Ward, 1998), and the Campaign for Nuclear Disarmament and Rock Against Racism in the UK (Goodyer, 2009; McKay, 2005).

Buried within these various accounts of music in political movements, whether in the West or East, are assumptions about how exactly music performs the role ascribed to it – and indeed what that role actually entails.

One approach treats music as an expression of political causes and movements. The music is seen to embody particular sentiments, typically, but not exclusively, contained in the lyrics. These are deemed to coincide with the political goals of the participants. Music constitutes a primary source: a way 'seeing' into the inner life of political participants. So, Brian Ward (1998: 6) explains, in his study of music's relationship to the civil rights movement in the US, that the music 'offers a glimpse into the state of black consciousness and the struggle for freedom and equality' at a given moment. The alternative approach is to present music as the *cause* of political participation. Sabrina Petra Ramet (1994: 1), for instance, opens her edited collection on music in the Soviet bloc with the claim that music is 'an unexpectedly powerful force for social and political change'. She goes on: 'Music brings people together and evokes for them collective emotional experience to which common meanings are assigned.' But although both approaches generate a wealth of material on music's presence within social movements, the underlying assumptions are rarely stated explicitly, theorized in detail or tested empirically. There have, however, been some attempts to provide a more systematic account of how music – as organized sound – prompts (or contributes to) political participation.

In *Acting in Concert*, for example, Mark Mattern (1998) distinguishes between different types of political action, arguing that music's role varies according to which is involved. He identifies three variants: deliberative, pragmatic and confrontational. Each posits a different relationship between music and action, and indeed a different role for music, but the key determinant is the political context. The latter he defines according to the relationship between the contending parties. Where confrontation refers to a situation of stark opposition, pragmatism refers to one in which the participants simply pursue their immediate interests, and deliberation to one where an attempt is being made to realize a common identity. Mattern argues, taking case studies of each type of political context, that music is used differently, depending on the character of the conflict. This approach is valuable in that it avoids sweeping generalizations about music's role, and it forces us to think about the political context. But in putting the emphasis on context, Mattern presents music as a conventional 'form of communication', in which what it communicates is determined by the structure of the political conflict, rather than by the particular character of the sound itself. 'Music reveals', he writes (1998: 15), 'constituent elements such as beliefs, assumptions, and commitments that define the character and shape of the community.' In other words, music is primarily a cipher for existing relations, rather than playing a direct part in them. Mattern presents music as a message, inscribed in the lyrics of the songs. Thus, although Mattern seeks to theorize music's place within political action, he does so in such a way as to reduce its role to that of functionary in the political cause. It serves to communicate or convey what the political context requires. His concluding sentences read: 'Music is a communicative arena in which various political actors can pursue multiple, often contradictory, agendas in which there are no guarantees of a positive democratic outcome. It is one political terrain among many' (ibid.: 146). Music here is viewed in primarily instrumental terms, as a means to a pre-determined end.

Other writers concerned with music's role in political participation are prepared to accord it a more active, expressive role. Ron Eyerman and Andrew Jamison (1998), for example, echo Mattern in their reference to the political context and to music's capacity to act as a form of political communication. They differ from Mattern to the extent that they invest music with more than the ability to convey messages. They describe music as 'a kind of cognitive practice' (Eyerman and Jamison, 1998: 7). So where Mattern sees music as expressing the political realities of particular conflicts, Eyerman and Jamison view music as contributing to the constitution of those realities and to providing a resource by which the logic of collective action (to *not act*) can be challenged. But while music is allocated a special role by Eyerman and Jamison, it remains subservient to the wider political context. It is the social movement that gives meaning to cultural expression, and music becomes one of 'the resources of culture' that contributes to 'the action repertoires of political struggle' (ibid.: 7).

While Eyerman and Jamison see music as a vehicle for the collective memories that underpin social movements, and musicians as 'truth bearers' to the causes that are fought (ibid.: 21–4), it is never quite clear how music and musicians perform these roles. Or put another way: the role is understood in retrospect only; music is important because music *was* important. Little or no attempt is made to establish how music embodies collective memory or when musicians become truth bearers. Why was it Bob Dylan or Phil Ochs, but not any of the other, now forgotten performers, who are seen as decisive in the story that Eyerman and Jamison tell? Such a question requires closer scrutiny of the way in which music works *as music*. For both Mattern and Eyerman and Jamison, their primary concern is with the social movements, and with the explanatory problems they pose. Music is a necessary, but secondary consideration, and hence they develop only a weak link between sound and social action. Music becomes just another form of political communication.

There are writers who have tried to identify music's specific contribution to political participation. They are typically those who begin with the music.

Thomas Turino (2008) is one such exception. It is through music, argues Turino (2008: 2), 'together with other public expressive cultural practices . . . that people articulate the collective identities that are fundamental to forming and maintaining social groups.' He is dismissive of the idea that other forms of communication can fulfil this function, in part because of the range of feelings and experiences that music is peculiarly adept at conveying and because of music's (and the arts more generally) ability to imagine new realities (ibid.: 15–18). Where Mattern has a political typology, Turino has a musical one. He distinguishes between 'presentational' and 'participatory' music. They are differentiated by the way in which musicians and audience relate to each other on a number of dimensions. The participatory performance entails 'no artist-audience distinctions', whereas in presentational performances the roles are clearly distinguished. In the latter the artist performs *for* the audience; in the former they perform *with* them, and in so doing forge new social relations (ibid.: 35). Turino's approach seems to yield an account of music's specific contribution to action, at least in the case of participatory performances.

The problem with Turino's approach, however, is that while he draws our attention to the politics of musical performance, he does not show how these politics connect to those on the street. Or more accurately: he does not make the connection very persuasively. Towards the end of his book, he turns his attention to the role of music in Nazism and in the civil rights movement. He characterizes the Nazis's cultural policy as exploiting music's participatory potential. Massed singing in particular, he argues, served to inculcate a sense of unity around the Nazi programme and to eliminate individual self-doubt, and to bolster collective courage in the case of the civil rights movement (ibid.: 210 and 215). This is important in that it attributes power to the music itself, but in doing so it eliminates the context. The music provides essentially the same resources to each movement. Turino's useful distinction between presentational and participatory music moves us closer to appreciating the particular function played by music in social movements, but at the loss of their distinctive politics. So, it would seem, that those whose focus is on the social movement have little to say about music, and those whose focus is on the music underplay the politics.

Music as action as participation

There is, however, a possible escape from this state of affairs. It follows Turino in that it places the emphasis on the music, or at least gives it equal weight, but it diverts from him in that it places this emphasis on music's specific political contribution. Where Turino's approach allows participatory music to serve fascism and civil rights, this alternative approach connects music directly to one particular political outcome: social democracy.

Before *Bowling Alone*, the book by which he is most commonly known, Robert Putnam wrote *Making Democracy Work*. In this earlier project, Putnam asked why some regions of Italy developed strong democratic traditions, where others did not. Many factors account for the variations, but key to Putnam's explanation is the presence (or absence) of trust. It is trust that underpins the reciprocity and cooperation upon which self-government depends. Variations in levels of trust, according to Putnam, are connected to the existence (or absence) of 'civic associations'; it is these that form the bedrock of relations of trust and good government: 'the more civic a region, the more effective its government' and the more egalitarian its society (Putnam, 1993: 97).

These civic associations can take many forms. As Putnam (ibid.: 90) argues: 'taking part in a choral society or a bird-watching club can teach self-discipline and an appreciation for the joys of successful collaboration.' Although it is mentioned in conjunction with bird-watching in this quotation, music features prominently in Putnam's account of 'civic-ness' – local bands and choral societies are a key measure of the level of trust in a community (ibid.: 97 and 115). Furthermore, Putnam is quite clear that the connection runs in a particular direction. It is not good government that produces civic associations; it is the other way around; it is the civic associations that produce the good government. The same is true for economic well-being: 'economics does not predict civics, but civics does predict economics' (ibid.: 167).

This theme reappears in his subsequent book, *Bowling Alone*, where the focus is on 'social capital' rather than 'civic associations', although the two perform very similar functions. They both help to sustain political engagement. For example, Putnam (2000: 405) notes that participation in high school music groups correlates with civic engagement in later life. But Putnam says relatively little about why music has the effects that he attributes to it, until, that is, the end of book, when he is looking for solutions to the civic malaise he sees befalling the US. Then he begins to speculate that '[s]inging together does not require shared ideology or shared social or ethnic provenance', and hence is capable of constituting a sense of community that would otherwise not exist (Putnam, 2000: 411). On this basis, he argues for more 'songfests' and 'rap festivals' as a way of generating social capital.

Putnam's proposals may be lightly sketched and speculative, but they are not without foundation. In nineteenth-century Germany, choral and music societies fed directly into the political life of the country (Blanning, 2008: 283). More than a hundred years later, Ruth Finnegan observed how the musical life of an English town provided a means to creating and controlling the world inhabited by the performers. 'To be involved in musical practice', she has written (1989: 329; her emphasis), '*is* to be involved in social actions and relations – in society'. Chronicling the history of popular music in England, Dave Russell (1987: 222) has described the part played by music in social order and social relations: 'choirs and bands offered endless opportunities for basic sociability, and sometimes more.' This 'more' could take the form of rebelling against the social order. In his account of working-class intellectual life, Jonathan Rose (2010: 199) quotes one concert goer as saying in the early 1900s: 'After most recitals I came away with my head in a whirl, and my emotions and feelings in a state of tumultuous rebellion.'

The idea that music is important to the development of civic and political attitudes continues to circulate, and even to be enshrined in public policy. In the UK, the Music Manifesto's 'Sing Up' initiative (see chapter 2) is an inheritor of these earlier ideas. They are present too in the introduction of *El Sistema*, the Venezuelan initiative to tie musical performance to social engagement, into schools and communities in England. But while these examples take us closer to the idea that music provides for a form of social engagement, we remain some way from a full understanding of how an event like Live 8 works and how, more generally, music enables political engagement. While music is capable of linking people socially and politically, it does not mean that every instance of musical performance works in this way or has the same effects. Music's capacity to enable engagement is contingent on other factors. It is these to which we turn now.

Orchestrating engagement: organization, legitimation and performance

In research that I conducted with colleagues at the University of East Anglia (Hague et al., 2008; Street et al., 2008) we identified at least three elements to the construction of music's capacity to engage. We labelled these 'organization', 'legitimation' and 'performing participation'. Our argument was straightforward. For musicians to persuade others that the cause they represent is worth following, they have to be regarded as credible or authoritative voices. They have to be deemed legitimate representatives. Secondly, there have to be processes – forms of organization – that enable musicians and political actors to work together. The discrete worlds of music and political activism have, in some way, to be linked. And finally, there has to be some means by which the music not only conveys the message or sentiment of the movement or cause, but also motivates it.

Organization

Jürgen Habermas, Nancy Fraser and others have focused on the infrastructural conditions that make the public sphere possible. A similar approach is needed to account for the link between (particular forms of) music and (particular forms of) politics. The impression created by many of the stories told about music's link with politics, as we saw earlier, is that the two just 'happened' upon each other, or that they are drawn together by the 'spirit of the times'. While such narratives pay considerable attention to the political conditions and context, they do not typically include an equivalent account of the conditions and context of the music. As Christian Lahusen (1996) has pointed out, the conjunction of musicians and movements requires a variety of forms of capital, not least financial, but also social and cultural capital for the link to be forged. Live 8 cost £11 million to stage. In other words, in understanding music's role in participation, we need to appreciate the infrastructural arrangements that make it possible.

Legitimation

Just as Habermas focuses on the role of art critic in creating the conditions for deliberation within the public sphere, so Eyerman and Jamison fashion a similar role for musicians as 'truth bearers'. But where Habermas maps the emergence of the critic, attributing it to different institutional and market developments, Eyerman and Jamison say very little about how the musician acquires the authority to act as 'truth bearer'. The fact that they are 'popular' is not a sufficient condition of political credibility. There are many performers who are popular, but whose political views are either not sought or not taken seriously. (*The Spectator* magazine once asked the Spice

Girls for their views on the EU and European integration. This was a satiri-cal gesture, not a sign of respect for the girls' insights into the Maastricht Treaty (Sebag Montefiore, 1996)). The capacity to speak has to be pro-duced; it can neither be assumed nor derived from general claims about popularity. The generation of this capacity, it might be suggested, is a product of mediation, in particular that of the ways in which the press and broadcasters report, represent or use musicians as 'authoritative' sources on political issues.

Performing participation

Although some musicians make speeches and some sign petitions, these form a relatively small part of events like Live 8 or movements like Rock Against Racism. Much more significant are the performances they give. If Live 8 does indeed constitute a form of political participation, then the musical performances must also feature in the story. The political acts being described are those that occur when people strum guitars and sing, as well as when they shout slogans or deliver polemics.

Such claims are not as odd as they might first seem. They chime with Habermas's account of the emergence and character of the public sphere, and the role he ascribes to art and culture. The freeing of art and culture from pre-existing forms of power is part of the process by which a critical public is produced. But in observing this, we have to be wary of reducing art to political 'communication' or 'cognitive practice', in which its exis-tence as sound or images (rather than words) is ignored or overlooked. There is a real danger to reducing music to a form of literal communica-tion in which the pleasures that it generates and the forms in which it operates (as sound and rhythm, as well as words) are obliterated. If music has a role in political participation, our understanding of it must acknowl-edge its particular qualities and attributes *as music*. In other words, in writing about the musical performances that make up events like Live 8, we have to do more than report the words spoken or indeed the lyrics sung. We need to acknowledge the other gestures and forms of expression that constitute the event. Jane Bennett (2001: 131 and 110–30), for example, talks of how music, particularly through its rhythmic patterns, can 'ener-gize' our moral sentiments. The repetition within songs and the experience of singing, she argues, enchants us and conjures up new meanings, identi-ties and collectivities. In a similar vein, Simon Frith (1996) argues that to like a piece of music, to respond to it, is to share the ethical values it encodes. Both Bennett and Frith suggest that music does more than reflect our moral and political sympathies; it actively engages them. In making her case, Bennett sets herself against those writers (like Theodor Adorno, 2002, or Jacques Attali, 1985) for whom the repetitive character of popular music is what kills its capacity to inspire political engagement or rebellion. The point is not which of these competing claims is right, but rather that both sides take seriously the power of music, and both believe that music engages with our system of values; that aesthetic values are also political values. To this extent, understanding music's place in political participation means, at the very least, asking how it seeks to move those who hear and perform it. We return to these arguments in later chapters.

From Jubilee 2000 to Live 8

In this final section, I want briefly to show how these three elements came together in Live 8. Live 8 was the culmination of the campaign for debt relief that began with Jubilee 2000 in 1996. Jubilee 2000 created a loose coalition of organizations, all of which were committed to relieving developing nations of the debts they had incurred in their dealings with the developed nations (Mayo, 2005: 172ff). It was formally wound up at the end of the millennium, but its legacy continued in the guise of bodies like Jubilee Debt Research and Make Poverty History (MPH), and its personnel re-emerged to carry on the campaign within organizations like Oxfam and Bono's DATA (Debt AIDS Trade Africa). Key to all that follows is the acknowledgement that the conjunction of music and politics is not a product of spontaneity, but of hard work and planning, of networks and various forms of capital.

Organization

Throughout its existence Jubilee 2000 wrestled with the problem of how to get its message across (Mayo, 2005: 176). As one of its leaders commented: 'It's not apartheid; we don't have Nelson Mandela behind bars. It's a really hard issue to make visual' (Ann Pettifor, *Rolling Stone*, 11 November 1999). In an attempt to heighten its profile, Jubilee 2000 (as is now common practice with many NGOs) committed resources to liaising with celebrities, particularly those in the music business. They established celebrity liaison posts (more often, and more respectfully, known as 'artist liaison'), the responsibility of which was to persuade musicians or their managers to support the cause. Many of the phone calls made by the artist liaison offices went unanswered, but one musician in particular became interested. This was Bono, who was himself already sympathetic to the cause (not least because of his involvement in Band Aid and Live Aid several years earlier), but he, like all such celebrities, was inundated with calls (interview, Jubilee 2000 organizer, 2006; interview, Richard Constant, 2006).

From these tentative beginnings, Jubilee went on to establish an informal music industry steering group. Two key figures on this were Richard Constant, a senior executive in the Universal Music Group, and Marc Marot, Managing Director of Island Records, U2's label. The presence of these two powerful music industry players was crucial to developing a strategy for recruiting musicians and for creating networks into which Bono was drawn (interview, Jubilee 2000 organizer, 2006).

One example of how this network operated was revealed at the 1999 Brits Awards ceremony (the British music industry's equivalent of the Oscars). Jubilee 2000 was honoured with the Freddie Mercury award. Previous winners had been War Child's *Help* charity record and Elton John's charity single, 'Candle in the Wind'. In 1999, Bono made the nominating speech and Muhammad Ali accepted the trophy on behalf of Jubilee 2000. From that moment onwards, Jubilee 2000 became 'fashionable' in the music industry, and the organization had no further difficulty in recruiting musicians (Jubilee 2000 Report, 2000; interview, Jubilee 2000 organizer, 2006; interview, Richard Constant, 2006). As the *Guardian* economics journalist, Larry Elliott, commented: 'Suddenly, debt relief is all the rage' (*Guardian*, 26 April 1999)

Behind the event was, however, a complex sequence of meetings, the first of which involved tying Bono into Jubilee (Jubilee 2000 Report, 2000). This meant getting the agreement not just of the singer but of his band too. It also meant elaborate negotiations with the British Phonographic Industry (BPI), the organizer of the Brits, and most crucially ITV, the television company that owned the broadcast rights (interview, Jubilee 2000 organizer, 2006). A similarly complex story can be told about the moments when musicians and causes become allied. Live 8, for instance, involved political negotiations between the Band Aid Charitable Trust and the Prime Minister's Office, the Treasury, the Department of Culture, Media and Sport, and the London Parks Authority. It also required global negotiations between political and bureaucratic actors in seven other major cities (interview, Harvey Goldsmith, 2006). These were supplemented by further negotiations with broadcasters, together with arrangements for an immense array of logistical issues, incorporating arrangements for sound mixing, lighting and so forth (*Entertainment Design*, November, 2005). The cost of running the event had to be recouped through sponsorship, rights' deals and merchandise sales (for accounts, see: http://www.live8live.com/docs/accounting.pdf). A standard contract was issued to all musicians in which they signed away all rights – performance, visual and merchandise – to the Band Aid Charitable Trust (interviews with Harvey Goldsmith and John Kennedy, 2006).

This tells only a part of the story of the organization of Live 8, but it serves to establish the general point: a great deal of capital of various kinds has to be invested in creating such an event. The capacity to generate political engagement is dependent on this investment, and much else besides.

Legitimation

Behind these stories of negotiation and networking is a longer running one of legitimation. Bob Geldof once remarked of Bono and himself: 'debt relief . . . turned a couple of Paddy pop stars into economists' (*Rolling Stone*, 11 November 1999). More likely, it might be contended, *media representation* of Bono and Geldof turned them into 'economists'. Jubilee and Live 8 were heavily dependent on the mainstream media to help constitute the musicians as authoritative representatives of their cause. Many years later in an interview with *Q* magazine (Odell, 2005: 106) Geldof reported that the editors of the leading national newspapers referred to him as 'Mr Africa'.

There are a number of dimensions to this legitimation process. At one level there is the 'popular' legitimation of the stars; that is, the way in which Geldof and others are represented as speaking for the people or popular conscience. This was evident in almost all elements of the UK media. On the day of Live 8, the *Independent* (2 July 2005) devoted its front page to an open letter from Geldof to the G8 leaders. The *Sun* (2 July 2005) produced a 'souvenir 8-page pull out', which carried a headline quote from Geldof: 'I can't wait for the world to come together to cry out for Africa.' One month earlier, on the day that Live 8 was announced, the *Daily Mail* (1 June 2005) led with: 'Geldof's encore for world's poor'. Each of these papers suggested that Geldof spoke for the 'people' on behalf of the 'poor' of 'Africa'; he was the 'people's' representative, their voice, their conscience.

The media representation of Geldof and Bono also characterized them as 'experts' on debt relief and Africa. Geldof was, for example, commissioned by the BBC to present a series of programmes on Africa. The *Independent* (15 July 2005) ran this headline on its world news pages: 'Geldof rates UN four out of 10 on Africa.' The obvious implication was that

Geldof's views on the United Nations were worthy of serious attention. Meanwhile, the *Guardian* (16 June 2005) described Bono as: 'The Irish rock star, who arguably has done more than any other to ensure that the cause of Africa gets on the agenda of the US administration.' There were, of course, dissenting views (Yasmin Alibhai-Brown, *Independent*, 6 June 2005; Janet Street-Porter, *Independent*, 2 June 2005; John Harris, *Observer*, 5 June 2005; Paul Theroux, *New York Times*, 15 December 2005), but the general coverage tended to endorse the claims of the pop stars to be authoritative and representative spokespeople.

It was notable too that the coverage of Live 8 in 2005 was of a different order to that given to Live Aid twenty years earlier. Then *The Times* (15 July 1985) gave Live Aid low-key coverage: 'Live Aid, the global rock show seen by an estimated 1,500 million people in 160 countries is expected to raise nearly £50 million for famine relief.' The first person quoted was not Geldof, but Live Aid's accountant. For Live 8, it was the stars who received the media's endorsement for their efforts, couched in explicit and implicit claims that they had the authority to speak. As Geldof and Bono came to represent the official voice of Live 8, other voices were silenced. It was reported that, when an NGO pitched an article on African debt to the *Daily Telegraph*, they were told: 'We only want it if it's from Bono or Bob Geldof' (interview, CAFOD staff member, 2005). Or as Geldof himself acknowledged: 'the celebritization of politics means it's [a humanitarian crisis] not worth covering unless some c*** like me takes an interest' (Odell, 2005: 108). This process is compounded by the decisions, such as that taken by New Labour to create The Commission for Africa, and to give Geldof a leading role on it (Williams, 2005).

Performing participation

In a sense, the cultural politics of Live 8 were simple. There was a single criterion, at least as far as the leading figures were concerned. As with Live Aid, the selection of artists to appear at Live 8 was based only on their market size. Any political values that might be encoded in their music was of no significance. Indeed, Geldof ridiculed those musicians who wanted their music to be seen in political terms. He once described The Clash's music as 'just Pure Nonsense for Now People' (*Rolling Stone*, 5 December 1985: 60). Geldof was dismissive of the idea that African bands should appear at Live 8 because they were *African*; they should only appear if they were *popular*, and they weren't. As Geldof said: 'For all their great musicianship, African acts do not sell many records' (*Guardian*, 28 December

2005; also interviews with Harvey Goldsmith and John Kennedy, 2006). At the same time he welcomed the appearance of the re-formed Pink Floyd because it 'helped the American audience take the event more seriously' (*Daily Telegraph*, 23 June 2005). While this may appear as a statement of fact, it does, of course, disguise a political judgement, one that promotes a particular populist vision, that was itself much criticized (see for example Moeletski Mbeki, *Mail on Sunday*, 3 July 2005). It shaped the form of the political engagement just as surely as did the processes that organized and legitimated it. Bono and Geldof set their cause to music, and in doing so gave it a particular resonance.

Conclusion

This chapter has begun and ended with Live 8, but it has been about a more general issue: music as political participation. Such an idea depends first upon how participation itself is to be understood and how its boundaries need to be extended to encompass cultural activity, and to move beyond instrumental action to achieve specific ends. But the idea is not just about definitions. It is about how music can animate or mobilize political participation. This is why Robert Putnam insights into the way music generates social capital are important. Finally, the argument developed here depends upon the way that particular conditions allow for music to perform its political function. Many agents are involved in this process, and as we shall see in the next chapter, the actual combination of them produces quite different forms of cultural politics. With Live 8, we saw how its organization, legitimation and performance invested it with power and with a particular politics. In the next chapter we look at a quite different combination and a quite different politics. We look at the example of Rock Against Racism. Both are cases of music being used to animate political participation.

5

Fight the power: music as mobilization

In his book *The Progressive Patriot*, the musician Billy Bragg (2007: 242) argues that Rock Against Racism was the key to his political and musical education: 'attending the Carnival Against the Nazis [in 1977] was the first political act I ever undertook and it was, in its way, as significant as seeing the Clash at the Rainbow'. Bragg is not alone. Others accord Rock Against Racism (RAR) pride of place in their biographies, a moment when their passion for music and their sense of justice found common cause. But RAR is not just the stuff of personal histories; it is also allotted a role on a larger stage. RAR, it is suggested, drove racism from the streets of the United Kingdom. This is a lot to claim for a movement whose motivating force was supplied by music and musicians. This chapter is about RAR and about the question of whether (and how) music can change the world. It is a partner to the previous one; it too looks at how music can become implicated in political action, but it differs in one important respect: where Live 8 was organized from the top down, RAR made use of local networks and initiatives.

While Billy Bragg is happy for RAR to occupy a prominent place in his personal biography, he is reluctant to accord it a wider importance. Musicians, he argues, are not able 'to change the world', but they can 'bring people together for a specific cause, to raise money or consciousness, to focus support and facilitate an expression of solidarity' (2007: 247). This is a widely shared view, not just of RAR, but of most cases of music's involvement in politics. But is it right? In the last chapter we saw how music can be used, at elite level, to pursue political goals and to enable a form of political participation. Can we also see it as a means of mobilizing mass movements and challenging racial prejudice? Can music and musicians actually forge popular movements, and if so how? In what follows, I try to address these questions, looking at the way other writers have tried to account for RAR and raising larger questions both about music's capacity to mobilize people and about the problems of writing a history of such movements. Is it possible to recover the evidence that might tell us – one way or the other – what RAR achieved? How do we write the history of moments that were fleeting and undocumented, that have only a fragmentary presence in the archives, and that seemed to exist only in the moment and in fallible memories and inflated mythologies?

Rock Against Racism

Without wishing to pre-empt the competing narratives that lay claim to RAR, it is necessary to sketch briefly the outlines of its story. Although RAR has existed in many forms in many different countries, my focus here is on the UK variant. RAR emerged in the late 1970s, at a time when the racist National Front (a forerunner of the British National Party) was gaining in strength (Walker, 1977). RAR was founded in 1976 by a group of activists, several of whom were associated with the Socialist Workers' Party (or International Socialists, as they were known until 1977). The founding moment, according to almost every history of RAR, is a letter that was sent to the weekly music press. It followed reports of on-stage remarks by Eric Clapton at a concert in Birmingham, at which the guitarist spoke in defence of Enoch Powell. Powell had been a Conservative MP for Wolverhampton, and was famous for a speech he had delivered in Birmingham in 1968, in which he warned that, if immigration – by which he meant non-white immigration – was not curtailed, he foresaw 'the River Tiber foaming with . . . blood'. Powell, who was a government Minister, was sacked by Edward Heath (Dabydeen et al., 2007: 377–8). According to Robin Denselow (1989: 138–40), Clapton's outburst received only minimal coverage, and there are few first-hand accounts of what was said. Nonetheless, the news was sufficient to provoke a letter to the music press.

Written by Red Saunders and six others, it said: 'When we read about Eric Clapton's Birmingham concert when he urged support for Enoch Powell, we nearly puked.' They went on to remind Clapton that 'half of your music is black. You're rock's biggest colonist.' And they ended: 'You've got to fight the racist poison otherwise you degenerate into the sewer with the rats and all the money men who ripped off rock culture with their cheque books and plastic crap. We want to organize a rank and file movement against the racist poison in music' (quoted in Widgery, 1986: 40). The letter elicited some 600 expressions of support, and offers from many bands to perform for the cause (Dawson, 2005: para. 17; Denselow, 1989: 140).

Clapton's outburst, however, was not only the event that inspired RAR. It combined with punk appropriation of Nazi insignia, and with incidents at the Reading music festival in 1976, when beer bottles had been thrown at the reggae artists U Roy and the Mighty Diamonds. Placards saying 'Go Home' were also waved. Earlier the same year David Bowie had arrived at Victoria Station and made a gesture that was interpreted by some as a Nazi salute (Widgery, 1986: 41). The evidence is not clear-cut (Buckley, 2000: 290). It was true, however, that Bowie had given interviews in 1974 and 1975 in which he had evinced some sympathy for a stricter social order and had said that 'Adolf Hitler was one of the first rock stars' (quoted in Buckley, 2000: 289). Whatever his views or his gestures, such incidents helped to fuel concern about the direction in which rock was moving.

But while Clapton's remarks provided the catalyst for RAR, the larger context was, of course, provided by the National Front (NF). Formed in 1967, the NF was a coalition of various elements of the extreme right. Its racist politics assumed greater mainstream prominence in the 1970s, when it fielded nearly 100 candidates in the second of the two 1974 General Elections and 176 candidates in the 1976 local elections, winning considerable local support in some areas of Britain (Walker, 1977: 174–5; 198–9). It was this rise in support for the NF that provided the underlying rationale for RAR.

Following the publication of the letter to the music press, a small number of gigs took place around the country. The first of these was in December 1976, when Carol Grimes and Matumbi performed at the Royal College of Art. These relatively small-scale concerts were characteristic of much of RAR's contribution. There is considerable disagreement, though, about how many such events were organized under the RAR banner. Paul Gilroy puts the figure at two hundred; Ashley Dawson, Lucy Robinson and Dave Renton estimate that it was three hundred (Gilroy, 1989: 164; Dawson, 2005: para. 1; Robinson, 2007: 112; Renton, 2006: 175). Simon Jones (1988: 99) claims that eight hundred gigs took place over three years. However many gigs were actually organized, much of the work was done by fifty or so RAR clubs (Widgery, 1986: 101). RAR also published its own paper, *Temporary Hoarding* from 1977 onwards. RAR only developed a national profile in 1978, when it held two big festivals, both in London – the first in Victoria Park, the second in Brockwell Park. Each attracted some 100,000 people. One of the key features of these events, and many of the smaller ones, was the presence of black and white musicians on the same bill and often on the same stage. The last of these large national events was held in Leeds in 1981.

The growth in RAR's profile coincided with the formation, in late 1977, of the Anti-Nazi League (ANL). The emergence of the ANL adds a further complicating factor to the narrative history of RAR. The ANL was an alliance of the SWP and other political groups, including members of the Labour Party. It provided considerable support to RAR, on which the latter came to depend. However, ANL and RAR had different agendas and were even, according to Paul Gilroy (1989), at odds with each other. Again, the role assigned to ANL in the history and effect of RAR is a feature of the competing perspectives. What is less controversial is the claim that the ANL became a key player. Some 250 branches were formed, who between them distributed 9 million leaflets and sold 750,000 badges (Robinson, 2007: 113). The ANL, drawing on SWP resources, was responsible for many of the most distinctive badges ('Teachers against the Nazis', 'Students against the Nazis' etc.) and banners. Dave Renton (2006: 175) estimates that RAR and ANL together prompted some 500,000 people to become involved in anti-racist campaigning. And for one of RAR's leading lights, the ANL was crucial to defeating the NF: 'If such a campaign as the ANL and RAR had not been launched in Britain, there is every reason to suspect that the mid-seventies electoral surge of the NF might have been sustained' (Widgery, 1986: 111). This is a view echoed by David Renton (2006: 128ff), author of a detailed history of the ANL. David Widgery points out that the racist right in France, which was active at the same time, but which did not attract similar opposition, continued to grow.

Certainly, the period of RAR's expansion and prominence coincided with the decline of the National Front. In the second General Election of 1974, the NF fielded 90 candidates and attracted 0.4 per cent of the national vote. In 1979, the year Mrs Thatcher was elected, the NF fielded 303 candidates and secured 0.6 per cent of the vote. By 1983, they could muster only 60 candidates and a meagre 0.1 per cent of the vote. It is true that the newly formed BNP also stood in 1983, but its 54 candidates were recorded as having received 0.0 per cent of the national vote (Yonwin, 2004: Table 1). While the collapse of support for racist politics might be attributed to RAR and to ANL, there are those who contend that it was the triumph of Thatcherism, and its right-wing agenda, that accounts for the demise of the NF. Again this, like much of the story that I have recounted so far, is also the subject of debate between the competing perspectives on RAR. It is to these to which we now turn.

Telling tales

The competing accounts of RAR's relevance and achievements are part of a much wider range of stories. Some of these emerge in the telling of rock music's history, some in recounting its involvement with politics, and some, more narrowly, in trying to recapture the specifics of RAR.

RAR and musical history

Although RAR attracted large audiences and was important to the careers of a number of rock acts, it is accorded only a modest part in rock's official history. It does not warrant mention, for example, in Hanif Kureishi and Jon Savage's (1995) *Faber Book of Pop*, and only a passing mention in Paul Friedlander's (1996: 257) *Rock And Roll: A Social History*. There are exceptions. Reebee Garofalo's history of popular music (1997: 325–8) devotes several pages to RAR, even though his book is formally about the history of US music. Garofalo's contribution is, it should be pointed out, unusual in its emphasis on politics. He portrays RAR as capturing the political loyalties of punk fans for the left, and as extricating them from the racist right. Garofalo is an exception even among books dedicated to telling the story of music in the 1970s only. Julie Burchill and Tony Parsons's (1978) *The Boy Looked at Johnny*, written during the emergence of RAR, makes a passing – slightly dismissive – reference to RAR: 'who would have *dreamed* that Rock could be anything *other* than Against Racism?' (1978: 88; their emphasis). Greil Marcus's (1989) compendious re-interpretation of punk, *Lipstick Traces*, gives little if any attention to RAR. The other major history of punk, Jon Savage's (1991) *England's Dreaming* accords RAR a larger role. For Savage, RAR was one element of the racial and other politics that fuelled punk, a movement which he saw as attracting racist as well as anti-racist fans (Savage, 1991: 334). It was therefore important to the genesis of RAR that punk icons like Johnny Rotten spoke against the NF in *Temporary Hoarding*. But while there might be a musical side to the story of RAR's rise, Savage (1991: 392–5) attributes the main responsibility to the SWP.

Not everyone saw it like this. In his survey of political music, Robin Denselow (1989) grants greater significance to the musicians, particularly to the links forged between reggae and rock and to the contribution made by the Clash, Linton Kwesi Johnson, John Lydon, Jimmy Pursey and Tom Robinson. He represents RAR as a broad coalition that had music at its core. In particular, he emphasizes the political contribution made by reggae, a genre for which political commentary was the generic norm, and one for which politics was seen as a source of solutions as well as of problems. Denselow (1989: 142–4) contrasts this with punk's unfocused political anger. While he concedes that the SWP made a contribution, he argues that RAR was central to challenging the NF and to exposing the failure of the then Labour Government to provide a political focus for anti-racist politics (see also, McKay, 2005). For Denselow (1989: 152), RAR's unambiguous achievement was to show 'that musical idealism was still possible now that rock music had become very big business'.

RAR and political ideology

Others are less sanguine about the 'musical idealism' of RAR, seeing it instead as one of several competing ideologies. For example, Dave Laing (1985: 110) describes RAR's founding statement as an example of 'Old Leftism', with its commitment to a 'realist' politics tied to a Marxist truth. RAR, he suggests (1985: 111), might have played a more creative and imaginative role if it had worked ideologically to create a different interpretations of the same 'reality'. For Laing, music's political potential lies less in what it 'says' about a particular situation, and more in how musicians as workers can challenged the systems that organize the production of their art (ibid.: 126–7). Paul Gilroy is similarly concerned with RAR's ideology. But in contrast to Laing, Gilroy reads RAR's ideology more sympathetically, particularly in contrast to the position adopted by the ANL.

Gilroy (1992: 148) draws a contrast between the two parties to the alliance. He associates RAR with 'the institutions and associations of socialist local government', while the ANL he links with 'far left groups, particularly the Socialist Workers' Party'. The latter he sees as being organized around class consciousness and the slogan 'Black and White Unite and Fight', the former he connects to the rise of an anti-racist movement in Britain, articulated in such publications as Race Today and Searchlight, and taking the form of small local groups (Gilroy, 1992: 153–5). RAR, with its focus on music and youth, is seen by Gilroy as challenging the traditional SWP line on class struggle and capitalism (ibid.: 156). RAR, according to Gilroy (ibid.: 157), presents racism, not just as a feature of racists, but of state institutions and practices; hence the need for it to be challenged more generally. He portrays RAR's anti-racism as a populist coalition in which racism was exposed and challenged through the cultural complexities contained in music. Gilroy (ibid.: 158–9) cites a Temporary Hoarding essay that celebrated Elvis Presley as evidence. He sees in punk, and in punk's borrowings from reggae, challenges to 'racist nationalism and nationalist racism' (ibid.: 162). Gilroy (ibid.: 164–7) also celebrates RAR's visual style, particularly as it appears in Temporary Hoarding. For him, the slogans, banners and badges gave a distinctive form to RAR's politics, creating a stark contrast to those of ANL. The latter he sees as losing the broad account of racism, and of prioritizing an anti-Nazism that dwelt upon racism's fascist origin; anti-Nazism took precedence over anti-racism (ibid.: 172–4).

While Laing and Gilroy draw different conclusions, they both share the view that RAR has to be understood as an ideological intervention and as a product of the political traditions from which it derived. They are not the only ones to see RAR in terms of its ideology. More recently, Lucy Robinson (2007: 113–16) has criticized RAR for its failure to address the politics of sexuality – in particular, for failing to recognize gays among the NF's targets, for failing to include British Asians, and for failing to engage directly with racism *in situ*, providing only middle-class entertainment instead. This catalogue of failures, whether legitimate or not, derives from a perspective which sees RAR as the representation of a political ideology, and locates those failures – or in the case of Gilroy, its successes – in the character of those ideologies.

RAR and cultural politics

For Ashley Dawson (2005), RAR is to be understood in terms of its cultural politics. Dawson (2005: para. 18) shares Gilroy's critique of ANL and its bracketing of racism with fascism (and Nazism), rather than existing UK state politics and practice, but he (ibid.: para. 2) is more concerned with RAR's contribution to 'polyculturalism' – a term he borrows from Vijay Prashad (2001) and which is to be contrasted with 'hegemonic multiculturalism'. The latter deals with 'neatly bounded, discrete cultures'; the former with cultural 'permeability and dynamism'. Dawson attributes RAR's special value to its ability to open up a 'new terrain of politics predicated on engaging with the spontaneous energies of subcultural creativity' (Dawson, 2005: para. 3). This was achieved through the 'transnational affiliations' that RAR was able to inspire through the bands it recruited (ibid.: para. 4). For Dawson, RAR is a site, not of ideology, but of cultural messages, which are contained within the song lyrics, the stage gestures and the banners.

Seeing RAR as a vehicle of polycultural expression also means taking a view on its accompanying political organization. Dawson characterizes this not as the political vanguardism of the SWP, but rather as 'self-organization' (ibid.: paras. 8–13), a form of organization that explicitly rejects the SWP's democratic centralism. Where Laing sees RAR's key actors as adherents of 'old leftism', Dawson represents them as inspired by a new cultural politics, drawn from a combination of politicized art movements such as constructivism, surrealism and situationism, and the 'celebratory blend of aesthetics and politics that characterizes the Caribbean carnival tradition' (ibid.: para. 22). This cocktail, suggests Dawson, helped to forge a generation of white youths who 'came to admire Black culture, to hate racism, and to view Britain as a mongrel rather than an ethnically pure nation' (ibid.: para. 2). While Dawson differs from Laing, Gilroy and Robinson in his emphasis on the cultural rather than the political, he shares with them a view of RAR as the bearer of ideas. Indeed all the interpretations we have considered so far tend to treat RAR as the embodiment of ideas, rather than as an organization. Dawson is a notable exception in this respect.

RAR as an art and social movement

Max Farrar (2004: 229), who describes RAR and ANL as part of 'one of the major social movements' of the 1970s and 1980s, is another who breaks this pattern. For him, RAR is part art movement and part political organization. He (ibid.: 229–30) talks of RAR as the 'creative vanguard', with ANL providing the organizational resources and knowledge, which together provided for: 'The explosion all over the country of RAR reggae/punk gigs, where dreadlocked blacks and safety-pinned whites enthusiastically shared the same space for the first time and effectively expelled both the nazi regalia and actual Nazis from the movement.' This coalition of art and politics is, for Farrar (2004: 233), a product of political precursors like Big Flame, who were, in turn, the inspiration for such things as the Leeds Coalition Against Racism and Fascism (founded in 1974), and of cultural precursors such as Bob Marley, Peter Tosh and Linton Kwesi Johnson, who fused cultural activity with political commitment.

RAR as an enlightened populist movement

Farrar's narrative coincides in many respects with that offered by the late David Widgery, one of RAR's founders and the author of the first major account of its existence, *Beating Time* (1986). This book was both an attempt to capture the passion of the moment and to reflect upon the context that brought it into being. Despite Widgery's own links with the SWP, his narrative presented RAR as a form of enlightened populism. He (1986: 8) described RAR as 'a rank-and-file movement of the ordinary, the unknown and the unkempt', 'inspired by socialism, punk rock and common humanity', and set against the background of both immigration and racism in

Britain. He insisted that RAR achieved this without state or media help. He represented RAR as a direct product of the rise of racism (symbolized by the antics of Clapton and Bowie) and of the initiative of 'an off-the-wall bunch of left-wing arties outside the leadership of any of the established organizations' (Widgery, 1986: 40). RAR's founding conference in January 1977, he (1986: 59) claimed, 'pulled together a caboodle of oddballs who were going to work together a lot more imaginatively and explosively than the worthies of the conventional anti-racist platforms.'

Although Widgery was careful to place RAR within a specific political context and trajectory, he was also keen to present it as a work of cultural politics. Like Farrar and Dawson, he placed RAR in the tradition of politically engaged art; in his case, represented by artists like Paul Robeson and Billie Holliday, and of artistic and other traditions that saw the political in the personal and in the imagination (ibid.: 53). RAR, Widgery (ibid.: 56) wrote, 'cured the schizophrenia between Marxist politics and modern culture . . . Black music was our catechism . . . our experience had taught us a golden political rule: how people find their pleasure, entertainment and celebration is also how they find their sexual identity, their political courage and their strength to change.' He believed in the capacity of music to break down barriers, citing in support of his belief Aswad, the Adverts and Carol Grimes. His most telling example, though, was Sham 69, a band then linked with a racist following. RAR's decision to sponsor a show with Sham 69 was seen as a deliberate challenge to the racist elements attached to the band. For Widgery (ibid.: 80–1; 83–95), concerts of this kind were RAR's political battleground; the Carnivals were RAR's message. Without RAR, the ANL would not have succeeded; and without punk, RAR would have amounted to little (ibid.: 114).

RAR as enlightened political leadership

Widgery's view of RAR as an enlightened populist movement is in marked contrast to Dave Renton's (2006) perspective, which places RAR within the history of the ANL and under the guidance of the SWP/International Socialists. For Renton, RAR is the story of SWP strategy and politics. He talks (2006: 46) of how '[t]hose members of the International Socialists who provided some of the leadership of Rock Against Racism in 1976 were drawn from a particular layer.' But he does concede (ibid.: 46) that they were a different breed of IS activist: they were relatively young, worked in the International Socialist print shop and were 'not always the most orthodox of Leninists'. And he acknowledges (ibid.: 48ff) the importance of

David Widgery, who he sees as a maverick whose friends were outside the SWP and whose interests in music and art inspired RAR. Despite this, Renton retains a commitment to a traditional notion of political leadership. 'But cultural styles, alone,' he writes (ibid.: 50),'build no movements. That requires people. Even once a style had developed which would make possible a fusion of radical music and politics, there was still a need to win the support that Rock Against Racism and others could then shape'.

At the same time, Renton (2006: 47) does not see RAR as being subsumed within SWP, but as the two enjoying a relationship that was 'reciprocal, with SWP shaping RAR, but with the latter influencing the former in its thinking on populist politics'. In a similar way, he represents the ANL as a broad alliance, in which the SWP had a central organizing role, but not a dominating one (ibid.: 76ff; 96). This notion of a mutually beneficial alliance is key to Renton's story. It is designed deliberately to challenge Gilroy's picture of conflicting political agendas, interests and ideas, and to play down the role of RAR and to play up that of the ANL and SWP. In his defence, he quotes (ibid.: 105) Peter Hain, now a Labour MP and then best known as an anti-Apartheid activist, as saying that 'The SWP brought Rock Against Racism. Without the SWP there wouldn't have been enough energy'. But Renton adds (ibid.: 112–13), somewhat ruefully, that the party failed to benefit from its involvement in terms of membership and its message.

RAR and party politics . . . and cultural politics

It is interesting to read the competing claims made for RAR against the most recent study of the movement. This is Ian Goodyer's Crisis Music (2009). He is one of the few to note (2009: xii–xiii) how difficult it is to write authoritatively about a movement like RAR. These problems are partly practical – the absence of comprehensive archives – partly problems of historiography – how do you write the history of a movement which is experienced in the sounds carried on the air? – and partly theoretical – how should we understand the formation and organization of such an entity, one that lacks the formal structures of a social movement, let alone a party? His answer, at least in respect of the latter, is to see RAR as a form of cultural politics, itself a product both of currents within the political left (inside and outside the SWP) and of emerging forms of politicized culture.

Goodyer brings together cultural and political narratives in his portrait of RAR. He attributes RAR's emergence to the changing terrain of left politics, away from traditional industrial struggles (and the Labour Party's inability to make this move), and towards the politics of the new social movements and the issues – like racism – to which they responded. But he also sees RAR as a product of changing attitudes within the left to popular culture, these being themselves a legacy of the politics of the 1968 generation, of anti-fascist art in Germany, of UK subcultures and of the Notting Hill Carnival (ibid.: 2009: 12, 93). But, like Renton, Goodyer believes that these attitudinal changes only assumed political importance through the intercession of the SWP. Not only did the party provide logistical support, it also supplied key personnel, network links to the ANL and theoretical and political insight (ibid.: 22ff). In making this case, Goodyer (ibid.: 23–4) gives voice to those in the SWP who were sceptical or critical of Widgery's enlightened populism, which they felt glossed over the key political and class realities. He also acknowledges the criticisms of those, like Lucy Robinson, who question the too easy fit made between punk and anti-racism. Such critics point to the racism of some punks, and to the musical styles (disco) and audiences (British Asians) that were marginalized by the movement.

Goodyer (ibid.: 51) prefers to see RAR 'as one element within a much wider-ranging attempt to shift the ideological balance within the British left and British society'. His contention is that RAR was neither a front for the SWP, nor was it directed by it. While the leading lights of RAR were SWP members, they held no formal positions within the party, and it was not clear that the party itself was always fully aware of the support it was giving (the internal party papers, according to Goodyer (2009: 67), say virtually nothing about RAR). Goodyer paints a picture of networks being forged in which favours were granted – including the use of IS/SWP printing and typesetting facilities – but in which no formal agreement was in place. This was partly because RAR did not conform to the standard model of political activism, particularly when compared to the ANL, and partly because of the disparate politics and backgrounds of those who belonged to it.

Unlike some other RAR historians, Goodyer pays close attention to the role of music itself in the way RAR operated. In particular, he takes up Paul Gilroy's suggestion that punk offered 'an oppositional language' through which anti-racism could be expressed. Goodyer shares this sense of punk as voicing radicalism, but he also cautions against punk mythology, in which the claims of actors like Malcolm McLaren, or writers like Jon Savage or Dick Hebdige are taken as gospel. Not only does he point to the London-centric nature of much of the discussion, he also notes the petit bourgeois economy on which punk was founded, and to the mixed motives that might account for some artists' support (ibid.: 88–9). In a similar vein, he highlights the politically ambiguous messages that could be taken from punk, and which could be used by racists (The Clash's 'White Riot', for instance). Such ambiguities do not, however, detract from his central claim: that music conveys messages, and can form the basis of political alliances. He talks of how reggae, for example, created the conditions for a 'cultural coalition' around 'counter-cultural dissent' (ibid.: 91–2). For Goodyer, this capacity was a product of the sentiments contained in the songs, the experiences attributed to its performers and the political context (police harassment of Anglo-Caribbeans).

These connections and models, as Goodyer notes (ibid.: 98ff), were themselves a product of a disposition to see culture as a site of politics. This disposition has a long and complex history, which Goodyer traces through currents in Marxist historiography – the work of E. P. Thompson and Christopher Hill – and through the politicization of folk music – by way of Ewan McColl and Peggy Seeger. In short, Goodyer's account of RAR, by far the most sophisticated of those available to us, knits together the specific and the general. The specifics lie in the sensibilities and associations of the RAR's founding members, the general in the wider political context: the trajectories of left thought and the politicization of culture. But I am still left with a question: while, in retrospect, we can see how RAR fits into the political and cultural history of its times, and how particular contingencies – Eric Clapton's outburst – prompted its formation, we are still left to wonder both about the character of its organization and its capacity to energize those who joined its ranks, and especially the extent to which music played a part in the mobilization of the movement.

Picking up the pieces

While they vary in the detail they offer, almost all the previous accounts tie RAR to particular political agendas, and view it as a form of ideological intervention in a debate about racism and how it might be tackled. In other words, there is a pervasive tendency to reduce the music to ideology and the movement to strategy. RAR emerges, in these narratives, as a function of a political vacuum left by others (most notably, the Labour Party), as a challenge to some (the National Front), and as travelling companion to a third party (the SWP). Only Goodyer raises questions of how in practice RAR operated – indeed, how it succeeded as a political movement (one of the first RAR festivals depended on Pink Floyd lending their sound system).

And while Goodyer, like Widgery and Denselow, invests the music with the capacity to convey key political messages, it becomes a bearer of the meanings attributed to it, rather than the author of them. We are left to wonder how RAR actually came to move people, and to what extent the music – as organized sound – did the moving. Was it the case, as Simon Jones (1988: 97–9) suggests in a brief discussion of RAR, that reggae introduced the possibility of 'being "political" within youth culture'? These are large questions, and ones to which I return later in this book. What I want to do here is to signal some of the ways in which we might get closer to answering them.

In one sense, the issues raised by RAR are those that afflict all attempts to explain any social movement, and are most familiarly associated with Mancur Olson's (1965) 'logic of collective action'. This highlights the disincentives for rational actors to commit to political action, the results of which will neither depend on their contribution nor benefit them exclusively. The logic suggests that we are better off *not* participating in this case. If we have some reasonable expectation of a return on our efforts (i.e. if the policy has a direct and exclusive benefit to the participants), then the logic points to participation. Most social movements are like the first case. A campaign to end racism will benefit everyone who is affected by racism in its many forms, whether or not they take part in the movement. This weakens the incentive, according to the logic of collective action, to commit time and effort to the cause. So it is that social movements develop strategies designed to counter this logic, by reducing the cost of participation or by providing other benefits which are exclusive to participants. Asking people to attend a concert is an example: the demands are minimal (they do not risk getting arrested or abused in the street) and the benefits are obvious – they get to hear music they like.

But this is not the end of the story. If it were, we would be talking about charity fairs as well as political movements; or about how every concert has the capacity to be a rally. There are two issues here. The first has to do with the performers, the second has to do with the audience. As a social movement, you have limited resources – for the same reason that people may be reluctant to participate, they are even less likely to give money (if they could afford to). The music that people will turn out to hear on a wet Saturday has to be attractive – there have to be names they recognize. Well-known bands, by definition, command a high fee – which the movement cannot afford. So the movement has to offer other incentives – they have to guarantee a large audience (who might buy the band's latest record), but for that they need name bands, and for that they have to ensure media attention, and for that they need a large audience, and for that they need name bands. . . . Or they have to touch the conscience of the performers, so they play for free or expenses anyway. We will discuss how they do this in a minute. What we should note first is that, in the case of RAR, this logic did not operate with quite the same force or in the same way at the local level. The local gigs typically would not involve name bands, but instead newly formed bands. When local RAR groups wanted bands to perform, they could offer them a minimal fee, but more importantly they could offer them a venue and an audience, both of which were highly valued. But while the incentives for local and national action are different, they both have to deal with the (dis)incentives which Olson's logic identifies.

What social movement theorists also point to, as they wrestle with the logic of collective action, is the part played by the 'framing' of the cause (Snow et al., 1986). The logic of collective action not only works against participation, it also works against finding out why it might be worth participating. This is because in itself a grievance is not sufficient to explain participation; what matters is 'the manner in which grievances are interpreted and the generation and diffusion of those interpretations' (ibid.: 466). How things seem is as important as how things are. It is not enough just to have an 'interest' in a cause or in a policy outcome. We all have a multiplicity of interests, some of which we recognize, some of which we do not. How we perceive our interests is not a matter of fact, but, as Anne Swindler (1986) has argued, a matter of cultural mediation. It is against this background, in which the 'logic' of participation cannot be assumed, that claims are made for the particular contribution to be made by music and musicians, as we saw in the previous chapter (Eyerman and Jamison, 1998; Mattern, 1998; Turino, 2007). Writers like Ron Eyerman and Andrew Jamison have been engaged in this same attempt to meet the challenge set by the logic of collective action. Musicians become part of the process of framing an issue by bearing witness to it. But Eyerman and Jamison say little about what music itself contributes to countering the logic. How does music *as sound*, rather as part of a more general culture, contribute to the mobilization of political action? The answer, I want to suggest, lies in the capacity of music to contribute to what Jonathan Githens-Mazer (2008: 45) describes as the three key elements necessary for participation in any social movement: '(1) injustice or "moral indignation"; (2) collective identity; and (3) agency, the sense that sustained collective action will be able to alter conditions and politics it seeks to address'.

RAR, music and political mobilization

A musician involved in RAR described how the movement educated him about racism in Britain: 'We had no idea about race and racism – what we learned, we came to know through the music'. Someone who had been at one of the big RAR carnivals admitted that he was never a punk fan, but recalled how RAR nevertheless managed to engage him politically: 'it was quite worrying, the rise of the National Front in the 1970s, and the political elites said that it was terrible, but nothing was put forward like a positive alternative to it . . . My memory of going to the marches, like 1978 in Victoria Park, [is] arriving in Trafalgar Square and the relief of seeing thousands of people . . . The music felt angry and there was an emotional alternative. . . .' In these personal narratives, we see the practicalities of political engagement being linked to its emotional pull. The music was not incidental, but a way of making sense of the politics.

But this reading of the music as 'angry', of its capacity to teach and to give a political focus to participation, was not simply a feature of the chords and the choruses of the songs. It involved seeing and hearing music as a political experience in itself. Red Saunders, one of RAR's founders who had a background in agit-prop theatre, said that the aim of RAR was 'not only to use the music as a weapon but also the environment and the atmosphere: a palace of throbbing anti-racist propaganda! We've made up the best banners you've seen, twenty foot long with huge lettering in yellow on red, red on green, plus lots of six foot blow-ups of kids dancing in clubs, enjoying themselves' (*The Leveller*, January 1977: 12–13). The aim was to create gigs that both visually and aurally provided an aesthetic and effective alternative to the depressing possibility of a bleak nation ruled by the National Front. In Leeds there was a weekly RAR club that hosted local and national bands. The local RAR committee assiduously decorated the corridor to the club with day-glo and homemade banners. They would not let a single punter in until all was ready. The RAR activists saw the music and the venues as providing more than entertainment, and more than straightforward political information or ideology.

Whether or not they succeeded, these RAR activists were working with a prior assumption: that music, or at least their kind of music, could constitute a political experience. And this assumption was itself a part product of the mediation of music and musicians. Just as the media constituted Bono and Geldof as 'experts' on Africa and legitimated them as representatives of the popular conscience, so a similar process occurred with RAR. But where for Live 8 it was located in mainstream media, for RAR the key intermediary was the music press. During the 1970s, the music papers – and the *NME* in particular – became increasingly politicized. This was not just a matter of the music and musicians that were covered, nor just of the critical perspective adopted; it also involved the direct reporting of conventionally political events (Gorman, 2001; Renton, 2006: 115). The overall effect was to represent musicians and music as inescapably political. The music press became a source of political education. This was a function most explicitly performed by RAR's house journal *Temporary Hoarding* (Farrar, 2004: 229). David Widgery described the paper as providing 'dub Marxism'. In reporting the political to its readers and in politicizing music, the media and the activists also contributed to a further process: the political evaluation of music. This entailed the decoding of music as a political statement or expression of political value. So it was that when Roger Huddle booked Carol Grimes for the first RAR event, he explained that she played 'RAR's kind of music' (Widgery, 1986: 42). There was, from the beginning, a thought that RAR's politics had a distinct sound. It was not the sound of 'glam rock', for which Widgery (1986: 64; also 66 and 110) had considerable disdain. It was music that belonged within the 'black music tradition'. This was an ideological claim, one that drew upon a particular reading of music and its politics, one in which 'authenticity' was identified in particular sounds and associations.

The counterpoint to RAR's belief in the link between music and political values was provided by Bob Geldof. Geldof valued the music and musicians he hosted at Live 8 in terms of their commercial reach and their inclusivity (terms he took to be interchangeable). RAR saw its music in more exclusive terms; they sought out music that could be traced to distinct struggles, performers and audiences, and whose political claims were realized in its associations and performance style. RAR refused to accept the argument that the political value of music was realized only once it had been validated by the charts. The pages of *Temporary Hoarding* were taken up with debates about what kind of bands or music could legitimately speak for RAR. Being 'popular' was not enough; it might even be a hindrance.

Music was not just a bearer of political values; it was also a form of organization. It was often the case that the journalists were also musicians or organizers of gigs. The idea of RAR as a grass-roots movement was also a statement about the link between culture and politics. Widgery's distaste for 'glam rock' was not just an aesthetic judgement, but also a political one, in that glam rock represented the worst excesses of a corporate, centralized music industry. What punk represented was the reclaiming of music for the people. In *Temporary Hoarding*, the London office underlined the movement's DIY, decentralized ethics. They encouraged local fans to 'make your own conflict grafix for the show. You do the lay out – put the pics and words together – and we'll put it on a slide for you – all you need can be ripped out of papers and zines' (*Temporary Hoarding*, Spring 1978). Many of the bands that graced RAR gigs were unknown outside of the locality – some of them had been formed only weeks before the event.

RAR's organizational contribution extended to providing an opportunity for bands to perform. As Mark E. Smith of The Fall explained: 'RAR were the only people giving us gigs and we didn't have an agent; I was still working at the time' (interview, BBC Radio Manchester, National Sound Archive). RAR 'struck bargains where a band's desire for exposure was exchanged for an explicit stand against racism' (Watson and Leslie, 2001). RAR was constituted by the intersection of musical and political networks. The sociologist Nick Crossley (2008: 89) has mapped the way in which punk emerged from 'the social network of key actors'. For Crossley (ibid.: 90 and 94), the social network represents another device for countering the logic of collective action by helping to pool resources and to reduce the risks of participation. He draws parallels with the role played by black churches and colleges in the formation of the civil rights movement. RAR can be seen as another example of this thesis. RAR sat at the intersection of political and musical networks – local musical and political scenes – constituting the infrastructure and political capital necessary for the movement to flourish. Just as the RAR founders embodied the intersection of politics and culture, so did those who drove RAR forward in cities like Leeds, Sheffield, Manchester and Liverpool. In Manchester, there were well-established cultural networks, including Music Force from the early 1970s and the people responsible for the Deeply Vale festivals. These networks were able to incorporate RAR, which itself had offices at Manchester Polytechnic. In Liverpool, by contrast, it was the predominantly political networks formed by organizations like Big Flame that were able to create a platform for RAR. Sometimes it was less organized than this. One of the people involved in RAR in Sheffield said: 'I don't remember any formal network – just people you knew, gig-listings and posters . . . In Sheffield there wasn't a huge political motivation. It was on the back of music scene that was already vibrant. If you went to a gig, chances are there was a RAR logo. It was by default that people were there for the political movement . . . The music we were listening to was attached to the movement.' Even in the absence of clearly identifiable networks, there were informal links that allowed the political and cultural dimensions of RAR to coalesce.

As with Live 8 so with RAR, these networks are key to creating what can often seem to be 'spontaneous'. As Crossley observes: 'feelings do not suffice to make movements' (ibid.: 94). This is not to say that emotions are irrelevant, only that they work through and within organizing structures and networks. One of RAR's slogans was 'N[ational] F[ront] = No Fun'. Creating a sense of fun was one of RAR's avowed aims, but it could not be achieved by injunction alone. An *NME* reviewer of the first RAR gigs at London's Royal College of Art wrote that it turned into 'much more of a party and much less of a gig . . . it was the kind of jam where every one embraces afterwards – not because the music was so great but because of the feeling. A lot of people made new friends and some of them curled up right there on the floor together to sleep' (*New Musical Express*, 25 December 1976). RAR capacity to create fun owed much to its awareness of the carnival tradition and of various art traditions. It also owed much to the political and cultural networks to which it was connected.

Conclusion

I began this chapter wondering about the capacity of music to mobilize people, taking as my example the case of Rock Against Racism. Here was an instance of music seeming to take on the guise of a political movement, and of being able to make a real political difference. We began by looking at how RAR's relatively simple story has been told in many different ways, but almost always, it seems, in terms of its formal politics and its relationship to the SWP and ANL. These are clearly important elements in the RAR narrative, but they are not the only ones.

There were two omissions. The first was caused by a lack of attention to the logic of collective action. Olson's argument raises real questions for anyone who wants to explain the formation of RAR. And as we saw, in looking at RAR in these terms, we could see how music and musicians played some part in countering the incentives for apathy. But there remained the second omission: the question of what exactly music and musicians contributed to RAR and how this contribution is to be understood. For this, we looked at how – in terms of the activists – music was able to communicate, organize and move people in its name. For RAR, music conveyed a message about anti-racism and about the NF, but it also provided a platform from which this message could be heard and it created a desire to participate in its efforts. Many intermediaries were involved – from the music press to the cultural and political networks. Together, these many contingencies and processes made it possible to think about how music might move people to act politically.

RAR and Live 8 are prime examples of the way in which music and politics can be harnessed in the service of a cause. My argument through these last two chapters has been that, for all the differences between the two examples, there is a need to look beyond the sentiments and ideas that they articulate to the means by which they are organized and legitimated, and to the styles in which they perform their politics. My argument has also been that, despite the tendency for the political story to dominate the narrative, music plays a key role too, and cannot be treated simply as an instrument or cipher of some larger political purpose. But in insisting on the importance of sound, in seeing it as political as well, we are forced to consider further questions about how music conveys or articulates politics. This is what concerns the next chapter, in which I discuss the interplay of music and history, and how music is implicated in our sense of the past and shapes our sense of the present and its politics.

6

'Invisible republics': making music, making history

Geoffrey O'Brien (2004: 53) writes in his remarkable memoir *Sonata for Jukebox*:

> In any event the knowledge that any music imparts is not necessarily of the world, or at least of this world. It is into other spaces, absent, imagined, seemingly infinite, that the hearer is initiated. The unknown melody secretes histories without names, voyages undertaken without a body, love affairs of mysterious intimacy in which the beloved remains unknowable. Here is generosity without motive – embodied in, say, a low tone sustained by Bing Crosby as if he were startled by the timbre of it as anyone else – or grief without bottom, a lament for the loss of what one has never, or not yet, known.

O'Brien's tribute to music's power to evoke hidden histories is what underpins this chapter, in which I look at how this power is harnessed to the narratives of political history. As Joshua Clover (2009: xiii) remarks: 'Lived history slips away. Of course. It is replaced with images and stories.' He (ibid.: 2) goes on to argue, songs 'may communicate historical experience'. My interest is in how music might construct our sense of history, and in the political meaning we invest in that history.

In 1997, the Smithsonian Institution in Washington released a boxed record set: the *Anthology of American Folk Music*. At first glance, this might have seemed like yet another example of worthy archival preservation. It was, however, much more than that. Intended only as a limited edition, the six CD set sold thousands of copies, despite its cost ($85), and it went on to top the *Village Voice* annual music critics' poll (Hoberman, 1998). But its sales figures and critical approval are mere details compared to the other claims made for it. The *Anthology* was celebrated not just as an extraordinary repository of American music, but as a key document in the narrative of a nation. It helped to constitute, in Greil Marcus's (1997) words, America's 'invisible republic'. This is no small claim. It gives music an importance, not just to the lives of individual fans, but to the fate of nations. How does music come to warrant this kind of investment, and can it bear its weight?

This chapter explores the ways in which music is seen to write history and to configure the constitution of countries. It asks whether such suggestions are entirely fanciful. I start with the example of the *Anthology*, before considering another case of music being used to imagine a nation and to mark a time: the Woodstock Festival of 1969.

Both the *Anthology* and Woodstock are recurrent figures in the mythology of music. In the Summer of 1999, for instance, the Meltdown festival devoted a night to Harry Smith and his *Anthology*. The show contained performances by Bryan Ferry, Nick Cave, Kate and Anna McGarrigle, Van Dyke Parks, and many others. Woodstock put in a reappearance in the so-called 'Second Summer of Love' in 1989, when the UK was gripped by rave culture (Clover, 2009; Reynolds, 1998). But understanding how and why music comes to mark the passage of historical time and to shape the imagination is not just a matter of revealing the context – of identifying the conditions and interests around specific moments. Nor is it simply a matter of 'reading' the politics of a piece of music or a film, any more than it is a question of seeing sounds and images as 'reflections' of their times. All of these play their part. There are vested interests in the writing of music's history, just as there are resonances in that music which conjure up past time and experiences. But there is also the possibility that the *Anthology* or Woodstock *write* history and *create* political traditions.

This chapter, therefore, is about both how politics is encoded in cultural texts, but also about the ways in which those texts are implicated in the constitution of political identities and histories. In doing so, it draws upon Benedict Anderson's (1983) notion of national identity as an 'imagined community', constructed by way of a set of cultural resources. Anderson speaks, for instance, of the role of mass singing in the constitution of national identity. National anthems are, he writes (1983: 132–3; emphasis added), 'occasions for unisonality, for the *echoed physical realization* of the imagined community.' The chapter draws too upon the now considerable literature on music's constitution of local and sexual identities (see Negus, 1996, for an early survey). But while these form part of the theoretical backdrop, my concern is more with the specifics of the link between musical experiences and imagined identities. How do the apparently ephemeral moments that music creates become part of much larger historical narratives. The answer to such questions are typically to be found in the work of a writer like Greil Marcus (1975, 1989, 1992, 1997). But it is present elsewhere. Michael Shapiro (2006: 131ff), for instance, talks of how America has been 'composed' musically, and how different musical forms have evoked different Americas. More recently, Joshua Clover (2009: 127) has written: 'pop music still manages to register at once the foreclosure of historical experience, and to develop forms, affects, and cultural schemas that cache within themselves the knowledge of what had been lost in that foreclosure.' What follows, I suppose, is a sceptic's rather cautious response to their eloquent investment in music's historical and constitutional power.

Anthology of American Folk Music

The *Anthology* was compiled in 1952 by a bohemian film-maker, poet, literary editor and discographer called Harry Smith. Drawing on the new possibilities offered by recording on vinyl, and hence the opportunity to sequence several songs on one side (compared to the single song per side of a 78rpm record), Smith brought together recordings made in the US in the 1920s and 1930s. The *Anthology* contains country fiddle tunes, folk ballads, church hymns and gospel chants, performed by people such as Uncle Eck Dunford, the Carolina Tar Heels, Doc Boggs, Blind Lemon Jefferson, Mississippi John Hurt, Furry Lewis and Sister Mary Nelson. The songs and tunes, eighty-four in all (nearly as many as there are performers), were recorded sometime between 1926 and 1932. They include: 'When the Great Ship Went Down', 'Mississippi Boweavil Blues', 'Old Shoes and Leggins', 'Fifty Miles of Elbow Room', 'White House Blues'.

As the title of the collection suggests, Smith was trying to draw a musical and social portrait of a country and its diverse peoples. It was, however, a very particular, personal picture. Smith demonstrated a taste for the weird and the bizarre, but he was not a folklorist, in the sense that he used only commercially recorded examples, discs made to make money. There are tales of revenge and murder, of lust and love; strange, bleak and funny accounts of lives lived in the cracks and on the margins of American society. Because Smith was not trying to create a musical typology, because he seemed more interested in the voices and the experiences they recounted than the formal sociological and musicological categories into which the singers fitted, listeners are forced to hear the music more as a noisy conversation than an exercise in formal archivism. In describing the *Anthology*, Robert Cantwell uses the analogy of the 'memory theater', a reference to the seventeenth-century idea as to how all human knowledge can be ordered and recalled. The key to the memory theatre was the sequence in which knowledge was arranged. Smith's compilation makes oblique reference to this 400 year old device, but Cantwell (1991: 374) makes it explicit: 'In the musical cosmos, then, the *Anthology* was a sacred narrative, reaching from origins to last things in a sequence of performances . . .'

The *Anthology*'s quirky character tells us something about Smith's aesthetic, but it does not explain why it has come to assume cultural importance. It does not explain why such a compilation, both in its original incarnation and in its later digital version, has been interpreted as constructing a narrative of an America in which the American dream is part ideal, part farce, part nightmare. To account for this, we need to know how music can (be seen to) evoke these visions and images. Certainly, music, like any form of historical evidence, does not simply recount the past; that past has to be reconstructed and interpreted through documents, rather than by them. Music poses particular (but not unique) problems of interpretation. To make the obvious point: the lyrics of a song cannot be taken as a straightforward revelation of experience; they are not, in this sense, oral history. The words are written to be sung, and as such are bound by rules of genres and rhyme, and in the singing, in the 'grain of the voice' (as Roland Barthes famously called it), many other possible meanings are set in motion. By way of illustration, you need only to listen to the first track of Smith's compilation, 'Henry Lee', and then to the covers of it by Bob Dylan, P. J. Harvey and Nick Cave, each one recreating the song anew.

The *Anthology* may be a historical document, but its meaning and significance are constructions of times, places and experiences. The *Anthology* does not just exist as one piece in the narrative of cultural history; it is part of the present as well as the past. Harry Smith's archival work was to be an inspiration to a generation of US folk performers. Cantwell (1991: 364) describes the *Anthology* as founding the 1960s folk revival, for which the *Anthology* was 'its enabling document, its musical Constitution'. Key to this claim is Bob Dylan, who told one interviewer many years later: 'I heard that record [the *Anthology*] early on when it was very difficult to find these kind of songs . . . That's where the wealth of folk music was, on that particular record. For me, on hearing it, was all these songs to learn. It was the language, the poetic language – it's all poetry, every single one of those songs, without a doubt, and the language is different than current popular language, and that's what attracted me to it in the first place' (interview with Serge Kaganski, *Mojo*, February 1998: 64).

The voices and songs on the *Anthology* legitimated a kind of musical personality and perspective. Dylan used those songs and characters, not just to produce his own cover versions, but to establish his own artistic persona. Dylan's use of the *Anthology* can be discovered in his first recordings, and thence on the *Basement Tapes* (recorded in 1967; released in 1975) and *World Gone Wrong* (1993). The songs and singers of the *Anthology*, according to

Greil Marcus (1997), were key to the voices that Dylan adopted and to the characters that populated his songs (and his relationship to them).

The story of the *Anthology*'s musical role does not end with Dylan. Smith's collection still features in accounts of contemporary music. Indeed, its moods and aesthetics continue to haunt a whole tradition of US music-making. The musician Beck revealed how he 'was immersed in stuff like the *Anthology of American Folk Music* when I was growing up. Of course, a certain amount of it was romantic and macabre and intriguing and fascinating. That faraway strange quality is definitely something I gravitated towards when I was younger. And I guess travelling through America, I realized that a lot of that strangeness is still out there, only it's maybe a little more frightening because it's alive here and now' (quoted by Barney Hoskyns, 'The shock of the old', *Mojo*, December 1998: 64–5). The rock writer Ben Thompson (1998: 93) has identified an entire genre, which he calls 'Woodchuck Nation' (a play on Abbie Hoffman's 'Woodstock Nation'), that sounds 'strangely familiar' to anyone who has heard the *Anthology*. Bracketed in this category are performers such as Sparkelhorse, Smog, Freakwater, Lambchop, whose music is a ramshackle, stumbling amalgamation of country and rock, in which eerie voices whisper about lost souls and dark secrets. The musical legacy of the *Anthology* is most vividly evoked in Mercury Rev's *Deserter's Songs* (1997), which includes a song called 'Holes':

> Holes, dug by little moles, angry jealous
> Spies, got telephones for eyes, come t'you as
> Friends . . .

Some sixty years earlier, Bascom Lamar Lunsford, a lawyer and singer whom Smith includes in his *Anthology*, sang 'I Wish I Was a Mole in the Ground', in which he tells of a railroad man who will kill you and drink your blood as wine. The two songs, with their strange mix of the whimsical and the weird, echo each other.

Greil Marcus, the *Anthology* and myths of America

So it is that the *Anthology of American Music* can be seen to run through the history of popular music, becoming a founding 'constitution' on the way – or at least that is what is *claimed* for it. But this narrative, in which the *Anthology* is both a musical template and authenticating source of a cultural and political identity, is itself a construct, a way of running together various histories and creating meaning out of them. It is an exercise in myth-making. This does not make it wrong-headed or incoherent; indeed, it is revealing of the importance that is attached to music. All music – all art – inhabits the mythical realm. But it does not follow that we should embrace all myths uncritically, however attractively or however eloquently expressed. It is in this spirit that I turn to look at one of the *Anthology*'s most articulate myth-makers, Greil Marcus.

Marcus is a hugely influential interpreter of popular music. Beginning with his book *Mystery Train: Images in America in Rock 'n' Roll Music* (1975) and continuing to one dedicated in large part to the *Anthology* (*Invisible Republic* (1997)), he has consistently linked music (and other art forms) to the wider political and historical landscape. And in doing so, he has created mythical narratives. Sean Wilentz (1998: 101) described him as a 'cultural historian-cum-mysterian'. For Marcus, popular music constantly makes and remakes the political myths and reality of 'the old weird America' (1997). It is also responsible for revealing 'secret histories' (1989). By this account, the *Anthology* is a crucial component of America's identity and history. Its importance lies in the way that it writes that history. Thus it is that Marcus suggests that Elvis Presley continues to haunt contemporary American culture many years after his death. Marcus (1992: xiii–xiv) talks of 'Elvis Presley's second life', a life which is lived as 'a great, common conversation, sometimes a conversation between specters and fans, made out of songs, art works, books, movies, dreams; sometimes more than anything cultural noise, the glossolalia of money, advertisements, tabloid headlines, bestsellers, urban legends, nightclub japes. In either form it was – is – a story that needed no authoritative voice, no narrator, a story that flourishes precisely because it is free of any such thing, a story that told itself.' These conversations and stories are, for Marcus, about the American dream.

In Marcus's book about the *Basement Tapes*, the 1967 collaboration between the Band and Bob Dylan, he talks of the musicians reconstituting the 'invisible republic' of the *Anthology*. He (1997: 21) argues that Dylan came to personify a democratic ideal; the singer 'embodied a yearning for peace and home in the midst of noise and upheaval, and in the aesthetic reflection of that embodiment located peace and home in the purity, the essential goodness, of each listener's heart'. Marcus connects Dylan's evocation of the American dream to that which earlier generations heard in the recordings collected by Smith. He (1997: 21) says of Dylan: 'this purity, this glimpse of a democratic oasis unsullied by commerce or greed' was what people in the 1950s and 1960s found 'in the blues and ballads first recorded in the 1920s and 1930s'.

For Marcus, the *Basement Tapes* connect to the *Anthology* through a common narrative which tells 'a story' and creates 'a map' of the invisible republic of the United States (Marcus, 1997: xiii). Of one song, 'Lo and Behold', he writes: 'A new nation, reclaimed in this song as if the country were still new, still unsettled . . .' (Marcus, 1997: 65). In connecting these sixties' recordings to the *Anthology*, Marcus describes them as representing 'a mystical body of the republic, a kind of public secret'. Acted out in this republic is a vision of 'democracy', but not a democracy of material resources and governance; it is instead a 'democracy of manners', in which 'people plumb their souls and then present their discoveries, their true selves, to others' (Marcus, 1997: 125). All of this is contained in the music, in the cadences of a banjo, in the bending of a note.

This investment of music with the identity and character of nations, with visions of democracy and invisible republics, is a constant theme in Marcus's writing. In *Mystery Train*, he describes the blues singer Robert Johnson as evoking a 'shadow America' (1975: 36). He says of the Band's songs that they 'bring to life the fragments of experience, legend, and artefact every American has inherited as the legacy of a mythical past', that they looked for 'the traditions that made new things not only possible, but valuable; a flight from roots they set a sense of place' (Marcus, 1975: 62 and 50). And of Elvis Presley, he says that the performer 'takes his strength from the liberating arrogance, pride, and claim to be unique that grow out of a rich and commonplace understanding of what "democracy" and "equality" are all about: no man is better than I am' (Marcus, 1975: 204). What Marcus is suggesting in each of these tributes is not just that images of America can be 'read off' the music, that the country is reflected in the songs, but rather that the music helps to *constitute* America, creating a sense of what it means to be 'American', and also that the pleasures of the music, the way it moves its listener, is bound up with their experience as Americans. Throughout Marcus's writing there is the sense that what matters are the submerged currents of individual and communal lives, and that music provides access to them. *Invisible Republic* talks of the 'mystery' of America, not as something to be laid bare, but rather to be recognized as part of the daily reality of American life. For Marcus, it seems that the songs *are* the country. American music re-incarnates the country described by Alexis de Tocqueville in *Democracy in America* in the eighteenth century (1988; Marcus, 1975: 22). The pleasures that the songs afford are part of a political narrative. Marcus hears in the sounds of pop and rock the traces of hidden histories and political beliefs that constitute a sense of national identity.

The *Anthology* is not linked to particular times and moments; it stands, like the Constitution, as a permanent testimony to the American dream.

In making this case, Marcus does not resort to the tools and resources of historical or social science research. Instead, he depends upon political rhetoric and aesthetic insight. And arguably, both are important to making sense of culture (and of how people respond to it). But there are, nonetheless, good reasons to be sceptical of the particular claims. Much of Marcus's argument rests on the assumption of a single, universal American dream, to which the music is always linked. It assumes, as it were, that Elvis was the King. Secondly, Marcus makes no attempt to give a specific context to his claims. His is a largely ahistorical account of music and its power.

Katherine Skinner (2006) shares this scepticism, noting that the *Anthology*'s canonization is a recent phenomenon. In earlier decades, it was overlooked by the historians of folk music. This neglect reflected the indifference that greeted its original release. Skinner (2006: 63) reports that it sold less than 100 copies a year in the domestic market during the 1960s and 1970s, and that many of the sales were to libraries, rather than the general market.

From Skinner's perspective, Marcus's own readings are a peculiar product of his own time and location; they emerge from the specific circumstances and interests that coalesce to attach meanings and significance to sound. By this account, Marcus uses the *Anthology* to claim membership of an 'imagined community' that gives him and his concerns a political coherence. As such his argument represents a powerful, personal testimony to the importance of music. But there is a question about whether it represents any more than that. This, though, is not a reason for discounting all attempts to weave history and music together.

Imagining a community

In the 1950s in Britain, jazz came to signify a certain kind of political affiliation for white middle-class suburban teenagers (McKay, 2005). This derived from, in Simon Frith's (1988: 22) words, 'the urge to "authenticity"', and its counterpoint, 'the strange fear of being "inauthentic"'. Robert Cantwell (1996: 314) ascribes something similar to the inner lives of Elvis fans: 'What did the fourteen-year-old know of the idiom and manners of the frankly erotic, unsentimental, passionate black underworld of New Orleans, Little Rock, or Memphis? Nothing: but rockabilly music, like the thief that doffs his clothes to baffle the guard dog, made it part of his life.'

To root music in these desires, to use music to claim others' experiences, is not to diminish its importance. It does, though, require us to qualify its claims to a transcendent universality, and to see how its magnificent myths are grounded in a grubbier reality. In making sense of the *Anthology* (or any piece of music), we need to think about the needs and interests that it addressed.

So, why did the *Anthology* come to be the recipient of so much cultural and political investment? Skinner (2006: 71) argues that a number of factors came into play, including the credibility lent by the Smithsonian's involvement, and by the rise of Americana as a musical genre. Cantwell (1991: 367) suggests that part of the answer lies in Smith's idiosyncratic principles of selection. Smith refused the obvious compiler's categories. He bracketed his choices under three headings: ballads, social music and songs. He rejected the traditional or typical categorizations – work songs, mountain songs, etc. – and in doing so focused attention on the voices and the stories they tell. This simple move made possible the larger narrative that people hear in the *Anthology*, the narrative of nations and peoples, but it also started the intergenerational musical conversation too.

Why people heard the *Anthology* as a particular union of politics and aesthetics is a result of the context in which they listened. The *Anthology* first emerged at a time when the politicized folk of the Weavers and other Communist sympathizers were being forced off the airwaves by Senator McCarthy (Denisoff, 1971). Left-wing culture appropriated the *Anthology* as an example of the 'people's spirit', but the compilation did more than simply embody a political populism. It also gave a particular aesthetic to those politics. As Cantwell (1991: 364–5) points out, the fact that the anthology appeared on long-playing records, which were typically reserved for classical music, bequeathed the music a distinct cultural capital. The music of the poor was 'reframed as a kind of *avant garde* art'. And, argues Cantwell (1991: 370–1), it was an art that engaged the aesthetic of those who were reacting against the impoverished imagination which television's emergence threatened to impose. In defining itself *against* the new video culture and *with* the avant garde and left populism, the music of the *Anthology* founded both an aesthetic style and a political vision, and it was this combination which legitimated Dylan's musical (and political) persona.

The context alone, however, is not enough. Just as Smith's refusal of the conventions of archival compilations made a certain kind of engagement possible, so did the type of song. Michael Denning (1997: 119) talks of 'the obsession with documentary and folk authenticity that produced the folk and blues purism of the "folk revival".' Against this was a different kind of vision summoned up by the Popular Front's more eclectic aesthetic, which Smith's collection exemplified. These specific aesthetics matter because of the kind of pleasures they produce and the different 'peoples' they evoke. Starkly put, folk music was associated (via the Seeger family) with communism, while the Popular Front had jazz (Denning, 1997: 283 and 329). The *Anthology* was caught up in these cultural political arguments, and as such its meaning and influence were inflected in the way it was used as a source of influence. The two notions of the 'people' at play are, first, that of the 'real' people in the workshops, those waiting to be organized by communism, for whom folk music is a form of social realism; the second notion of the 'people' is that of the 'folk', who in Cantwell's (1996: 368) words, 'live up on the mountain, telling tales, distilling whiskey, singing ballads, salvaging old washing machine motors, and playing the fiddle.' It is these 'folk' who inhabit the *Anthology*.

But what are they saying or experiencing? What do the songs tell us? The words of a song provide 'hard evidence' of a kind – they give clues as to what the song is about, and what the composer wishes to say. And there are, of course, many songs which address political issues or which are intended to generate a political response. The *Anthology* does contain the occasional reference to politics in the world outside the studio ('White House Blues', for instance), but to focus on these would be to overlook much else. Lyrics which appear to have no explicit political content may still convey a highly ideological message. The fact that the lyrics lack any direct political references is not evidence of an apolitical character. Simple celebrations of pleasure – like, say, Little Richard's song, 'Rip it up' – can contain implicit criticisms of a protestant work ethic and deferred gratification (Lipsitz,1990: 116).

Lyrics, argues Simon Frith (1988), exist in large part only to give the voice something to sing. In popular music, the voice invests the words with feeling, and hence with meaning. Contained in different versions of the same song (the same words, the same tune) are different visions, different narratives: alternative accounts of how the singer encountered their present predicament. How they do this is not just a function of technique, but of genre, of the conventions for articulating certain feelings. Thus, political anger can find expression in an open-throated roar or in a sweet falsetto. Whatever the rules, the voice serves to convey a character, to testify to an experience – to set up a narrative. Writing of the voices to be heard on the *Anthology*, Cantwell (1991: 375) suggests: 'They accompany us, like so many Virgils; they reveal in the *Anthology*'s eerie environment of whines, cries, shouts, growls and other weird vocal sounds, the path which our own traditions have taken, at the same time positioning our own voices in rela-tion to sounds lost, abandoned, or forgotten.' The voices collected on the *Anthology* have provided a way of singing and a way of seeing the world that Dylan, Nick Cave, Beck and others have, self-consciously or not, bor-rowed and reproduced. What they have taken is the outsider's perspective that the songs constantly evoke (the poor, the criminal) and the extremes of experience that they articulate (the rage, the lust). They have created communities in which these figures move and in which their emotions are expressed. These communities are also evoked in the associations estab-lished by the tunes. The *Anthology* contains melodies borrowed from France, Ireland, Scotland and from the continent of Africa, each carrying its own associations.

The claims for the *Anthology*, the way it is inserted within cultural history and cultural politics, make a powerful case for how we might link music to the wider political narratives by which we live. But as we have seen, this case is made in very different ways – from Greil Marcus's vaulting tales of invisible republics lived in the voices that Harry Smith collected, through to the more banal realities of political movements and alliances. As a fan, it is the former story that inspires me; at his best Marcus makes us hear music in new and exciting ways. As a social scientist, it is the latter approach that reins in my fan-like romantic excesses. And it is to this latter guise that I turn now, to another community summoned up by music: the 1969 Woodstock Music and Art Fair (as it was originally known). If the communities and pasts summoned up by the *Anthology* are those of the performers and those who have written about them, then those summoned up by Woodstock are products of a different process and poli-tics. Woodstock's place in the myths by which we live is established by multiple interests and their very different discourses.

Imagining the Woodstock nation

From the stage at Live Aid in 1985, opening the Philadelphia end of the media spectacle, Joan Baez announced to those watching: 'Good morning, you children of the eighties. This is your Woodstock and it is long overdue.' With her history of political activism, her career as a singer of radical folk songs and her association with Bob Dylan, it seems fairly clear what Baez meant. She did not mean: 'Here are some great rock acts; I hope you enjoy them.' She meant instead that Live Aid was a major cultural and political event, a revival of the spirit of 1960s cultural politics. Many years later, Bob Geldof (*Sun*, 28 January 2011) gave a sly twist to Baez's sentiment, when in an interview he said: 'There's a resonance to Live Aid. It was like Woodstock, but it was for a political purpose.' For Baez Woodstock *was* political. She was not just looking out at a sea of pop fans, at an audience; she was looking out at a political movement. Baez's 'Woodstock' was the moment when all the dreams of flower power idealism coalesced into a single gesture that was to define a generation. 'Woodstock' represented the triumph of peace and love. It was the Woodstock that the journalist Pete Hamill characterized as 'anti-authoritarian, anti-establishment, anti-war' (quoted in Garofalo, 1997: 380). The music, the musicians and the fans had somehow forged themselves into an alternative political community – a 'Woodstock Nation' – that stood opposed to the dominant ideology. And Live Aid, Baez appeared to suggest, offered the same prospect for the children of the 1980s. It was a blow against the empire of neo-conservative, materialist individualism then presided over by Margaret Thatcher and Ronald Reagan. And when David Widgery (1986: 90) described RAR as that generation's Woodstock, he meant something different again. As did Greil Marcus (1993: 380–1), when he suggested that the demonstrators in Tiananmen Square inspired themselves 'with images of Woodstock'.

Such pronouncements raise a number of interesting questions. Did Baez's audience, for instance, draw the same inferences as her? Would the crowd in Brockwell Park have shared Widgery's vision, or in China Marcus's? What did 'Woodstock' mean to them? After all, Live Aid took place almost a generation later and was being witnessed by many more people than either gathered at Yasgur's Farm or saw the movies. And if 'Woodstock' meant something to the Live Aid or the RAR audience, or to the Chinese students, does it mean the same thing now, in the twenty-first century? The answers do not lie buried in the earth in New York State. They live in the business of myth-making.

Remembering Woodstock

Woodstock lives on in a number of different guises and in a number of different places. It is not preserved and enshrined in a single form in a single place like a dinosaur in a natural history museum. Its history is notoriously fuzzy. There is, after all, no agreement as to how many people there were actually present. Was it 500,000 (Friedlander, 1996; Osgerby, 1998); or 400,000 (Ward et al., 1987; Clarke, D., 1998); or 300,000 (Larkin, 1993; Murray, 1989)? If there is no consensus as to the number of people attending, there seems little chance of a unanimous view on any other aspect of the event. And while, in principle, it may be possible to establish a more accurate account of how many people were there, it would not get us much closer to understanding Woodstock. 'Woodstock' exists not as a single historical entity, but in a multiplicity of incarnations. It signifies many different experiences and ideas and moments. What follows serves merely to illustrate the diversity.

Woodstock on the web

Woodstock lives today, as do many past events, as a website (http:// www.woodstock.com/1969-festival/). What is most obvious about current Woodstock websites is the aura of 'heritage' that pervades them. They both want to record the minute details of the performances that took place in 1969, and to evoke what they see as the spirit of those days, to evoke the bucolic pleasures of communing with nature and with each other. There are web pages devoted, for example, to preserving the venue (as, you might say, a site of special cultural significance) for future generations. Other websites advertise the memorabilia and memories of performers such as the Incredible String Band. At the Woodstock Store (www. woodstock69.com/woodstock_gift.htm) you can buy, framed or unframed, a 'Set of Original Single Day Woodstock Tickets', as well as Woodstock Zippo lighters and souvenir programmes of the event.

You can browse the memories of those who were there in August 1969 (www.woodstock69.com/woodstock_mem.htm), with their tales of the cold they endured or of their journey ('in my Fiat convertible'), or of giving up smoking at Woodstock (because the 'coolest' girl refused the offer of a cigarette). These memories are, though, firmly embedded in the present, in the importance Woodstock had for the lives lived now. Woodstock was, Diana Vincelli writes, 'a turning point in life'. Juan Morales says of Woodstock that it epitomized the 'social changes in human freedom and expression . . . we learned not to be ashamed of our bodies in the nude, we smoked grass to expand our horizons with the music, we spent time with our kids . . . it was LIFE!!' Susan Harnisch-Jones reports: 'If Woodstock did anything for me, it gave me STRENGTH to state my beliefs.'

Woodstock also exists as a utopian moment, never again to be attained: 'There was a feeling of community, a spirit of cooperation that touched everyone who was there. It may only have existed for a few days, but it lives on in some form in all of us' (Chris S.). Dr Jan Pitts explains that, for her, 'Woodstock was not a concert. This was a coming together. . . . Many people dropped out, stopped wearing and eating decaying animals, began to respect our setting.' 'In my mind', writes Jimmy Wage, 'Woodstock was the biggest time I've ever had and most likely will ever have in my life.' These accounts, written long after the event, are evidence of how Woodstock is imagined and recalled: as a utopian experience, as a turning point, and as part of present reality. In all of these, the music features remarkably little. Even those who played at the festival say little about the performances. The keyboard player of Sha Na Na remembers the 'COLD'. It is the political and social significance of Woodstock that animates the memories and the personal narratives in which it is located. The music is peripheral in one sense because, Jan Pitts points out, it was not what made Woodstock unique. The same music was to be heard at many other festivals that Summer. 'How could the music have had anything to do with it?', she asks, 'Some people never even found the main stage. . . . There was something much greater that pulled us together at Woodstock that day in August.'

Woodstock in the mass media

'Woodstock' has an altogether different existence in mainstream mass media (all the quotations that follow are taken from the British print media). It is a shorthand for describing any number of events in which people gather in large numbers, especially for festivals: 'China's answer to Woodstock'; 'a Woodstock-style happening organized by the Social Democrats in Bonn'; 'It's like Woodstock, only with advertisements'. When ex-President Bill Clinton addressed the Hay-on-Wye literary festival, he described it as 'the Woodstock of the mind.' 'Woodstock' also stands, as it did for memorialists on the web, for a life-changing cultural event – the Sex Pistols first gig, the opening of the club Shoom: 'the event that was the Woodstock of its generation.' And in this spirit Woodstock is used to mark the passage of music's history and of its audience. So Arlo Guthrie is dubbed a 'Woodstock veteran' or Joni Mitchell 'the darling of the Woodstock set'; eras and generations are marked by their relationship to it: 'the post-Woodstock, late-hippie, pre-Glitter period' or 'America's post-Woodstock generation', or 'Woodstock generation folkie parents.' Woodstock also stands for a specific aesthetic: 'Boho makes a comeback with a Woodstock vibe', wrote one fashion journalist; others described 'Woodstock bikinis' or 'Country Joe fringes'. In discourses on fashion, 'Woodstock' serves sometimes as a counterpoint, as a style to be avoided: 'ankle-length flares, which . . . won't make you look like a throwback to Woodstock'. The tennis player Andre Agassi is described as looking 'like he missed the last train to Woodstock . . . he's a tennis flower child gone to seed'. It is used to describe a film technique 'Woodstock-like split-screen'. It is even used to demarcate a musical aesthetic: 'Kula Shaker try to emulate Jimi Hendrix at Woodstock'; or a festival is described as 'a bit like Woodstock, only not so boring'. As this last quotation, and some of the others suggest, 'Woodstock' is not an unambiguously positive attribute. Dismissing the band Queen, one critic wrote: 'the whole point was that they were some camp old shambolic showbiz outfit miles removed from the true spirit of Elvis, the Beatles, the Stones, Woodstock, even Cliff Richard.' An unflattering review of Carlos Santana in *The Times* is headed 'Woodstock? It's still here, man'. Even if 'Woodstock' is not always a positive epithet in mainstream media, it remains an important marker of journalistic discourse.

Woodstock in the everyday

What is on the web or in the media does not translate seamlessly to those who consume these outlets. In 1999, thirty years after Woodstock, I conducted a simple survey of 150 university students to see what Woodstock signified for them. I asked them to write down the thoughts and associations that came into their minds when they saw the single word 'Woodstock'. I do not pretend that my sample was a representative one, but it produced some interesting results. One respondent wrote: 'Large rock festival in a muddy field, full of people like my Mum and Dad consuming drugs.' Others wrote about 'drugs' and 'hippies', and yet others about 'Snoopy's friend'. As with mass media, the music seemed relatively insignificant (and some of the artists they associated with Woodstock did not actually play there – Bob Dylan, for example).

My students' impressions of Woodstock chimed with those solicited by others. The BBC documentary-maker Pete Everett (1986: 100) was told by those who lived through the period: 'Everybody took their clothes off at festivals. At Woodstock and even at the Isle of Wight a lot of people took their clothes off. And it was all right.' Someone too young to have been there in 1969 writes on one of the Woodstock websites (www.woodstock69.com/woodstock_mem.htm): 'Woodstock is no longer a place, but let this place be sacred, for it is where it all came together for so many people. . . . It has nothing to do with drugs, or the music, or even Bethel, N.Y. It has to do with the people and their way of thinking, their way of loving and believing.' Woodstock exists here as a way of imagining the 'good life'.

Woodstock in pop history

It might be supposed that an important source of the popular and media mythologies of Woodstock are themselves a part product of the way the writing of pop history has constituted it (or ignored it). It is interesting to see how it features in such narratives. Some authors see it as a seminal moment in the legitimation of rock. Here is Colin Larkin (1993: 1209), author of a vast encyclopaedia of pop and rock: 'the festival totally changed the world's attitude towards popular music'. If the Monterey festival, continues Larkin, represented the 'birth of the new music revolution, Woodstock was its coming of age.' Others, like Charlie Gillett (1983: 403), saw it simply as confirming the status of rock's premier league, and as launching the careers of those still in the 'minor leagues'. The rock impressario, Bill Graham, once remarked: 'the real thing that Woodstock accomplished was that it told people that rock was big business' (quoted in Wiener, 1984: 104).

Yet others are keen to deflate the mythology. In *The Faber Book of Pop and Rock* (Kureishi and Savage, 1995), there is almost nothing on Woodstock, and what is there is pejorative: the 'Woodstock Nation' was 'a festival fantasy'; 'It [Woodstock] was so weak and stupid, and they believed it'; 'leftovers from the denimed Woodstock era'. *Rock of Ages: the Rolling Stone History of Rock and Roll* (Ward et al., 1987) compares Woodstock unfavourably to the 1965 TAMI Show, featuring the Beach Boys, James Brown and Gerry and the Pacemakers. But however badly Woodstock is treated in such books, its presence is acknowledged, where other similar events in the same year (Blind Faith in Hyde Park, a festival in Atlanta that attracted 140,000, and a three day festival at Newport) are overlooked.

Woodstock in social and political history

But if Woodstock has a mixed reception in the writing of music's history, how does it fare in histories of society as a whole? In summing up the twentieth century, Eric Hobsbawm (1995), once a jazz critic for the *New Statesman*, makes no mention of Woodstock. Jonathan Green (1998: 436), historian of the 1960s, warns of 'hyperbolic assessments' of Woodstock, preferring to see it as a mundane mix 'of dope and sex and rock 'n' roll . . . love and peace . . . self-sufficiency and vegetarian cooking', rather than as any kind of 'alternative culture'.

This tone is echoed elsewhere in other historical narratives, if it is mentioned at all. Tariq Ali's *Street Fighting Years: An Autobiography of the Sixties* (1987) contains no reference. George McKay's (1996: 14) *Senseless Acts of Beauty*, which tracks the Free Festival movement, plays down the impact of Woodstock, and quotes instead a remark from the *International Times* that 'Woodstock is the potentiality but Altamont is the reality.' In a similar vein, Nigel Fountain's (1988: 116) chronicle of the underground press reports one jaundiced commentator as saying: 'Woodstock . . . had a lot to answer for. It caused such damage everyone tried to emulate it . . .' While these critical references to Woodstock fit with the familiar cynicism that tends to accompany such ventures, there is a counter-narrative that also circulates.

Re-imagining the Woodstock nation

We began this brief survey of Woodstock's cultural presence with Joan Baez's address to the Live Aid audience. And we have seen the confused and contradictory set of ideas that circulate about what 'Woodstock' might signify. Before returning to the broader theme of how music allows us to imagine communities and their politics, I want to end by looking closely at what might be called the politics of representing Woodstock, given its enduring, if often marginal, place in cultural discourse.

For Michael Clarke (1982), Woodstock deserves a place in a very different narrative, one that recounts the regulation of music festivals. Woodstock demonstrated to the authorities, according to Clarke, that a peaceful festival was a possibility. It served thereby to diffuse the moral panic that typically had accompanied the staging of festivals. Clarke (1982: 36) writes of how 'Woodstock was eagerly promoted as the festival of peace and love, a demonstration that large numbers of young people could congregate without violence and disorder despite the forebodings of the authorities and in the context of substantial youth participation in the anti-Vietnam War movement and the civil rights campaign in the USA.'

While Clarke locates Woodstock in a narrative of regulatory enlightenment, Reebee Garofalo (1992: 15) sets it in one of radical engagement. He argues that 'Woodstock was experienced as participatory, communitarian and non-commercial (indeed anti-commercial), with no great spiritual or physical distance between artist and audience.' Garofalo is not alone. Robert Hewison (1988), for example, saw Woodstock as clearing a space for practising the hippy ideal, providing both legitimacy and opportunity for the other ways of being. Bill Osgerby (1998: 89) too portrays Woodstock as instrumental in the formation of group identities that helped to sustain commitment to 'alternative lifestyles'. Garofalo contrasts the Woodstock nation's alliance of folk culture values and mass culture commercialism with the 'unabashed celebration of technological possibilities' that was Live Aid (Garofalo, 1992: 15). Woodstock humanized mass culture, while Live Aid was part of the international star-making system and was compromised by its commercial sponsorship by the Pepsi Corporation (Garofalo, 1997).

A third narrative that is applied to Woodstock is that of cynical commercial exploitation – Woodstock the product. Certainly Robert Spitz's (1979) account of the festival describes an event which, in contemporary parlance, was very cleverly 'spun', and in which the master spin-doctor was the Yippie activist Abbie Hoffman. Spitz (1979: 167) claims that Hoffman secured $10,000 from the organizers to promote Woodstock as a radical event. As he (1979: 164–5) tells it, Hoffman 'periodically descended upon the office [Michael Lang's, Woodstock impressario] shouting anticapitalist war cries', and in the end Lang realized: 'We need those cats on our side . . . They're pretty groovy guys to have around, and they have a direct line to the underground which'd be invaluable to us. If they're in our corner, we can't miss.' The message was reinforced by leaflets printed and distributed at the festival that quoted Eldridge Cleaver and Bob Dylan. Hoffman's spin eventually took the form of his book *Woodstock Nation* (1969). Spitz presents us with a picture of entrepreneurial endeavour and smart business practice. Writing many years later, Dave Marsh (1983: 349) recounts how Michael Lang refused to pay acts because the event was a 'free festival', despite the fact that they had 'collected more than $1 million on film rights, recording rights and ticket sales'.

A fourth narrative is built around the performances, and in particular the way they were captured in Michael Wadleigh's commercially released 1970 documentary. The film highlights moments which seem to symbolize the melding of politics and music: Country Joe MacDonald singing, with the crowd on chorus, 'I-feel-like-I'm-fixin-to-die rag', or Richie Havens hammering out the insistent 'Freedom', or Jimi Hendrix's rendition of 'Star Spangled Banner'. Charles Shaar Murray (1989: 195) described the latter as 'the stately unreeling of the melody derailed by the sounds of riot and war, sirens and screams, chaos and alarm'; and Richard Morrison (*The Times*, 8 February 2011) saw it as 'a political statement: an anti-Vietnam protest'. In between the acts, there were the stage announcements – about the birth of babies or the beauty of the audience or the free food. The songs and the rhetoric are used to constitute a sense of political community – albeit a partial one. Few women musicians were represented (particularly in the filmed record of Woodstock). Only two women performed solo (Melanie and Joan Baez), and the other women to be seen were Grace Slick of Jefferson Airplane and Licorice Mckecknie and Rose Simpson of the Incredible String Band. There was a similar absence of African-American performers. Sly Stone, with Richie Havens, was one of the few exceptions, and he was omitted from the final film (Garofalo, 1997: 234).

Woodstock, in summary, exists in multiple sites and in many different narratives. The meanings and discourses attaching to it contrast and clash. This is hardly surprising. What is important is how 'Woodstock' illustrates the role played by musical events in imagining past and present communities, past and present political stories. In doing so it helps to write a version of history and of the peoples who inhabit it.

Making history, making music

This chapter has been about how music has been read into history, and how history has been read out of music. The examples of the Woodstock festival and the *Anthology of American Music* reveal how music can be used to construct, in Greil Marcus's words 'secret histories' and 'invisible republics'. Even though Marcus's own rhetoric might test the credulity of the social scientist in us, it points to a view of music's potential to evoke, not just place and time, but experience. It is this latter – the structure of feelings, as Raymond Williams dubbed it – that underpins the passions upon which social movements draw.

Marcus's approach to music, and to writing about music, provides a way of seeing it as creating narrative by which identities – national, political, personal – are *realized*, not just 'expressed' or 'revealed'. In imagining the communities through music, we also *experience* them. As Simon Frith (1996: 273, his emphasis) writes: 'Whether jazz or rap for African-Americans or nineteenth-chamber music for German Jews in Israel, it [music] both articulates and offers the immediate *experience* of collective identity.' Music is not a symbol of identity so much as a way of living it.

As the Ukraine was struggling to create its own separate identity in the 1990s, and to break free from the legacy of the Soviet Union, nationalists found that traditional musical cultures – the folkloric – proved peculiarly inadequate to this task. They provided only nostalgia for a lost or utopian past. It was, instead, rock music that was the most potent symbol of nationalism. Catherine Wanner (1996: 140) explains that it was 'the ability to mimic the Western pop music tradition [that] lent some credence to nationalists' claim that Ukraine is an Eastern European country and does not belong in an "Asiatic Empire", as many independence supporters refer to the Soviet Union.' The Ukrainian performers, however, did not simply imbibe and regurgitate Western pop. They customized it to emphasize their 'Ukraineness'. And when these songs were played at a festival, Wanner describes how the divide between performer and audience broke down as the fans formed 'a human chain, encircling the singers on stage and each other. Some formed spinning circles of twenty or more people all holding hands. Others formed swirling chains . . . The soccer stadium [the venue] became the central town square as the "imagined community".'

In his book *1989: Bob Dylan didn't have this to sing about*, Joshua Clover (2009) weaves a deft narrative between changing musical fashion (from Black Power to Gangsta Rap, the Second Summer of Love, Grunge) and world changing events, such as the collapse of the Berlin Wall, the protests in Tiananmen Square. Music, suggests Clover (2009: 2), helped us understand the world: 'A song may communicate historical experience . . . what it means, how it feels.' History is relayed through music. Clover's ambitions for music's importance belong with the Greil Marcus school, but more importantly they represent another example of the persistent belief that music forms and informs our history and the communities which make it.

7

Sounding good: the politics of taste

The Ukranian nationalists who decided to opt for rock to evoke their collective political identity were making an aesthetic and a political judgement. So too did the Serbian students described by Marc Steinberg (2004), who rejected officially-sanctioned turbo-folk for a music that better evoked their antipathy to the regime of Slobodan Milosevic. This chapter is about how musical taste and judgement plays into politics.

On the day before the Live Aid Concerts in 1985, the academic Will Straw told a group of popular music scholars: 'I take it for granted that most of us here find the various charity projects tasteless, self-serving for those involved, symptomatic of existing geo-political relations and politically inappropriate, and that we never much liked Bob Geldof anyway' (Rijven et al., 1985: 25). Some years later Dick Hebdige offered a quite different view of Live Aid. It represented, he said, a strongly anti-Thatcherite critique of selfish individualism and appealed to a collective identity which challenged the libertarian politics of the time. Live Aid was 'the articulation of a different version of "common-sense" drawing on traditions of co-operation and mutual support, rooted in the human(e) values of good fellowship and good neighbourliness . . .' (Hebdige, 1988: 219). As it happens, Straw had more time for Hebdige's perspective than his comments might suggest, but what is important about both judgements is how they elided musical taste and political values. It is not just that music may, in the form of a protest song, convey political values. Judgements of, and responses to, music also articulate political ideas. We have already seen many such examples in this book. From the criticisms of Geldof's choice of performers for Live 8 to Rock Against Racism's arguments about what is truly anti-racist music, from music that gets censored by states to music that is subsidized by them.

There is a tendency, when it comes to discussing cultural choices of all kinds, to regard them as mere matters of 'taste'. This labelling does several things. It removes the choices from the realm of the rational – 'there's no accounting for taste'. It attributes them to the subjective: 'I just like it.' And it separates them from the political: 'you cannot arbitrate for taste'. On the other side, there are those – from across the political spectrum (from Roger Scruton to Richard Hoggart) – who contend that there are standards of cultural taste which need to be preserved and reinforced, in part as a bastion against what has become known as 'dumbing down'. This chapter examines these various assumptions by looking in detail at the processes by which 'taste' is expressed, processes which, I shall argue, are irrevocably political in a number of different senses. I am not the first to do this. Many others have pointed out the ways in which music has been policed by those who write about it, and in particular about how music journalism has been colonized by men, with important implications for how 'music' has been understood (McDonnell and Powers, 1995; McLeod, 2001; Toynbee, 1993; Whiteley, 1997). At root, such criticisms are about the politics of taste, and about the ideas to which they give expression. Writing of the musicians that Ruth Finnegan portrays in her study of music-making in an English town, Simon Frith (1996: 276) remarks: 'it was in their aesthetic judgements that they expressed their most deep-seated ethical views.'

Star ratings

We begin with the business of reviewing, and in particular with the awarding of stars or marks out of five (or whatever) that are accorded to records in magazines, newspapers and increasingly online. What is going on when a record receives such a ranking, whether from a professional critic or a consumer?

The use of stars or other schemes is now widespread, but it is not universal and nor is it uncontroversial. When the *Guardian* introduced a star system for its arts pages, there was a lively debate. There were performers who favoured it on largely pragmatic grounds: 'Performing at Edinburgh this year, I experienced at first hand how stars affect a play's success. A three- or four-star review is how you sell your show and draw your audience in. With so much choice, it's the only immediate way in this consumer culture to advertise your show.' And there were consumers who admitted to using the ratings: 'As a discerning movie-goer I admit to being swayed very much by the star rating system and only really consider seeing those rated four and five star.' Somewhat sheepishly, another punter admitted: 'I am ashamed to confess that I find the stars a useful first indicator' (*Guardian*, G2, 3 February 2004). Against these – sometimes reluctant – advocates of a star system stand those who think of it as vulgarizing and demeaning. The playwright David Hare, for example, described it as 'militantly philistine' (*Guardian*, G2, 20 January 2004). To understand what is at stake in such debates about the seemingly trivial business of rating works of art, we need to look back into the origin of such schemes.

A brief history of star ratings: from Christgau to Q

Robert Christgau introduced a version of the star system into his 'Consumer Guides' in the *Village Voice* in 1969 (Christgau, 1982, 1990 and 2000). He was being ironic in offering his pithy reviews in this form, especially when he attached a grading scheme taken from college education (A+ to E). He was mimicking, not emulating, the systems he drew upon. As he wrote in explanation of what he called 'criticism in a pop form' (i.e. 'compact and digestible'): 'The most essential component of this form was also the most controversial – the grades . . . Of course, what people hate about grades, even more than their arbitrariness, is their appearance of objectivity, of absolute authority' (Christgau, 1982: 4–5). He only pretended to 'absolute authority', of course. In fact, the grades signalled 'a private aesthetic response', and one guided by a 'populism' that set itself against inaccessability – hence a B for Captain Beefheart and the Magic Band's *Trout Mask Replica* (Christgau, 1982: 5).

The irony which accompanied Christgau's grading system was not apparent nearly two decades later when Q magazine was launched. The star system it adopted – 5*: indispensable, 4*: excellent, and so on – was functionality itself. As one of the founders of Q explained, the awarding of stars was meant as an independent statement of merit, not a whim of the reviewer. It was not a version of Christgau's 'private aesthetic response'; rather, Q was establishing the order of things. This is how the Q regime operated, according to one of the magazine's original editors: 'Dave Rimmer produced a review of a David Sylvian album. We'd told writers that the star-rating system meant that they had to stand aside from the music, because the review was not purely their opinion. Dave Rimmer's review came back with five stars and Mark [Ellen] and I said "No, sorry, David Sylvian does not rate five stars" . . . It caused a bit of a to-do, but I think we were actually right, because we put ourselves on the side of the readers rather than the writers . . . So we docked a star. They got the hang of it' (David Hepworth, quoted in Gorman, 2001: 324). For Q, the star system was seen to offer the same kind of service as was offered by *What Computer?* or any other consumer guide. (*PC World* explained in its general rubric: 'It's designed to give our readers an easy-to-find, quick-to-interpret assessment of a product's overall quality and performance.') Interestingly, as Colin Symes (2004: 186–7; 226) points out, it is not just popular music that is subject to these schemes of 'semiotic calibration'. Classical music has been rated in the same way in the record guides published from the 1970s onwards.

What stars mean

There is a sense in which both Christgau and Q were engaged in the same business. Both were adherents of market democracy, both were celebrating or serving the (relatively) free choice of consumers. They differed, though, in the conceptions of democracy they operated. Where Q wanted simply to *reflect* the consumer, Christgau wanted to *educate* them. This is a political difference, and one that separates the many diverse strands of liberalism. This difference can be seen to connect the criteria deployed by the critics (or at least that they publicly represent themselves as deploying) to a set of political values.

For Christgau, the criteria have changed over time. In the 1970s an A+ record was 'an organically conceived masterpiece that repays prolonged listening with new excitement and insight' (1982: 21). By the 1990s, it was 'a record of sustained beauty, power, insight, groove and/or googlefritz that has invited and repaid repeated listenings in the daily life of someone with 500 other CDs to get to' (2000: xvi). A dud (which is to be distinguished from a 'turkey'), by contrast, is 'a bad record whose details rarely merit further thought. At the upper level it may merely be overrated, disappointing, or dull. Down below it may be contemptible'. Although these criteria make no explicit reference to politics, they can be read politically. They accord with J. S. Mill's (1859/1989) notion of the 'higher values' that a good society is obliged to promote, or at least protect, in the name of liberty.

Where Christgau adopts the voice of cultural elitism, Q speaks for market populism. In the first edition of Q (October 1986), it was announced that a 5* was to be awarded to 'a record likely to be enthused-over by 99 per cent of sane humans.' Where Christgau makes music serve some higher goal, seeking to educate his readers in a particular aesthetic, Q's approach (because it too is imposing an aesthetic, even if this is disguised) is to reflect what it perceives as popular (i.e. Q readers') taste. 'Popularity' is, though, an empty category. 'A measurement of popularity', writes Simon Frith (1996: 48), 'is not a measurement of value.' What is key is the conception of 'the people' that underlies the judgement. For Christgau, the people need and deserve to be educated; for Q, they're to be given no more than what they already want. Q's approach is in line with wider trends.

Explaining stars

The emergence of stars as indicators of quality are, of course, not confined to music. Some of us, I suspect, are familiar – if not as familiar as we'd like to be – with their use in ranking restaurants (the Michelin star) and hotels. Indeed, Colin Symes (2004: 186) suggests that the use of ratings in music may be a legacy of the Baedeker travel guides. In the UK, hospital trusts, the bodies responsible for managing health care, have been evaluated and awarded a star grade, as have university departments for the quality of their research. The use of stars, then, might seem to form part of a general process, one that is often captured in the term 'audit culture' or 'audit society' (Power, 1997), and is now characterized as 'neoliberalism' (Couldry, 2010). Such developments have been seen as the logical and material consequence of the breakdown of traditional value structures and hierarchies. Where once institutions operated on the basis of trust and/or authority, they are now required to be 'transparent' and 'accountable'. The star system becomes one way of delivering on these new obligations.

But there may be yet longer-term processes at work, particularly in relation to the arts. These have to do with the modernization and rationalization of society. Max Graf (1947: 30), for example, linked the emergence of music criticism to the emergence of reason itself: 'Musical criticism is one of the forces that have molded the modern world, a tributary to the mighty stream of criticism that began to flow through Europe in the middle of the eighteenth century. Since then, criticism has participated in every phase of the formation of modern ideas. It has grown in strength along with the rising tide of the scientific, philosophical, and social ideas of the "Age of Reason".' This echoes Jürgen Habermas's (1992: 159–65) suggestion in *The Structural Transformation of the Public Sphere* that, with the emergence of capitalism and instrumental rationality, cultural *debate* gave way to cultural *consumption* and the celebration of 'free choice'. To this extent, the star system can be seen as a device designed to help consumers choose – as those participants in the *Guardian* debate suggested. Certainly, this is a logic expounded by the economist Richard Caves (2000), who sees cultural criticism primarily as a way of conveying market information to consumers. Stars reduce information costs.

While noting the logic that might yield the star system, it is important to recognize that not all media outlets have succumbed, and those who have do not apply it to all art forms – it is commonly used for music and films, but less often for books. Variations of this kind may be linked to the function that information plays in cultural consumption. Theatre critics are reviewing products that potential customers cannot sample, unlike music buyers, who can often hear things for themselves and are therefore less dependent on the reviewer. As the suppliers of key information, theatre critics are more powerful than music critics (although in the world of Twitter, even the drama critic's special claims are being eroded). A further factor is the relationship of readers to the critical views. A magazine like Q acts to serve consumers, where other outlets, such as Christgau's, see themselves as serving fans, or even citizens. As with the rationale for stars, so with the explanation for them: there is a political story to be told, one that has to do with political economy of culture.

Distributing stars

There is one final possible political issue: who benefits? Who or what gets to receive 5 stars or to be a dud? This is a hard question to answer, and I do not pretend to provide a full answer. What I can do, however, is illustrate what is at stake in the exercise of cultural judgement.

1. Christgau vs Q

Taking a year at random (1994) (and allowing for the fact that US and UK release dates may vary), I compared the albums awarded an A by Christgau (73) and those deemed the fifty best records of the year by Q. Of the 123 records listed, only 8 (6.5 per cent) appeared on both lists: Beck (*Mellow Gold*), Nirvana (*Unplugged*), Hole (*Living Through This*), Green Day (*Dookie*), REM (*Monster*), Neil Young (*Sleep with Angels*), Soundgarden (*Superunknown*), Beastie Boys (*Ill Communications*). Apart from the fact that they were all US artists, this result would seem to suggest a real difference between the criteria being applied by Christgau and Q. What this divergence might signify (and indeed whether it is true for other years and other outlets) requires, of course, much more detailed examination.

2. *The case of Uncut* (and Christgau)

Founded in 1997, *Uncut* was one among several monthly magazines offering interviews and reviews. Although devoting much space to music, it was unusual in that it gave almost equal attention to film. Looking at how it awarded stars over a five-month period (January–May 2005), it is possible to detect patterns in the way they are allocated, and to explore the distribution of stars across a range of cultural categories – in particular, debuts, new vs re-releases, and music vs other cultural forms. Table 7.1 represents the distribution of stars given to records, comparing those awarded to new releases and those to re-releases.

Of the 434 new releases reviewed, 2 per cent received a 5*; of the 441 re-released albums reviewed 7 per cent received a 5*. The comparison for 4* is: 38 per cent (new)/45 per cent (old); and for 3*: 48 per cent (new)/37 per cent (old). This suggests that, generally, re-released albums receive more positive assessment than new releases. This is not altogether surprising, given that the records chosen for re-release will tend to be those that have already 'proved' themselves; it is rare for an abject critical or commercial failure to be re-released. What is perhaps more significant is the concentration of assessment in the 3*/4* categories: 87 per cent of all new releases received 3* or 4*, and 82 per cent of all re-released records were given 3 or 4 stars. By way of contrast, consider Christgau's distribution of top grades. Between 1969 and early 2005, Christgau reviewed 12,682 records, of which 2,859 (22 per cent) received an A, and 4,003 (31 per cent) a B. While there is no easy translation between the two systems of grading, it would suggest that Christgau is a 'harder marker' than *Uncut* and less inclined to provide endorsement for the industry's products.

A similar pattern of positive endorsement in *Uncut* can be detected for books and films (see Table 7.2). 87 per cent of films received 3* or better and 91 per cent of books received 3* or better, albeit with a significantly higher proportion of films receiving a 5* (14 per cent) than were awarded to records. Books were similarly favoured; 13 per cent received 5*. There may, of course, be a simple explanation for the latter: fewer books are reviewed, and the pre-selection may involved a pre-judgement. The same, though, would not be true for films (given the relatively small number

Table 7.1. Albums reviewed in *Uncut*, January–May 2005.

	5* new/old	4* new/old	3* new/old	2* new/old	1* new/old
January	0/3	24/31	35/18	6/7	1/1
February	2/4	21/19	33/28	6/7	1/0
March	1/5	36/39	33/36	7/12	0/1
April	3/7	25/37	37/25	12/9	0/1
May	1/5	30/34	38/24	7/6	0/1
June	2/6	31/40	33/31	9/4	0/0
Total	9/30	167/200	209/162	47/45	2/4

Table 7.2. Films and books reviewed in *Uncut*, January–June 2005.

	5*	4*	3*	2*	1*
Films	17	53	33	12	3
Books	18	65	40	9	2
Total (%)	35 (14)	118 (47)	73 (31)	21 (8)	5 (2)

released each month). Nonetheless, the impression created is of a hierarchy of cultural quality with films and books at the top and music below them.

The other issue that I investigated was the treatment of debuts. Of the 9 records receiving a 5*, 4 (44 per cent) were debut records. Taking the case of a single month, 6/24 (25 per cent) of 4* records were debuts and 11/35 (31 per cent) of 3* records were debuts. Put another way: of the records getting 3*–5* (68), 21 were debut records, and of these 4 (19 per cent) got 5*, whereas only 11 per cent of other records got 5*. There is no such distinction for 4* records, of which 28 per cent were debuts, and 26 per cent second or later releases. While we cannot use this evidence to claim that any given debut record will do better than a second album (because we do not have the global figures for both), we can say that there appears to be a bias towards debut records in the awarding of 5*. By way of further comparison, taking a single year of Christgau's A+ records, only 13/92 (14 per cent) were debut records. Christgau, it seems, is less impressed by debut records.

The politics of the star system

If we assume that the awarding of stars matters, and if we note the divergences between the signals transmitted by Christgau and Q and *Uncut*, then we should, at the very least, give further attention to the particular processes, actors and institutions that deliver these messages. It does appear that there are indeed radically different aesthetics at work. What the survey of *Uncut* seems to reveal is that – generally – the message being conveyed is of the 'high quality' of product: over 80 per cent of recordings are 'good' or better, and that this is a consistent monthly result. In other words, the attribution of quality would seem to serve the self-image of the industry. In respect of debut records, there is also the suggestion that the best is often embodied in the 'new'. Although, paradoxically, the distribution of stars also gives the impression that the past is more glorious than the present. The biases displayed by *Uncut* indicate both a commitment to market liberalism and to conservatism. The judging of music plays into wider political ideologies and is implicated in processes of challenging or sustaining them.

The politics of critical evaluation do not exist simply in the values encoded in aesthetic judgement. They are also institutionalized in the processes that produce those judgements. *Uncut*'s aesthetics, or the aesthetics of *Q* or Robert Christgau, perverse though it may seem, are not simply (or even) the product of an individual's evaluation, but rather of the system through which they are delivered. By way of illustration, I want to consider a particular means of delivering aesthetic judgement: the music prize.

The Mercury Music Prize

The viral spread of the star-rating system is matched only by the proliferation of prizes. There is almost no human activity (and many animal ones – think of those prizes for dogs, cats, horses, pigs . . .) that is not rewarded with a prize, and within the arts there is an apparently inexhaustible list of categories (recall the long list of awards made at the Oscars for almost every aspect of film-making). It does not require high levels of cynicism to see all prizes as devices for selling more products or tickets (or pedigree dogs). It is well known, and widely noted, that the awarding of prizes boosts the sales of those shortlisted and those who win. What is true for the Booker prize for novels is also true for the Mercury Music Prize (MMP). When Ian McEwan won the Booker Prize for *Amsterdam* in 1999 his sales rose by 455 per cent; when DBC Pierre won the same prize in 2003, his sales increased by 20,000 in the two weeks after the announcement. A similar benefit accrues to those who are merely nominated. In 1993, the year after the MMP was introduced, *Music Week* (18 September 1993) reported that sales rose by as much as 300 per cent for MMP nominees. Mercury nomination added sales to the relatively unknown Norma Waterson, Gavin Bryers and the Auteurs, but did little for U2, Oasis or the Spice Girls *(Music Week,* 21 September 1996). When Gomez won in 1998 their sales rose from 85,000 to 330,000 (*Guardian*, 8 September 2000). While these results are impressive, and indicate a possible major effect of the arts prize, they need to be kept in proportion. Up until 2000, *The Oprah Winfrey Show*'s Book Club had produced 28 bestsellers, with total sales of 20 million, earning publishers $175 million (*Guardian*, 4 January 2000).

But the impact of prizes does not travel in one direction. Prizes also influence business practice. Not only is a winner likely to receive preferential treatment from their proud company, but all future marketing will refer (as will reviews) to the prize. Black Star Liner were given more space and freedom by their record company after they were nominated for the Mercury, and as one of them commented wryly: 'When you're nominated, everybody wants to be your friend. Industry people who've never spoken to you before suddenly know your inside-leg measurement' (quoted in *Guardian*, 8 September 2000). Future industry signings will acknowledge the criteria apparently validated by the prize, as will media outlets in their coverage and in who/what they feature. The economist Victor Ginsburgh (2003: 100) has argued that prizes are 'correlated with economic success and may even influence or predict it.' Prizes do not just represent reward to an artist, but an influence on business and cultural policy. Of course, not all prizes have the same impact, partly because they differ in format and character. The Grammys and the Brits (music's equivalents of the Oscars) operate in quite different ways to the Mercury or the Polar Prize for Music (music's equivalent of the Pulitzer). Because my aim here is not to provide a comprehensive picture of music prizes and their impact, I will concentrate on the Mercury, if only to show how its political form shapes the judgements it exercises.

Background

The Mercury Music Prize was first awarded in 1992, with the winner receiving £20,000 (it was briefly raised to £25,000), and the other nominees receiving a smaller prize. The prime movers were Jon Webster, then Managing Director of Virgin, and David Terrill, then Marketing Director of HMV, who got the support of the BPI (British Phonographic Industry) and the record retailers' organization (BARD) (*Music Week*, 19 September 1992; Frith, 2004: 44). It was modelled on the Booker Prize for literature, but as one of the judging panel said of it, it served as 'a celebration as much as a calibration of British music' (David Sinclair, *The Times*, 16 July 1997). Its formal purpose was to identify the British or Irish album of the year. While its intention was to select the best of British and Irish music, its music business founders made no secret of the fact that it was designed to attract the attention of what the industry identified as 'lapsed' customers, people with disposable income who used to buy music but who were no longer doing so – or at least, were not buying new music (*Music Week*, 31 July 1993).

The prize was not designed simply to produce either a populist winner or market winner. That was the business of the Brits or the Grammys. It was important to the strategy for the prize that it had credibility and authority. This meant both that it had to be seen to be independent of the industry and to operate non-market criteria – to choose the best not the most popular. This strategy was embodied in the appointment of Simon Frith as chair of the judging panel, a role he has continued to occupy. Not only is Frith one of the most cited popular music scholars, he worked for many years as a music journalist and has developed close links with the music industry and cultural policy makers. Frith could, therefore, be seen as both independent and credible. The judges too have been selected to represent different aspects of the industry and to shore up the prestige sought for the prize. They have been drawn from all sectors of the music industry, and to have established themselves in respect of a specific expertise, and to be sensitive to the needs which the prize has to meet. Hence the tendency to invite *Time Out* journalists, rather than *NME* ones. At the same time, the jurors are charged with choosing the record of the year without reference to media hype, the previous career of the artists, chart placings or other such factors. The Mercury's calling card is that it is just about the music. It is a claim that is also necessary to legitimating the prize with those who fund and support it. Recognizing the interests of the industry means a certain kind of shortlist, one that reflects the diversity of its products. As Simon Frith explained: 'If we've got 10 heavy metal albums, they can't all go on' (quoted in the *Independent*, 15 September 1994). And the choice of winner, too, can also be seen to deliver on the industry's expectations. The much-derided decision to award the Mercury prize in 1994 to the dance band M People was viewed by insiders as a 'good choice' because it established that the Mercury was not just 'a rock prize' (*Music Week*, 24 September 1994).

The political economy of the prize

Put crudely, a prize is a device for generating media coverage. As Frith himself once explained: 'Their [prizes'] success is measured in units of publicity and this is where their problems start. For maximum publicity music award ceremonies must be televised. . . . The television programme is the peg on which newspaper previews (and sponsorship deals) are hung' (*The Scotsman*, 23 February 2000). Or as it was put to me when I interviewed the chair of a literature prize: 'It is showbusiness of a serious kind.' Hence, much of the planning and organization of prizes is directed to getting coverage and choreographing it. Prize and shortlist announcements are designed to fit broadcasting schedules, and the 'success' of prizes is measured in part by the type of channel and time of broadcast that any one prize secures – 'BBC2 provides a perfect audience', the Director of the Mercury Prize once said (*Music Week*, 24 September 1994).

The detailed reality is, of course, much more complicated (see English 2005 for an extended discussion of the prize economy). The MMP is the product of a number of different stakeholders. These include the prize's formal sponsors, which have, over the years, been Mercury Communications, Technics, Panasonic, Nationwide, and Barclaycard. The sponsor has a number of interests. Most prominent of these has to do with their brand recognition and reputation. They want media coverage, of a kind that plays into their brand and which reaches their target audience; and they want a prize that further enhances their brand. They also want a prize ceremony that can serve as a reward (a glitzy night out) to company executives and others.

Then there is the music industry, encompassing both record companies and retailers. They too want publicity, but crucially they want a shortlist and a winner that generates sales in their target markets. The shortlist is carefully constructed to encompass genres (including jazz, folk and classical, although these are not always present) and geographic regions. In return, all the main retailers, except for Boots and Woolworths, agreed when the prize was being founded to give window space to the prize (*Music Week*, 24 July 1993). A similar agreement was sought from the broadcasters, including those that cover the announcement of the short list and final ceremony, as well as those who simply carry the kind of music represented by the prize. The media strategy is designed to provide a 'shop window' (and possibly a passing, manageable controversy) (English, 2005). The organizers of the prize, including the judging panel itself, have an investment in the process. They may welcome controversy, because, on the one hand, it brings publicity, and on the other, it reinforces the idea that the prize (and the music it celebrates) matters. As one music executive told *Music Week* (16 May 1992), 'you have to have controversy. You have to have people disagreeing with the short list'. This links to the self-images of the judges, as people who want to be seen as autonomous and independent minded critics. How these various interests intersect is crucial to determining the character of the prize. And their interaction is a classic case of power politics in action. But before digging further into these politics, it pays to reflect briefly on the origins of the prize as a device for delivering aesthetic judgement.

A history of the prize

The proximate causes of the MMP lie, as we have seen, in the initiatives taken by record industry executives, drawing on the model forged by another cultural sector, and in response to a perceived market problem. But these local causal connections are themselves a product of wider changes, ones that make the 'prize' a solution to the 'problem'. The prize represents another of those devices for managing consumer information costs in a crowded market by signalling 'quality to consumers and thereby bring[ing] pecuniary gain to producers' (Caves, 2000: 196). There is nothing terribly new in this. Awarding the Northcliffe literature prize in 1930, the playwright Henry Granville Barker (*The Times*, 21 June 1930) explained its function: 'The work of the [prize] committee was one of the efforts which quality was making as a counterpoise to quantity. There was an enormous mass of literature which could not be read and which was not of high quality. This [prize] is an attempt on the part of a small body of people who, without conceit, might think themselves experts, to inform an otherwise uninformed public that here were works which deserved to be marked out from the others.' Nonetheless, even if the prize is primarily a marketing device, it plays an important role in establishing cultural 'value'. Prizes can contribute to a winner's sense of themselves as *artists*. When Suede won the Mercury, the band's Matt Osman said: 'It's extraordinary. The honour for us was really being nominated. For us, that meant that our music hadn't been judged on the clothes we wear, our shoes or the interviews we've given. But to actually win was beyond our wildest dreams' (*Melody Maker*, 18 September 1993). Osman's message was echoed by his colleague Brett Anderson: 'The point of this prize is not the money, it's the honour of being nominated' (*NME*, 19 September 1993). The prize can be seen as a form of the 'consecration' of art and artists that Bourdieu (1986, 1993; English, 2005: 31) sees as essential to an account of the production of culture.

But the emergence of the arts prize can be seen in a yet wider context – in particular, the emerging, capitalist economic order of the eighteenth century, and even in a much earlier era, in the drama and arts competitions of Ancient Greece (English, 2005: 1). The historian Linda Colley (1992: 90–1) records how in the mid-eighteenth century the Society of Arts, whose full name was 'the Society for the Encouragement of Arts, Commerce, and Manufactures in Great Britain', established prizes to reward achievements that advanced economic performance. Initially, there were prizes for producing dyes and growing trees, but these were followed by prizes 'for the most promising child artists and sculptors', and later for map-makers and others (Colley, 1992: 91–3). The prizes were part of a strategy for securing victory in commercial competition with the French, just as 200 years later, the CIA-funded Congress for Cultural Freedom instituted a prize for music as part of the cultural Cold War of the 1950s (Saunders, 2000: 220–1). Prizes have increasingly derived from the wider corporate interests of their sponsors. Chin-tao Wu (1998: 29) argues that corporations chose to sponsor arts awards because it gave them 'considerable cultural visibility, along with the appearance of being arbiters of society's taste.' Prizes generated by these larger issues became part of a world of prizes, where internal rivalries created their own incentives, partly as sponsors competed for the prestige that prizes accorded and prizes fought each other to claim prestige for themselves. The Orange prize for the best novel in English written by a woman, for example, was set up to challenge the male bias of the Booker, and to promote the image of a mobile phone company. This is how corporate interests and cultural politics become entwined.

Prize winners

We saw, in the analysis of starred reviews, the biases that seemed to operate in their allocation, and the tendency towards conservatism that could be detected. Is the MMP any different? There are any number of criteria that might be used to answer such a question, depending on what might be deemed a measure of 'conservatism'. For example, one such might be the preponderance of nominations on independent labels, as opposed to majors, on the assumption that the former represent 'innovation'. And in the first 10 years of the MMP's existence, 27 per cent of the 119 records nominated were on an independent label. But such a measure is to be treated with suspicion. There is first the question of what defines an 'independent', and secondly – and more importantly – there is no necessary correlation between originality and independent labels. As Dave Laing (1986) has pointed out, the commercial logic of independent labels tends to make them more conservative than the majors which can afford to take risks (and fail).

Here I want to concentrate on the treatment of debut records. The reason for this choice is, first, that it allows for comparison with the distribution of star reviews, and second, that it allows for reflection on the aesthetic values being applied by the MMP. Table 7.3 below records the number of debuts included in the shortlist and which of those that

Table 7.3. Mercury Music Prize – debut records in shortlist and as winners, 1992–2009.

Year (shortlist)	Debuts	Winner	Debut record (Yes/No)
1992 (10)	3	Primal Scream	No
1993 (10)	4	Suede	Yes
1994 (10)	1	M People	No
1995 (10)	7	Portishead	Yes
1996 (10)	3	Pulp	No
1997 (10)	2	Roni Size	Yes
1998 (12)	5	Gomez	Yes
1999 (12)	2	Talvin Singh	Yes
2000 (12)	7	Badly Drawn Boy	Yes
2001 (12)	7	PJ Harvey	No
2002 (12)	6	Ms Dynamite	Yes
2003 (12)	9	Dizzee Rascal	Yes
2004 (12)	5	Franz Ferdinand	Yes
2005 (12)	8	Antony and the Johnsons	No
2006 (12)	6	Arctic Monkeys	Yes
2007 (12)	9	Klaxons	Yes
2008 (12)	6(3)*	Elbow	No
2009 (12)	7	Speech Debelle	Yes
144	97 (67%)		12/18 (67%)

[*This is an example of the problem of determining what counts as a 'debut'. There were three side-projects by artists with established track records: Neo Neon (feat. Gruff Rhys of Super Furry Animals), The Last Shadow Puppets (feat. Alex Turner of the Arctic Monkeys), and Robert Plant and Alison Krauss].

were eventual winners. It needs to be noted that the length of the short list increased from ten to twelve in 1998.

It is noticeable that debuts feature prominently in both lists. The short-list, particularly in the latter years, includes a high proportion of debuts, with debut records more often than not winning the prize. In comparison with the stars awarded in the print media, the MMP is much better disposed towards debut releases than either Christgau or *Uncut*.

It might be tempting to conclude, on the basis of what we have seen, that the MMP represents a radical aesthetic compared to the conservatism of the print media – whether Christgau, *Q* or *Uncut*. This may be true, but it is not proven by the statistics. This is because it rests on an assumption that what is new (i.e. a debut) is also innovative (i.e. radical). Clearly, this is not necessarily true. The 'new' might also be 'innovative' or it might conform to the market's need for *the appearance of innovation*. Equally, those debuts awarded 5* or A+ may be innovative in ways that the debuts which win the MMP are not. No amount of statistical data will, in itself, resolve these questions. They depend on more detailed, qualitative (literally) analysis of the records involved. For what it is worth, however, it does seem that the MMP has succeeded in identifying innovation, if by that we mean the highlighting of new musical trends. The awards to Portishead, Roni Size and Dizzee Rascal would serve to support this contention.

The politics of deliberation

If it were the case that the MMP made better decisions, in the sense that it identified quality and innovation more effectively than did reviewers in magazines, how might we explain this? One thought might be that the people taking the decision are better qualified or more insightful than those awarding stars and grades. But often they are the same people, and in any case it would be very hard to validate any such distinctions. More plausibly, it might be argued that collective decisions are necessarily better than individual ones. Certainly those who advocate deliberative democracy (Fishkin, 1991; Miller, 1992) or the 'wisdom of crowds' (Surowiecki, 2004) might be disposed to make such a case. But even they concede that larger numbers *in themselves* do not guarantee better decisions, and there are others who argue that collective decision making is more likely to result in compromise and mediocrity than innovation (Riker, 1982). This debate is vast and complex, and there is little or no point engaging with it here. However, it is worth asking how Mercury jurors go about their business, and to see whether their behaviour suggests enlightened, deliberative rationality or collective irrationality (as compromise around the second best/least worst).

For many journalists who write about the Mercury (and indeed other such prizes), it is the latter characterization that dominates. Here is Nicholas Barber writing about the MMP in the *Independent on Sunday* (5 September 1999): 'The judges will pick a name out of the hat, safe in the knowledge that no one could argue logically whether the choice they've made is the right one or the wrong one.' This is a variant on the familiar journalistic trope when discussing the MMP. The jurors, it is assumed, are being forced to compare the incommensurable – jazz vs folk vs hip hop vs indie rock. . . . And the argument is that because there is no rational way to determine whether one record is better than another, then whatever takes place in the jury room must be deemed entirely random. But this criticism is itself incoherent. Such judgements are made every day at all levels of society (by consumers in supermarkets and by ministers in Cabinet meetings), and while it may not be possible for those decisions to be reduced to a formalized arithmetic calculation, that does not make them irrational. It does not make them perfect either, and their quality depends on the process as much as the individuals involved.

Even those who participate in the judging tend sometimes to represent it as a form of collective madness. Judging is, according to Simon Frith, chair of the MMP panel, 'a process which ignores political influence, but is passionate, fairly crazed and based on personal choice' (*Music Week*, 24 September 1994). On another occasion he explained: '. . . once you get in that [jury] room and start fighting it out, you forget everything that's gone on outside and you become wrapped in this internal world' (quoted in the *Independent*, 15 September 1994). And this closeted world fits with other descriptions of the experience. One Mercury Music Prize judge told me: 'If you're talking about an album and you just realize that nobody else is getting it, you might as well give up.' But while I do not doubt these accounts as accurate reports of the experience of judging, it does not follow that we have to accept them as explanations of what is happening.

Prize jury deliberation, like all forms of decision making, are affected by the application of particular decision rules, by the distribution of power and by the ideals which inform behaviour. As Kenneth Shepsle and Mark Bonchek (1997: 177, their emphasis) argue: 'The decisions a group reaches . . . depend not only on the degree to which group members reveal or mis-reveal their preferences, but also on the way they conduct the actual decision making. And all those other things, likewise, are influenced by the voting method we adopt. A group decision surely reflects member preferences. *But it also reflects much more.*' Applied to prize committees, this approach focuses our attention on such things as the administration of the meeting and the voting procedures. Changes in the rules, about the number of nominations on the shortlist or about what categories need to be represented, can affect the outcome. Adopting different procedures produces different results. And procedures are necessary in order to generate a collective decision within inevitable time and other constraints.

How the meeting is chaired, how the agenda is set, how the vote is taken: all of these have profound and decisive effects upon the outcome of any meeting. It seems unlikely that prize committees are the exception to this rule. As part of the research I conducted on the MMP, I also investigated book prizes. One book panel chair used a system of elimination, excluding those books deemed to have no chance of winning, while another introduced a point scheme, whereby each judge gave 6 points to their first choice, 5 to their second, and so on. Some used a secret ballot; others an open ballot. One panel chair decreed that every juror had to come to the meeting with just one nomination. And as one of his jury complained, this meant 'no open minds. No voting, just majority decision and no lingering' (John Sutherland, *Guardian*, 6 October 1999). Simply resolving the decision by voting does not just eliminate discussion, it introduces biases. As rational choice theorists and others have pointed out almost all majorities are in some sense fictional (Arrow, 1951; Dahl, 1956; McLean, 1987). They are the artificial product of decision rules, and different rules produce a different 'majority' choice. Reflecting on one experience of judging a piano competition, Charles Rosen (2002: 106) commented: 'The reason for the lamentable misjudgement was a flawed voting system used that year.'

More interestingly perhaps, majoritarian judging systems, or ones that model themselves on democracy, may produce culturally conservative decisions. As one prize organizer told me: 'One of the things I've noticed is that a slightly experimental novel . . . which is doing extremely well, and then . . . when a major flaw is pointed out, then another judge will say "funny you should say that, because there's that very awkward chapter . . ." and steadily it builds up, . . . whereas the lesser novel hasn't got any obvious flaws [and] manages to get through.' Knowing this a chair, by virtue of their power, can organize discussion and decision making so as to avoid the 'populist' compromise – 'a Roddy Doyle-type decision', as it was put to me.

A variation on this approach was adopted by Simon Frith in chairing the MMP. His concern was to get a deliberative decision; that is, a decision that was not simply the aggregate of individual jurors' preferences, but was what they collectively thought (what Jean-Jacques Rousseau meant by the 'General Will', which he contrasted favourably with the 'will of all'). This deliberative approach is nicely captured by Mercury juror David Sinclair's description of how Gomez's *Bring It On* became the eventual winner: 'It seemed such a frail contender when it first found its way on to the shortlist of 12 albums and was initially derided in some quarters as unauthentic, retro blues-rock. But over time *Bring It On* gradually revealed a wealth of detail in the production . . .' (*The Times*, 18 September 1998).

Frith resisted the use of votes in order to get people to think about the 'sense of the meeting' and not just to promote their own view (email to author). In such a setting 'advocacy' becomes key, because jurors have to persuade others to see one record as being the one 'we' all identify as the best. Indeed, Frith has argued that the skills of the advocate are crucial to the outcome: 'What matters is less comparison than advocacy. It's a pity that no one outside the judging room will ever hear the wonderful case made (by the same judge) as to why first *To Bring You My Love* and then *Maxinquaye* should win the prize; that no one else will get to applaud the speech that swung it for Portishead' (*Guardian*, 15 September 1995).

Advocacy is not just a matter of skills of putting ideas into words, it is also a matter of the authority that certain languages command. If the debate about the relative merits of a piece of music is conducted on musicological criteria, those with access to the appropriate language and terms will be at an advantage. What appears to happen is that certain languages and rhetorics are organized into the discussion and some organized out. This may be symptomatic of the fact that different cultural professions work with different critical discourses. This argument is made by Frith, both in his capacity as a Mercury judge and as a writer on aesthetics (Frith, 1996). The background of the judges is reflected in the way they approach the task of judging: 'the way music journalists operate is that they tend to operate in an exclusive fashion, in other words a lot of critics seem to focus on things that only a few people are going to like – exclusivity, whereas if you work in radio you're more interested in trying to put an audience together' (interview with author).

Judging becomes, therefore, a matter of decision rules and of advocacy, mediated by the authority accorded to certain expertise and refined by particular acquired skills. Here are some of the Mercury judges discussing their experience. The musician Anne Dudley described her (vain) attempt to persuade her fellow judges to vote for the Manic Street Preachers' *Everything Must Go*: 'It really did attempt to break new ground in terms of its arrangements. It was a fantastic sound – the clarity of the texture, very interesting use of strings . . . I couldn't really get the others to agree with me. They kept saying "Sounds like Queen to me". Well, what can you say? Well, *yes*, it does a *bit* . . .' (*Guardian*, 10 April 1998; her emphasis). Another Mercury judge, explaining the decision to give the award to Talvin Singh, said that Singh's 'record works as a movement in the classical sense. The composers on the panel, for instance, admired it for that reason. They want to know how the overall concept is expressed and how well it sustains. They talk about note and key changes' (*Guardian*, 10 September 1999). Yet another Mercury judge recalled how, although the jury was not much impressed by one jazz record, they were impressed by the fact that the judge who was 'the real jazz expert' liked it, and as a result were persuaded to put it on the shortlist; in the same way, they acknowledged that the 'classical' composers [on the Mercury] have a better ear for the classical stuff' (interview with author).

The business of judging music or arts prizes generally is profoundly political. It is a consequence of the constitution of the procedures and of the distribution of power (coded as cultural capital of various kinds). It is political too in the sense that the decisions that are reached about what is worthy of the prize are themselves politically inflected. Juries can make conservative or radical decisions; they can be populist or elitist. And what they are also doing, and this may be even more important, is that they are setting the criteria by which 'quality' or 'value' is to be assigned. Juries are not simply processing a decision via pre-established criteria or procedures. They are creating those criteria and procedures in terms of some notion of 'the good'.

Amazonia: the revenge of the citizen critic?

In discussion of modern mass media, there is an emerging (if much disputed) conventional wisdom that new media are causing the replacement of traditional, professional journalists by the civic journalist (Allan, 2003; Atton, 2002). And although it has received less attention, the same might be claimed for cultural journalism. Sites such as Amazon now provide the opportunity for anyone to offer their opinions on the music for sale. And not only do these reviews remain permanently attached to any given item, the aggregated rankings of the citizen critics come to represent a populist equivalent of the star grades and the prizes. More importantly, artists and their companies regard the reviews on Amazon as key to their success (so much so, it seems, that one academic author resorted to bestowing glowing praise on his own books, and offering withering condemnations of those of his rivals). The technological opportunity created for the citizen critic is complemented by the software built into sites like Amazon which allow for the construction of a 'customer profile' and for targeted recommendations: 'you bought Laura Marling, so you might be interested in Beth Orton. . . .' Or 'Customers who bought Beth Orton, also bought Martha Wainwright and . . .'. The net effect of all of this might be to eliminate the need for professional critics and prizes. And what then would the politics of judgement entail?

New media analyst Mathew Hindman (2009: 55) has introduced the word 'Googlearchy' to our vocabulary. He uses it to describe an online world in which the winner – in this case Google – takes all, and in which, rather than the open network that the internet seemed to promise, we get high degrees of concentration around key search engines. Although iTunes and Amazon are not search engines, their online presence has a similar dominance in respect of the marketing of music (Hindman, 2009: 86; Castells, 2009: 86; Strauss, 2003). Important though this market dominance is, my concern here is with the rather more specific issue of how the politics of taste are being changed.

Chris Anderson (2004) used the example of Amazon in expounding his take on 'the long tail'. According to this, the new retail business model involved selling less of more. Amazon offers an apparently inexhaustible range of products, catering for every taste. In such a world, the market in music, books and other products is no longer dependent on selling a lot of a few items. But while this apparent wealth of choice might be welcomed because it engenders cultural plurality, it does require that choice provides for diversity, rather than many variants of similar things. And it may be that the combined effect of citizen reviewers and customer profiling is to reduce plurality and cultural experimentation. It may lead people to choose more of the same.

I do not think we are yet in a position to assess in detail the effect of the nets. Although research is emerging on how consumers use the new retail outlets and how peer-to-peer recommendations operate, we have relatively little knowledge of the particular effects of new systems of retailing and evaluating (Liu and Shih, 2005; Wikstrom, 2009). It will not be long before we do, and we will then be able to add the impact of new media into our account of the politics of taste.

Conclusion

This chapter has been devoted to the devices by which value is attributed to music. We began with the use of star ratings, before considering the case of the music prize and ending with the new media variants. Each could be seen as a product of the political economy of their times, providing forms of evaluation that were required by the political and commercial interests organized around culture. But as we went on to see, each also could be seen to enshrine an aesthetic which itself could be interpreted politically – the degree to which systems of evaluation celebrated the radical and innovative or the familiar and conservative.

But why does any of this matter – or more pertinently, why does it matter in a book about music and politics? There are two parts to the answer. The first returns us to the general assumption, one that has been referred to throughout, that culture is important to the capacity of peoples to engage with each other and with politics. Insofar as critical evaluations are, as Frith suggests, also ethical ones, and as such bear upon political life, then reflecting on these judgements – on what they consist in and how they are made – has a wider relevance. This leads to the second part: the different politics that inform such judgements. Anyone interested in the relation of music and politics needs to be attentive to the ways in which value is attached to music. This is both because that value is in part a political one, and because the processes that attribute value are themselves forms of political organization.

This chapter has, I hope, shown how different institutional designs produce different value systems, but more than this: that in making judgements we are positioning ourselves in different relations to each other. We saw this in the enlightened elitism of Christgau, as compared to the market populism of *Q*. While both claim to speak for, or on behalf of the people, they conceive of their constituencies in quite different ways. And this difference may be revealed in the extent to which prizes or reviews predict or cause *success* or reward *talent* (Ginsburgh, 2003); in the extent to which they serve the market or the public.

8

Politics as music: the sound of ideas and ideology

The music that wins prizes or is awarded five stars is music that is deemed 'good'. However compromised or imperfect the processes that lead to such judgements, they give expression to an important aspect of the consumption of all music, indeed of all culture: the act of discrimination. 'The essence of popular culture practice', writes Simon Frith (1996: 16), 'is making judgements and assessing differences', and in discriminating people realize their own identity and differences (ibid.: 18). Tastes and standards may vary wildly, but they are all driven by a desire for some notion of the best. This is because music matters, and because aesthetic discrimination entails more than an expression of taste. It is a question of morality and identity. This view is widely shared. As the conservative philosopher Roger Scruton (1974: 248–9) writes: 'The relation between moral and aesthetic judgement suggests that standards for the validity of the one will provide standards for the other. To show what is bad in a sentimental work of art must involve showing what is bad in sentimentality. To be certain in matters of taste is, therefore, to be certain in matters of morality: ethics and aesthetics are one.'

Frith and Scruton, in joining aesthetics to ethics and identity, become part of a long-established tradition, in which music becomes a central feature of the way lives are lived and assessed. It is a tradition that places music at the heart of politics, but it is also a tradition that has been largely neglected, at least by those who study political thought and action. This chapter revisits this tradition, and explores the claims it makes for music's political role.

From almost the first recorded writing on politics, music has been present as a key component of the good society or as a topic upon which it was necessary to comment. This is no longer true. Indeed, it is remarkably rare to find mention of music, or sound more generally, in any work of contemporary political theory. This, as we shall see, is partly explained by the character of political theorists and partly by the character of political theory. In the first half of this chapter, I trace the place of music in political thought, to account for its marginalization, and to point to those writers who are engaged in a process of re-instatement. If the first part is about music in politics, the second half is about politics in music. I want to look at how political ideas – particularly the notion of conservatism – can be ascribed to music and what it means to describe a piece of music or performance as 'conservative'. The chapter ends by linking the two halves together by considering how music embodies and articulates political thought and action.

There is, within the history of political thought, a tradition of writers who have indeed attempted to identify the peculiarities of music and its place in political and social life. Without pretending to do full justice to their arguments, I sketch some of these below, in order to see how the connection between sound and politics may be drawn.

Music as morality: Plato and Aristotle

In arguments that are now nearly two and half thousand years old, Plato insisted that types of music could be distinguished morally as well as aesthetically, and that music of a lesser quality (and its popular celebration) was a danger to the social order. As he warned: 'For a change to a new type of music is something to beware of as a hazard to all our fortunes. For the modes of music are never disturbed without the unsettling of the most fundamental political and social conventions' (Plato, 1961: *Republic*, 424b–c). Music was not a peripheral aspect of society, a matter of light relief; it was central to the way society was ordered. For Plato (1961, *Laws*, 669c–e), rhythm, melody and lyrics shaped social relations. Or less prosaically, music had the capacity to work upon the soul and to bring harmony (Plato, 1961: *Timaeus*, 47c–d). As Charles Taylor (1992: 115) explains: 'The good souls enjoy order (*kosmos*), concord (*xumphonia*), and harmony (*harmonia*).'

Because music was of such importance, it was necessary for judgement to be made about its particular qualities. It was not just a matter of taste. For Plato, such decisions had to be made by those capable of so doing. To grant authority to those who were unaware of the relevant aesthetic distinctions or who were incapable of making such distinctions would be to allow 'the sovereignty of the best' to be replaced by 'the sovereignty of the audience' (Plato, 1961: *Republic*, 424b–c; see also *Protagoras*, 347c–d; *Laws*, 700a–701c). Music was too politically important to be left to the people. For Plato, according to Austin Harrington (2004: 10), the role of art was to enlighten citizens 'to the eternal beauty of the cosmos, alongside the eternal truth sought by philosophers, and the eternal justice sought by statesmen and lawgivers.' Art was not to be valued for its own sake; it represented a skill whose function was to serve these higher goals. If this skill was misused, however, as might be the case with music, it could unsettle 'the most fundamental political and social conventions' (*Republic*, 424).

Aristotle continued the tradition of his teacher. Like Plato, he linked musical quality to morality, judgement and order. His *Politics* ends with a discussion of the moral qualities of music and its place in education. He asked: 'Must we not rather regard music as a stimulus to goodness, capable of having an effect on the character?' (1962: Bk 8, Ch. 5). 'In music moral qualities are present,' he explained, 'represented in the very tunes we hear' (Aristotle, 1962: Bk 8, Ch. 5). For Aristotle, as with Plato, musical education was important to the wider political order. Its purpose was to enlighten and to lift its beneficiaries above the lot of other mortals: 'Musical exercises . . . should be pursued only up to the point at which the pupil becomes capable of appreciating good melodies and rhythms, and not just the popular music such as appeals to slaves, children and even some animals' (1962: Bk 8, Ch. 6). Moral education was intimately linked to music and an appreciation of its qualities. Music formed manners and hence social conduct.

In such arguments, we hear not just the claim that music is an important feature of the good life, but that discrimination between forms of music is not simply an expression of taste; it is a matter of morality and political order. It is music's moral character that forms the basis of, and reasons for, identifying excellence in it. Plato and Aristotle make explicit what is entailed in the notion of 'excellence' and how it might be discerned. Plato and Aristotle provide a rationale for both the promotion and the censorship of music. This moralizing of music is not exclusive to the ancient world. It is a recurring, if by no means consistent, feature of the ways in which music is valued in political thought. But what is also evident is that not all political theorists have attributed importance to music and sound. It pays to consider briefly those who are indifferent to music.

The sound of silence: Hobbes, Mill and Marx

The tradition of political thought that we associate with Ancient Greece, at least in its treatment of the arts, has been largely neglected by those writers who have tended to define the modern era. Thomas Hobbes, John

Stuart Mill and Karl Marx had little or nothing to say on the subject of music. As far as I can discern, Hobbes makes no reference to music (although there is a spoof webpage that documents the band he formed in 1652, Thomas Hobbes and the Pessimists). John Stuart Mill did, at least, acknowledge music's existence, but he gave it no detailed attention and consigned it to the general category of 'amusements' (Mill, 1972: 155). Mill treated music as a 'diversion', as something that we can take or leave. It was a 'taste' which must be recognized, together with many other such preferences, in a free society: 'Nowhere (except in some monastic institutions) is diversity of taste entirely unrecognized; a person may, without blame, either like or dislike rowing, or smoking, or music, or athletic exercises, or chess, or cards, or study . . .' (Mill, 1972: 136). Putting music in such company and consigning it to the category of a 'taste' is indicative of its marginal status in Mill's argument. Far from being central to political order, music could safely be ignored.

Marx too had little to say on music's political importance, although his theories have, of course, had a profound impact on the way music is studied in other disciplines. From a collection (mis)titled *Marx and Music* (Qureshi, 2002), it would seem that Marx mentioned music only once – in the *Grundrisse* – and then just to make a point about the definition of productive labour. This solitary reference is quoted several times, by different authors: 'the piano *maker* reproduces *capital*; the pianist only exchanges his labour for revenue. But doesn't the pianist produce music and satisfy our musical ear, does he not even to an extent produce the latter? He does indeed: his labour produces something; but that does not make it productive labour in the *economic sense*; no more that then labour of the madman who produces delusions is productive . . .' (quoted in Qureshi, 2002: 8; Marx's emphasis). Marx was no more willing than Mill to treat music as important to our account of the ordering of social and political life. While we should be wary of generalizations about authors as different as Hobbes, Mill and Marx, their indifference to music owes something to their conceptions of the political subject and the political order. For them, the citizen is marked by their interests and ambitions, and the political order is to be understood as a product of these. Politics is seen in largely mechanistic terms, or as Charles Taylor (1992: 197) suggests the picture of world is constructed with 'building blocks'. And while Mill and Marx conceive of humans in developmental terms, the route taken is not dependent on art, but on scientific knowledge and instrumental control. Only those writers who break with this tradition allow a place to music and sound.

Music as language and emotion: Jean-Jacques Rousseau

Robert Wokler (2001: 37) once wrote: 'Rousseau is nowhere so politically inflammatory as when commenting on music.' He was 'inflammatory' precisely because of his assertions about the relative qualities of forms of music, and the way his arguments, and those of his critics, touched on more than matters of taste. They were arguments about morality and politics. Rousseau, in other words, echoed Plato and Aristotle in viewing music in moral terms and according it social importance. What he added was a sense of music's relationship to identity and emotion, and their place in the formation of human society.

A substantial part of Rousseau's collected writings was taken up with music, and his reputation in his own lifetime owed much to his pronouncements on it (see Rousseau, 1998). These aspects of Rousseau's work do not traditionally feature in the way he is taught and studied (for exceptions, see Dugan and Strong, 2001; O'Dea, 1995). It is notable, for example, that when the political scientist Andrew Gamble (2004: 13) evokes Rousseau in a discussion of Bob Dylan, it is Rousseau on alienation, not Rousseau on music, that he refers to. And yet one of Rousseau's essays, that on the 'Origin of languages' (written in 1761), has as its subtitle 'In which something is said about melody and musical imitation'. In this essay, Rousseau argued that music's power is greater than that of the other arts because it generates the feelings directly: 'sounds act on us . . . as signs of our affection, of our sentiments' (Rousseau, 1997: 288, 292). Music's power to evoke our sentiments forms part of Rousseau's general thesis about human nature, language and the philosophy of history.

Music matters because, for Rousseau, it reveals humans as 'sentient, thinking Beings' (1997: 248), allowing us to pass from a time in which communication served only to satisfy physical needs (to indicate the location of food and water), to one in which it orchestrates our collective, social existence. In this transition, communication moves from the visual to the aural arena and becomes less a matter of providing directions and more one of expressing emotions and establishing bonds. The language of sound and hearing caters for social, collective needs, by which he meant 'moral needs, the passions'. As he wrote of our ancestors: 'Not hunger nor thirst, but love, hatred, pity, anger wrung their first voices from them' (1997: 253). For Rousseau, our humanity is realized in the sounds we make and hear. This is not just an observation about the evolution of human society; it is a claim about how music is tied to politics. The emotions, particularly compassion, find expression in the way sound becomes the basis of organized co-existence. C. N. Dugan and Tracy Strong (2001: 353) characterize Rousseau's argument like this: 'In a world with no musical language for politics, no one can hear'.

Accents and intonations enable humans to convey their feelings. Language, by this account, is not used instrumentally to serve specific functions, but as a way of expressing passions and feelings. These are fundamental to social existence and predate the emergence of reason. This, said Rousseau (1997: 282), is why the passions of poetry precede the reasoning of prose. Singing evokes the passions through the way it accents sound (Rousseau, 1997: 255): '. . . cadences and sounds are born together with syllables: passion rouses all of the [vocal] organs to speech, and adorns the voice with their full brilliance; thus verse, song, speech have a common origin. Around the fountains . . . the first speeches were the first songs: the periodic and measured recurrences of rhythms, the melodious inflections of accents, caused poetry and music to be born together with language . . .' (Rousseau, 1997: 282). For Rousseau, music articulates the emotions: 'melody expresses plaints, cries of suffering or of joy, threats, moans' (Rousseau, 1997: 287). Rousseau is not talking about mere mimicry; music is not simply a mirror held up to reality or to the soul. The voice does not directly imitate the emotion, but makes it present: 'A musician who tries to render noise with noise errs . . . teach him that he must render noise with song, that if he wished to make frogs croak he would have to make them sing' (Rousseau, 1997: 288). In this sense, music is revelatory: 'Music . . . brings man closer to man and always gives us some idea about our own kind' (Rousseau, 1997: 292). Or as Dugan and Strong (2001: 349) put it: 'music makes a world present'.

Rousseau's theory places music at the heart of the social order as the means by which humans come to know themselves and each other. In doing so, he, like Aristotle and Plato, also introduces the issue of musical quality. The quality of music is not a matter of 'taste' (as Mill would have it); it is linked to moral quality. In Rousseau's case, the normative element is captured in the distinction he made between melody and harmony. Sounds as melody are the source of beauty and pleasure; it is the truly human form of expression. Harmony adds little, and indeed may dull the musical pleasure (Rousseau, 1997: 286). It is melody that gives force to expression. And just as written languages, compared with sung stories, 'lose force as they gain in clarity', so songs in which harmonies dominate tend to be 'dreary' with 'a slow succession of drawled and shouted sounds, devoid alike of sweetness, measure and grace' (Rousseau, 1997, 264–5 and 296).

The contrast that Rousseau makes between harmony and melody is not only a matter of musical aesthetics, but of politics. He links different political orders to different sound and music. He contrasts the free, public speech (melody) with 'the buzz in the Sultan's council chamber' (harmony) (Rousseau, 1997: 299). The same thought is found in a passage from Herman Hesse's *The Glass Bead Game* that Murray Schafer (1994: 7) quotes: 'the music of a well-ordered age is calm and cheerful, and so is its government. The music of a restive age is excited and fierce, and its government is perverted. The music of a decaying state is sentimental and sad, and its government imperiled.' And a contemporary version of this idea is captured in Liu Li's (2011: 32) suggestive view of the role of whispering in the exercise of power: '. . . this is how ideology reigns – through whispering. Unlike the coercive shouts, yells or screams, the ruling whisper wields a hegemonic soft power and sneaks into our social unconscious without being questioned.'

What is important about Rousseau is that music becomes a vital aspect of human communication that is directly implicated in forms of political order. Music is not merely a tool for reflecting upon and arguing about such an order; it is also entailed in the creation of that order. Our responses to music, our uses of sound, are ways in which we know ourselves and relate to others.

Music as consolation and desolation: Friedrich Nietzsche

Friedrich Nietzsche, whose writings sit on the border between philosophy and politics, looked back – like Rousseau – to Ancient Greece for his account of music's importance to the human condition. As he did so, he echoed Marx's vision of the desolation caused by modernity, but he differed from both Marx and from Plato in his understanding of the world and of art's place in it. Rather than Marxist revolution, he sought romanticism (Geuss and Speirs, 1999: xiii). This was to be found in recovering the fundamental importance of art – 'art – and *not* morality – is the true *metaphysical* activity of man' (Nietzsche, 1999: 8; his emphasis). Rather than the categorical knowledge and morality that Plato attributes to music, Nietzsche argued for the importance of instinct and against Platonic essentialism (Geuss, 2005: 206ff), although this insight was not fully realized in 'The Birth of Tragedy', the essay in which he develops his account of music and which I discuss here (Nietzsche, 1999). Music is profoundly connected to a sense of identity, albeit a sense that is shattered in the musical experience.

All art, for Nietzsche, is forged in the competing claims of Apollo and Dionysos (ibid.: 14), but music is afforded a special status, and Wagner a yet more special one, because his operatic works allow for the re-birth of tragedy. Wagner speaks to the tragedy of human existence, not simply as an idea, but as an experience. As Raymond Geuss and Ronald Speirs (1999: xx) explain, Nietzsche took the view that 'collective music-making is the form of art that brings us as close as it is possible for us to come to the experience of the basic truth that our individual identity is an illusion.' The Dionysiac is experienced when subjectivity is caused 'to vanish to the point of complete self-forgetting' (Nietzsche, 1999: 17).

Music is blessed with special powers, beyond those of the sculptor or epic poet (ibid.: 30). Like Rousseau, Nietzsche imagined music preceding language, reaching beyond even the realm of experience summoned up by the lyric poet: 'whereas lyric poetry depends utterly on the spirit of music, music itself, in its absolute sovereignty, has no *need* at all of images and concepts but merely *tolerates* them as an accompaniment' (ibid.: 36; his emphasis). Language 'only touches the surface of music'. Music's power lies in its ability to 'give birth to *myth*' (ibid.: 79), and hence brings the listener to inhabit the tragedy which is, for Nietzsche, the great truth of human existence.

As Geuss and Speirs (1999: xvi) point out, 'The Birth of Tragedy' is devoid of politics. However, it was intended to fit within Nietzsche's wider thoughts and, in particular, his deep distrust of democracy. To this extent, his remarks represent another element in the tradition of thought that places music at the heart of political and social existence, and hence connects him to the twentieth century's most influential exponent of it, Theodor Adorno. Nietzsche serves to illustrate how music can be implicated in the most profound of human experience, and as such fuel the politics that respond to that experience.

Music as control and negation: Theodor Adorno

While his aesthetic judgement and his social theory are far removed from both Rousseau's and Nietzsche's, Adorno shares the view that music is integral to the social order and that aesthetic distinctions express political and moral values. Where Adorno diverges most evidently from Nietzsche is in his debt to Marx and to the revolutionary response to the experience of the modern. Adorno places music within a particular political economy, that of capitalism. His theory of music's connection to politics is about its role both as a commercial product of a culture industry and as a challenge to the dominant system of production.

For Adorno, popular music (including jazz) was to be understood, like Hollywood films, as an artefact of mass production. It is a commodity which has been standardized, so that each pop hit is the same length, has the same verse-chorus structure, expresses the same sentiments – 'the eternal sameness of hit songs', as he wrote in 'On the contemporary relationship of philosophy and music' (Adorno, 2002: 135). The trick is that while being standardized, such songs *appear* as individual and different. It is this illusion that provides a mechanism of ideological control and of profit. Not only are films and songs manufactured to a formula, but contained within these formulaic products are encoded instructions about how to live and what to expect from life, all directed to compliance with, and acceptance of, the capitalist system. In his essay 'On the Fetish Character in Music', Adorno wrote of how music 'inhabits the pockets of silence that develop between people molded by anxiety, work and undemanding docility' (Adorno, 2002: 289). Music, therefore, performs for Adorno a vital function in pacifying those who might otherwise challenge the system under which they live. It does this, not by means of propaganda, but by penetrating deep into the sources of pleasure. The pleasures of music are part of the problem, and no part of the solution.

Against this critique of contemporary culture, Adorno constantly posits an alternative set of musical experiences that serve as a critique of the dominant order. This critique, though, is not evoked through the simple beauty of idyllic utopias or through socialist propaganda set to show tunes. In his discussion of 'National Socialism and the Arts', he described as 'infantile' those who believe that, in an ugly world, art should seek to evoke images of beauty and harmony. Instead, said Adorno (2002: 381), art should confront its audience with the ugliness. Only in confrontational art can the link between 'music and philosophical truth' be maintained (Adorno, 2002: 380). Or as he argued in 'On the Social Situation of Music', music is, like critical theory itself, 'under the same obligation as theory to reach out beyond the current consciousness of the masses' (Adorno, 2002: 394). This is not a call for 'politically committed art' (which, according to Richard Leppert (2002: 71), Adorno saw as 'preaching to the saved'), but rather for an uncompromised aesthetic. Nor is it an unqualified celebration of 'classical music'. Adorno famously accuses Wagner's music as speaking 'the language of Fascism, quite apart from the plots and bombastic words' (2002: 375). He merely demands music that represents 'the true societal interests against the blindness, spite and conventionalism of the actual audience' (Adorno, 2002: 380).

What Adorno represents, therefore, is an account of music's political importance, not as propaganda or manipulation, but as the disruptive power of sound itself. The politics cannot be 'read' off the views of the composer or performer; nor are the political values inscribed in the lyrics (in the manner of a political manifesto). Rather, Adorno suggests we must consider the direct effects that sound has upon us – the musical equivalent of a fingernail scraping down a blackboard. Their social theory and their musical aesthetics may be radically different, but this view of music forges a bridge between Adorno and Rousseau.

Adorno, like Rousseau, Plato and Aristotle, places much emphasis on the qualities of music. While the moral economy with which Adorno operates is very different to that of the others, it still trades on the idea that, in distinguishing between examples of music, we are marking more than taste; we are establishing and judging forms of action. And like Rousseau, Adorno places music within the process by which social relations are produced and reproduced; more particularly he places it within the antagonisms of capitalism. In so doing, he provides a way of addressing the questions raised earlier about *how* music operates within systems of compliance and resistance. What Adorno offers is a way of making sense of the role music plays in organizing political resistance and protest, whether in the Soviet bloc or in the civil rights movement, through aesthetics as much as through rhetoric. As a result, the continuities with earlier accounts of music's relationship to politics become evident. While what is valued in music, and how it is valued, may differ, the sense of its particularities remain. From this perspective, music shapes our sense of the world and our response to it.

Re-birth of a tradition

These writings on music's links to politics have been largely ignored by political studies, either through the marginalization of the writers who represent the tradition or through the select reading of their oeuvre (the Rousseau of the Social Contract, rather than of the Origin of Languages). However, in recent years there have been a number of writers who have sought to bring music back in.

This is evident, for example, in Jacques Attali's account of the politics of 'noise'. Attali (1985: 6) recalls Rousseau when he writes: 'In noise can be read the codes of life, the relations among men.' And he recalls Adorno when he adds (1985: 6) that 'any theory of power today must include a theory of the localization of noise and its endowment with form.' For Attali, as for Adorno, the commercialization and commodification of music has resulted in its 'banalization': 'popular music and rock have been recuperated, colonized, sanitized' (Attali, 1985: 109). And again as with Adorno, this is not simply a matter of regret, but a sign of significant social change, which can only be resisted through what he calls 'composing'; that is, in 'the permanent affirmation of the right to be different' (Attali, 1985: 132).

While the US political theorist Jane Bennett sets herself against Adorno's critique of mass culture, she remains wedded to the thought that music shapes our sense of ourselves and our world. She echoes Nietzsche in her emphasis on the power of art to enchant. Her main concern, though, is with how our attachments – our moral and political commitments – are motivated. Her argument is that our sentiments have to be 'energized'; they require an 'embodied sensibility' (2001: 131). It is not enough just to view something as unjust or unfair. We have to *feel* this sense of injustice or unfairness. This is where 'enchantment' comes into play: 'To be enchanted', she writes (Bennett, 2001: 4), 'is to be struck and shaken by the extraordinary that lives amid the familiar and the everyday.'

Her account of enchantment begins and ends with sound, and with an analysis of the value and effect of repetition, the very thing that Adorno and Attali most suspect in mass culture. The repetition of songs and the experience of singing, suggests Bennett, can conjure up the meanings, identities and collectivities that enchant us and motivate our commitments. Bennett (2001: 133) detects in music the 'sonority' of language – in its (literal) sound effects. Drawing upon Deleuze and Guattari (1987), and echoing Plato, she wants to see chants and refrains as giving 'sensory access to the cosmological . . . dimension of things' (Bennett, 2001: 166). Through singing, through the rhythms of repetition, Bennett argues, we are connected to others and enchanted by our world. She claims that this effect provides the motivation we need to act on behalf of others. Music, in this sense, mobilizes politics. While Bennett finds political hope within the music that others dismiss, she shares with them the sense that music's effects are profoundly political.

As with the other writers we have considered, Bennett's argument, rather than reducing music to a footnote to the political process, or an appendage to political ideas and values, makes it an integral part of them. What this account suggests is that music connects with political ideas, investing those ideas with emotional significance.

From music to ideology

But if music is more than a footnote to politics, and if it does more than reflect ideas and values, and if it actually embodies them and the feelings that accompany them, then how does it do this? Or rather, what does it mean to talk of the politics of music in this constitutive sense? I want to answer this question by looking at a rather more specific issue: what it means to describe music in political terms, as Adorno most famously does in labelling Wagner's operas as 'fascist'.

In *Performing Rites*, Simon Frith makes the distinction between culture that reconciles people to their circumstances and culture that seeks to transform those circumstances. This latter form must, says Frith (1996: 20; his emphasis), 'challenge experience, must be difficult, must be *unpopular*'. The idea that music can do this, that it can issue challenges or forge reconciliations, lies at the heart of the political tradition I have discussed above. But it also begs a question. What distinguishes music that can do these things? What follows is an attempt to address this question, not, as many have been tempted to do, by looking at music that constitutes 'resistance' or 'rebellion', but rather the opposite, music that encourages compromise and reconciliation. This is music that is typically attributed to the 'mainstream' and is equally typically ignored, music that is assumed in some way to be 'conservative'. What does it mean to call music 'conservative'?

In his *A Dictionary of Political Thought*, Roger Scruton (1982 : 90) defines 'conservatism' as: 'The political outlook which springs from a desire to conserve existing things, held to be either good in themselves, or better than the likely alternatives, or at least safe, familiar, and the objects of trust and affection.' How does such a disposition translate to music? This seems straightforward enough. We know what it means to talk of 'conservative music'. We mean those songs whose sentiments accord with a conservative political agenda. Here are Asian Dub Foundation on their fellow musicians, The Prodigy: 'The Prodigy thought it was cool to call a record "Smack My Bitch Up": that is political. It's deliberately political and deliberately conservative' (quoted in the *Independent on Sunday*, 19 March 2000). We are familiar too with the ways in which musicians associate themselves with conservative causes, or more often, with the way conservative politicians appropriate music to their cause. Presidents George Bush and George W. Bush attracted musicians who were seen in some way to represent the status quo – country performers like George Jones and Alan Jackson. Then there were the musicians who supported the Iraq War, and who were deemed conservative or reactionary by their anti-war opponents – singers like Toby Keith and Charlie Daniels.

In a similar way, conservatism is identified in the sentiments of songs. In 2006, the *New York Times* (25 May 2006) published a list of the 'Conservative Top 50', which included The Who's 'Won't Get Fooled Again', The Beatles's 'Taxman', The Rolling Stones's 'Sympathy for the Devil', U2's 'Gloria' and the Sex Pistols's 'Bodies'.

But 'conservatism' is not just attributed to individuals and ideologies; it is also attributed to entire genres. Most familiarly, country music is described as 'conservative', partly because of its propensity to look back, both lyrically and musically. It celebrates the old ways and the old days. However misguided such attribution may be, country is not the only genre so designated. Heavy Metal is seen in a similar way. This is the journalist Fiona Sturges, reviewing Alice Cooper: 'The years pass slowly in heavy metal. Whereas most contemporary music is required to assimilate new ideas and modify its sounds, this essentially conservative genre has remained locked in a timewarp for decades' (*Independent*, 21 August 2000). So too is indie rock: 'the music within carries all the traits of credible alternative rock – lots of reverb, distorted guitar, sections that jump suddenly from quiet to loud and back again – while remaining essentially conservative' (*The Times*, 28 January 2011). The same clichéd labelling is also applied to the music industry. Michael Bracewell's '. . . a deeply conservative and male-led industry' is typical (*The Times*, 28 October 2000). Or of a conductor: Riccardo Muti has been called 'conservative and even dictatorial' (*Daily Telegraph*, 17 March 2011).

Implicit in all the associations made between conservatism and music, is the equally familiar, radical Other: the radical songs, musics, genres, even industries, which are assumed to challenge the status quo, that innovate and liberate. Here are three examples of journalists celebrating that radical Other: '. . . wouldn't you rather hear playful, outgoing and chaotic music than the sterile, measured treadmilling of most indie-rock?' (review of The Beta Band's *The Beta Band*, *Mojo*, July 1999); 'Asian Dub Foundation's resistance to [the] celebrity myth is as radical as their music. Instead of seeing pop success as a credit card to buy cocaine, champagne and front-row seats at fashion shows, they are committed to grass-roots activism' (Nicholas Barber, *Independent on Sunday*, 19 March 2000); '. . . the Cabs [Cabaret Voltaire] spent 25 years battling against conservative pop attitudes' (*Guardian*, 26 May 2000). But although it is easy to find examples on either side – celebrating radicalism, condemning conservatism – there is, within all these familiar, stock responses, much ambiguity, confusion and contradiction. We need only to think of the battle for the soul of Bruce Springsteen's 'Born in the USA', in which liberals and conservatives claimed it for their side, or the debate that has plagued hip hop throughout its history. Rob Young (*New Statesman*, 31 March 2011) argues that the tension between conservatism and radicalism lies at the heart of English folk music.

Many of the political labels tell us more about those doing the labelling than about that which is being labelled. But does this mean that attributing political values to music is always in vain? Or can we identify something more substantial, something more than the prejudices inscribed in lyrics? And if so, what does it mean to call a sound or rhythm or melody 'conservative'? What is going on when the industry is labelled as 'conservative'? What is being identified in the description of 'conservative guitar-rock classicism'? Or of a conductor that they are 'temperamentally conservative' in their 'dislike of atonal music'? Or of a music festival as 'conservative, predictable, provincial'? In many such attributions, 'conservatism' is contrasted with creativity, but sometimes, though, conservatism refers to a moral coding of performers. The Pet Shop Boys were seen to represent a 'new conservatism' in their initial reluctance to come out as gay (Gill, 1995: 9). The Spice Girls were accused of promoting a 'conservative moral agenda' by their emphasis on respect for their mothers and for fidelity (Stuart Jeffries, *Guardian*, 11 August 2000). Audiences too may be described as 'conservative', where it is meant that they, like the industry and certain performers, are happier with what they know, and are reluctant to experiment. The journalist Nicholas Barber wrote of the Counting Crows that their 'full, crafted, professional sound prompts a pavlovian response from record buyers. After all, there is something reassuring about competent, conservative bar-room folk-grunge' (*Independent on Sunday*, 20 February 2000).

In the last example, an explicit link is being made between the 'conservatism' of the music and the 'pavlovian' reaction of the fans. The Counting Crows's music is being located in the mainstream and defined against the radical (autonomous/free-thinking) fringe. But, of course, this connection depends upon the way the key terms are defined. The mainstream, it is assumed, is composed of predictable and standardized products that neither offend nor shock. This would tend to suggest that the mainstream is conservative in the sense of being 'safe' and 'familiar'. But such a category and its definition does not automatically make it conservative. Radiohead, Bob Dylan, Sting, John Lennon, Lady GaGa, Madonna: they all inhabit the mainstream, but what would it mean to call them 'conservative'? Or to put another way, it would be equally suspect to label all those on the margin of radio schedules or in the indie sector as 'radical'. This is not just a matter of semantics. The mainstream is buttressed by its mediation – where and how it is written about, scheduled, etc. If the mainstream is conservative, it is because it is constituted as conservative. Labelling something as 'conservative' is to seek to deny it resonance and significance. But it involves more than this. Understanding how music is labelled is important to understanding the discourses that organize its consumption, but this is not the end of the story. We need to reflect critically upon these discourses and how they operate.

In evaluating music, according to Simon Frith (1996), we are not simply describing a disembodied taste or preference, we are giving vent to a feeling, a feeling which connects the aesthetic with the ethical. 'Not to like a record is not just a matter of taste', he writes (1996: 72), 'it is also a matter of morality'. But, he goes on, the connection of morals and aesthetics is not to be reduced to ideology: 'we don't, on the whole, arm ourselves with a grid of ideological consistency through which everything must pass before we feel it' (1996: 72–3).

For Frith, then, there is a connection between aesthetic value and moral values, but this does not map neatly or systematically onto a political spectrum. This suggests that in looking at what it means to label music as 'conservative', it is not sufficient or appropriate to simply 'translate' musical evaluation into judgement. Put another way, while, as Janet Wolff argues, 'there is a crucial sense . . . in which all art is political', it does not follow that art is 'merely politics represented in symbolic form', or that 'aesthetic judgement follows from political assessment.' Art may be criticized for the political interests that promote or produce it, or for the political values that it evinces, but this does not exhaust the range of aesthetic responses or the range of political meanings (Wolff, 1983: 66). A work of art can be politically radical and aesthetically conservative, and vice-versa. The last part of the chapter explores these two possibilities by looking more closely at what radical critics see as wrong with conservative aesthetics, and what conservative critics see as valuable in their aesthetic. In doing so, we recall the themes outlined in the first part of the chapter.

Radical critics and conservative art

Theodor Adorno and Max Horkheimer's famous essay on the culture industry (1944/79) draws attention to the conservative messages of the texts: 'Donald Duck in the cartoons and the unfortunate in real life get their thrashing so that the audience can learn to take their own punishment'; 'The tragic film becomes an institution for moral improvement' (1944/79: 138, 152). A similar ideological critique of conservative art drives Dave Harker's *One for the Money*, where he (1980: 86) questions whether the Beatles ever offered any kind of 'revolt'. Lyrically, musically and commercially, the Beatles were nothing special (unlike Dylan who, lyrically at least, broke convention and embraced confrontation) (Harker, 1980: 129).

These critics do not confine their critique to the articulated ideologies of the text, but look to the way in which an aesthetic is conservative. Adorno and Horkheimer (1944/79: 130) draw attention to the politics of 'style' : 'As late as Schoenberg and Picasso, the great artists have retained mistrust of style, and at crucial points have subordinated to the logic of the matter. What Dadaists and Expressionists called the untruth of style triumphs today in the sung jargon of a crooner . . . That which is expressed is subsumed through style into the dominant forms of generality, into the language of music, painting, or words, in the hope that it will be reconciled with the idea of true generality.' Style becomes a form of deception and distraction from the truth, a way of becoming reconciled to inequality and exploitation. So it is that Susan McClary (1991: 161) claims Madonna for a radical feminism by drawing attention to the singer's disruption of traditional (male) musical narratives, just as later in pop's history the Riot Grrrls are seen to do (Lynskey, 2011: 571ff).

Where Adorno and Horkheimer look to art to stand in opposition to daily routines and convention, so other radical critics look to culture to disrupt and unsettle, to ward off complacency. In *Performing Rites*, Frith (1996: 277) writes: '. . . I want to value most highly that music, popular and serious, which has some sort of disruptive cultural effect . . .'. The implications of this is that mass audiences will not follow, that their own conservatism will cause them to resist these alternative, disruptive cultures. Or as Greil Marcus once put it (1993: 367): 'To make true political music, you have to say what decent people don't want to hear.'

In his study of the independent sector of the music industry, David Hesmondhalgh (1999: 56, 55) speaks of 'aesthetic traditionalism' and describes the trajectory of the indie story as 'a move towards conformism and conservatism'. This discourse runs counter to that found in daily criticism to the extent that the indie sector is portrayed as, if anything, more conservative than the majors, but the terms of the criticism are the same: the failure to innovate or experiment, the embrace of tradition and nostalgia. Hesmondhalgh writes of the 'prevailing nostalgic classicism at large in indie culture'. In similar vein, Pete Symon (2001: 266) writes of 'the extent to which "indie music" ha[s] grown conservative on a wave of nostalgia'. Marcus (2000: 110) adds a final twist, defining nostalgia as 'the desire to reach back and touch the person you never were'.

Hesmondhalgh compounds this criticism of systemic conservative by linking it to a personal politics of a similar kind. He (1999: 56) accuses the indic sector of displaying 'a notion of personal and professional success indistinguishable from the aspirational consumerism of much of the rest of British society and a lack of interest in changing the social relations of production'. Like Harker (1980) before him and like many others since, Hesmondhalgh identifies a failure of political will and principle as a further source of criticism. But what Hesmondhalgh also shows is how the challenge to conservatism entails more than the attitudes and aspirations of musicians; it also implicates the operation of the music industry. His fascinating account of Rough Trade (Hesmondhalgh, 1997) documents the struggle to develop a genuinely radical, democratic business model.

In summary, then, radical critics, while not following exactly the same path mapped out by popular critical discourse, share much in their condemnation of culture as 'conservative'. It always is a condemnation, and it is one that applies to the politics and aesthetics of the culture, its performers and its audiences. But what is the basis of this criticism? Is it grounded in a particular politics, and is then adapted to deal with its different targets? Is the conservative critique reducible to radical politics? One way, albeit a slightly perverse one, of trying to answer this, is to turn attention to critics who are self-consciously and deliberately *not radical*, those who style themselves as conservative critics.

Elegantly conservative

Roger Scruton is, in the UK, the archetype of this category. Scruton has close political links with right-wing causes, is the author of *The Meaning of Conservatism* (1980), as well as *The Aesthetics of Music* (1999). He is also the author of *An Intelligent Person's Guide to Modern Culture* (1998). In this last book, Scruton (1998: 89) criticizes youth culture, and pop in particular, for being 'a culture which is largely indifferent to traditional boundaries, traditional loyalties, and traditional forms of learning'. He identifies (1998: 89) groups like Nirvana, REM, the Prodigy and Oasis as giving expression to words and sounds that 'lyricize the transgressive conduct of which fathers and mothers used to disapprove'. But despite these apparently familiar conservative complaints against authority or a lack of respect for tradition, Scruton has a more subtle criticism to make.

His argument is that these gestures of protest belie and encrypt a deeper concern: the inability to register real feelings. This, says Scruton, is because the music is 'externalized', by which he means that it does not issue from an organic musical form or aesthetic vision. He writes (1998: 90): 'Melody is synthesized from standardized units, which could be re-arranged in any order without losing or gaining effect. It is not that such music is tuneless: rather that the tune comes from elsewhere, like food from the supermarket shelf, to be heated in the microwave.' Scruton bemoans (1998: 93) the fact that 'Modern pop songs are meticulously put together, often by artificial means . . . .' Modern pop is 'the voice of the machine'; human sounds have been eliminated and the music 'discourses in the moral void' (1998: 91). These discourses are themselves inadequate and superficial: 'Modern pop rarely comes to a conclusion. The music bursts out, repeats itself, and then fades away. . . . There is, to put it another way, a lack of musical argument – a lack, indeed, of musical thought' (1998: 91).

Similar themes occupied the late Allan Bloom, another conservative critic, whose *The Closing of the American Mind*, was an obituary for the intellectual and moral development of his students. Appealing to the ideal of a Leavisite great tradition, he writes (1987: 81): 'as long as they [his students] have the Walkman on, they cannot hear what the great tradition has to say. And, after its prolonged use, when they take it off, they find they are deaf.' For Bloom, rock music works in precisely the opposite way to that which music should. It ought to be 'at the center of education, both for giving passions their due and for preparing the soul for the unhampered use of reason' (1988: 72).

It might seem at first glance that these criticisms by conservatives are completely at odds with those of the radical critics. And in many ways they may be, but note too the similarities, not just with the elitism of Adorno and Horkheimer, but with other critics too. Try substituting the words 'pop' or 'rock' as used by Bloom and Scruton, with the words 'conservative music'. The criticisms are similar. One reason for this similarity lies in the confusion over what it does in fact mean to describe something as 'conservative'.

Music as conservatism

Conservatives believe in tradition, but not necessarily in nostalgia. Scruton (1980: 40) argues that for conservatives: 'The power of tradition is two fold. First, it makes history into reason, and therefore the past into a present aim . . . Second, tradition arises from every organization in society . . .'

Hence, conservatives are disposed – rather than being ideologically committed – to resist change (and to be suspicious of innovation, experimentation etc.). But this disposition is not mindless, not simply the product of a knee-jerk prejudice. It is instead, a response to a distinct world view, one in which the tensions between individual and community, between good and evil, are an ineliminable aspect of social existence. Conservatives criticize liberals and radicals for their doomed attempts to resolve this tension politically by either postulating a free individual (the liberal) or an all-embracing community (the radical). For the conservative, 'evil and suffering are inseparable from existence, and wisdom lies therefore not in massive utopian schemes for abolishing them, but in modest proposals for containing and minimizing their impact' (O'Sullivan, 1987: 97). This is a view that issues in a limited politics of compromise.

Such conservatism is to be distinguished from dystopian fascism, which seeks a resolution in some pre-industrial arcadia or in a 'final solution'; it is also a rejection of cultural nationalism insofar as it presupposes a single harmonized community. As T. S. Eliot (1975: 305) noted in his discussion of culture: 'the unity of culture, in contrast to the unity of political organization, does not require us all to have only one loyalty: it means that there will be a variety of loyalties'. Equally conservatism rejects a politics of principle, which presumes a fully rational and coherent account of society. Such an assumption results in dogmatism, where the conservative favours pragmatism (Robertson, 1985: 65). And finally, conservatism need not be conflated with a neo-conservatism or neo-liberalism that places capitalism at its centre. Such views may be opposed by conservative pragmatists who suspect the emphasis on material and consumer values, and who see these as alien to the conservative moral order (O'Sullivan, 1987: 101). Michael Oakeshott (1962) described this tradition, not as a programme or ideology, but as a disposition, as a set of intuitions and attitudes that incline us to resist change, and to treat innovation with suspicion. Underpinning this is a moral position which rejects instrumentality, the idea that people or policies are to be treated simply as means to an end. Out of such arguments comes Oakeshott's defence of 'friendship' (Oakeshott, 1962: 177): a friend is 'somebody who engages the imagination, who excites contemplation, who provokes interest, sympathy, delight and loyalty simply on account of the relationship entered into. . . . the relationship of friend to friend is dramatic, not utilitarian'.

Drawing attention to these different conservative traditions might seem like a detour. It is not. It is central to the discussion here. If we see 'conservatism' as a pragmatic disposition, born of a social view built upon an assumption of inevitable tension and a mistrust of glib or dogmatic reasoning, then we might see it also as elitist and suspicious of populism. As such it might accord with a critique, in Scruton's words (1982: 109), of 'philistine consciousness', and the utilitarian and materialist order to which it appeals. Conservatism of this type is closer to the critical discourses of radicals and liberals. Put crudely, the conservatives and radicals might listen to different music, but they value it in similar ways. More crucially, in valuing music they treat politics and aesthetics as intimately entwined.

Conclusion

This chapter has covered much ground: from the politics of ancient Greece to the aesthetics of modern conservatives. But the distance travelled is less than might at first appear. What I have tried to show is that there is a well-developed, if sometimes submerged, tradition of political thought, that has accorded music a central place. This place derives both from the sense in which music plays a part in our constitution as moral beings and in our constitution as political ones. In responding to, and in evaluating, music we do not just give expression to our tastes, but to our political values and ideas. Music is, to this extent, part of the way we think politically.

In his fascinating study, *Neuropolitics*, William Connolly (2002: 20) describes the 'micropolitics' that 'operates below the threshold of large legislative acts and executive initiatives', but which connects to them. And he goes on to argue for the importance of film in our micropolitical thinking. My suggestion is that sound and music are similarly important to such processes.

9

One more time with feeling: music as political experience

When doing an earlier research project, I came across the Infernal Noise Brigade (INB), a musical collective dedicated to promoting political action. Their example has stuck with me ever since, and especially during the writing of this book. Sadly, the INB no longer exist, but while they did, they were to be seen – or more importantly, heard – at many of the rallies and demonstrations organized by the anti-globalization and anti-capitalist movement. With their collection of drums and other instruments, the Brigade would not just accompany the marchers; they would choreograph them. They would change the mood and tempo of the demonstrations by altering the rhythm. They represented themselves as 'a tactical mobile rhythmic unit consisting of a majorette, medics, tactical advisors, rifle-twirling contingent, flag corps, and percussionists' (quoted in Whitney, 2003: 218). Their aim was 'to provide entertainment, energy and support' for the demonstrators, but it was also to introduce 'music of a disorienting or ecstatic nature into sterile political discourse' (Whitney, 2003: 218–19). The Brigade was not just intent upon supplying an accompaniment to marching feet, but generating a new kind of political feeling; creating a new world through the 'subliminal disruption of time' (Whitney, 2003: 226).

The Infernal Noise Brigade was not alone. In New York, there was the Hungry March Band and in France, the Musicale d'Intervention. Each one was an incarnation of the potent mix of rhythm and resistance. And what each represents, at least for the purposes of this chapter, is an example of how musical and political experience become one.

The focus on experience helps to answer a crude, but crucial question: what, in the end, does music *do*? If we are to make any claims for music's political importance, this question has to be addressed. Politics is about making a difference, whether maintaining the status quo or changing it. It is about the circulation and use of public power. This does not mean that ideas, thoughts and values are peripheral or irrelevant, but it does mean that for those ideas to be deemed 'political' they must have consequences for the way people think and act in response to the exercise of public power.

This is to make considerable demands of music. There are any number of ways in which music affects the private world of individuals, and even perhaps the exercise of power within those worlds – the complex interplay of love and romance, of personal relationships of all kinds. But to make these the substance of politics is to extend its definition to breaking point. It makes everything 'political', and in so doing empties the term of significance. While the feminist slogan 'the personal is political' is an important polemical device that opens up use and abuse of power in the home (and elsewhere) to scrutiny and challenge, it too is premised on the thought that designating something as 'political' has particular consequences. It makes it the legitimate focus of organized public action, whether by groups, movements, parties or governments. In saying this, it does not follow that 'politics' be understood only as that activity which takes place within formally designated institutions and forums. An understanding of politics that does useful work – that avoids the exclusivity of the traditional account and the inclusiveness of some postmodern versions – means adopting a rather different perspective.

This is to return to the introduction of this book, where I drew attention to Colin Hay's (2007: 61ff) argument against conventional definitions of politics that focuses upon a particular *domain* only (the business of govern ment). Hay preferred to define politics by reference to its specific *content* and to the involvement of choice, agency, deliberation and social interaction. For Hay, politics describes a combination of identifiable alternatives, over which actors can have an effect and upon which they can reflect within a social setting. This definition is inclusive, but not so inclusive as to make everything 'political'. Rather it establishes that politics occurs in realms outside of the formal and public arenas, but is distinguished from those activities that are devoid of social interaction or are attributable to 'fate' or beyond human agency. In shifting the site and the character of politics, Hay (2007: 75) opened up the possibility that political participation could take the guise of everyday conversations, the 'micropolitics' that I referred to at the end of chapter 8, and which William Connolly (2002: 107) describes as 'a cultural collectivization and politicization of the arts of the self.'

How does this view of politics affect the way we imagine its relationship to music? The answer lies in the extent to which music, and the pleasures (and pains) it brings, articulates ideas that people have about their common existence and about their relationship with each other. It also lies in the capacity of music to inspire forms of collective action, and to provide for the social interaction that underpins that action. We may enjoy music for all manner of reasons; it may matter to us in an infinite number of ways; but these many features do not in and of themselves make music political. For it to be politically significant, it has to make a particular contribution to a specific form of collective action or public life; it must touch public power. And for it to be able to do this, it must be able to *do* things in the world. For those who see music as pure and autonomous – as sound that signifies nothing, the suggestion that it acts on the world is nonsense. Indeed for those – like J. S. Mill – who categorize it as a distraction, its impact is minimal and trivial. But for others, in that tradition that we associate with Plato, Rousseau, Nietzsche, Adorno and Attali, music does indeed act on the world and those who inhabit it. These claims are those derived from introspection and are kept aloft by the eloquence of their supporting rhetoric. How might we persuade the sceptic, in particular the sceptical political scientist, that music matters, that music *is* politics. Can we show that were it not for music certain things would not have happened, certain ideas not conceived, certain grievances not aired, certain injustices not challenged – or left unchallenged. As Bruce Johnson and Martin Cloonan (2009) have forcefully argued, there is a dark side to music – it has not always been allied with the angels; it has been associated with evil as well as good. But whatever music's associations, the question remains: does it make a difference?

The power of music

We know of the musicians and musical movements of whom it has been claimed that they made a difference – those who played for Rock Against Racism or Live 8, and those East German musicians who inspired the rebellion that saw the collapse of the Berlin Wall (Pekacz, 2008; Wicke, 1992). We may well disagree as to the extent (or indeed the fact) of this effect, but the theories and methods of political science have established an approach that allows us to know. We have a relatively sophisticated means of attributing responsibility to individuals and movements, of explaining how they obtain power and how they exercise it. It may be that the features to which we draw attention are different in the case of musicians than they are in the case of formally designated political actors, but these differences are merely of degree, not of type.

Where this question takes us to much less familiar and reassuring ground is when we ask whether sounds, rather than the individuals who produce them, can *do* things. Or perhaps, more cautiously, whether sound makes a peculiar and particular contribution to events like Live 8 or the collapse of the Berlin Wall.

The issue we are wrestling with here is whether there is anything special about music. This type of claim forms part of Brian Barry's (2001) reflections on multiculturalism. As we saw in chapter 2, he argued that the only grounds for state support for culture should be that which was intrinsic to it – those features that made it 'excellent' when compared to other works of culture. The fact that it might serve some other purpose – to represent cultural identity, to provide for social inclusivity – created no prima facie case for its support. Or rather, it puts it on a par with all other means to those social and political ends. What sort of argument might be involved here? It has to be one in which music is claimed to do something that cannot be achieved by other means. This means more than simply providing a cultural explanation for thought and action, but a cultural explanation in which music has a distinct and unique role. How might such a case be made?

The most obvious first move is to turn to the ideas and arguments of those for whom sound is an independent variable in accounts of human action. There is now a wealth of literature on the effects of music on individual and collective behaviour. Julian Treasure's (2007) *Sound Business* is one example. Treasure is the chairman of a 'strategic sound consultancy', and a passionate advocate for the importance of music (and sound more generally) to the organization of the human environment and to the behaviour that occurs within it. He recounts experiments in which researchers vary the tempo of music played in the background in restaurants or stores. The faster the rhythm the quicker the diners eat or the customers shop; the slower the music, the more tardy the diners and the shoppers. Treasure recounts too how wine-buyers respond to the nationality of the music they hear – playing French music increases the sale of French wine (Treasure, 2007: 138–9). He discusses the use of sound in the branding of companies – the 'sonic logo' (ibid.: 159). He talks of how changing the auditory architecture of the workplace changes the levels of stress felt by the workforce, their absenteeism and their work rates (ibid.: 184). He writes of how sound 'gets to our feelings and moods', and how in doing so it can make us more or less disposed to act as volunteers or to make us anti-social (ibid.: 135). He recalls the case of Austrian shopworkers who threatened to strike in protest at the Christmas music they were forced to endure and which, they said, exercised a form of 'psychological terror' and made them aggressive (ibid.: 185). He draws no explicitly political conclusions from this evidence, but they are implied in the sense that music, and those who determine its form and use, have power over those who hear it. Another, systematic academic study of the kind of evidence that Treasure provides is offered by Susan Hallam (2001), whose survey is entitled 'the power of music'.

The darker uses of sound to manage behaviour are documented by Johnson and Cloonan (2009). They point not just to the use of music to torture victims, but also such things as the Mosquito Ultrasonic Youth Deterrent that emits a high pitched scream designed to clear teenagers, whose ears are still able to detect the sound, away from public spaces. Here the connection between politics and sound is made explicit, but as the instrument of politics, and not as the particular features of sound itself. For that, we might be tempted to look to neuroscience.

Research by neuroscientists and psychologists has identified the ways in which the brain responds to music. Daniel Levitin (2008: 191) writes: 'The rewarding and reinforcing aspects of listening to music seem . . . to be mediated by increasing dopamine levels in the nucleus accumbens, and by the cerebellum's contribution to regulating emotion through its connections to the frontal lobe and the limbic system. . . . Music is clearly a means for improving people's moods. Now we think we know why.' 'Music', he continues, 'taps into primitive brain structures involved with motivation, reward and emotion'. Music's special capacity to operate on our brain is revealed, suggests Levitin (2008: 231), in the ability of people with Alzheimer's disease to recall songs from their youth, even as all other memories are lost. Musical experiences are 'tagged' neurologically as important.

Hard science's account of the impact of music might not suggest any direct political implications. However, writers like Connolly, in developing an account of the micropolitics of affect and identity draw upon neuroscience in order to understand better how thought processes and culture are mixed. He adopts the term 'neurocultural' (Connolly, 2002: 3–8). And while he is more interested in film than music, he does discuss how 'sound, rhythm, movement, and image . . . communicate affective energies to us' (ibid.: 13). Such thoughts echo those of Jane Bennett, whose work was mentioned in the previous chapter. Such theorists, and others like them, are intent upon incorporating cultural experience into political thought processes. One way of exploring this further is by considering how music might play into political deliberation, into thinking about the relationship between ourselves and others.

Music and deliberation

In his book *Reflective Democracy*, the political philosopher Robert Goodin (2003) ponders the process of deliberation. If we are to argue for deliberative democracy, as many are tempted to do by the perceived inadequacy of systems of representative democracy in which voters merely register preferences, then the issue becomes what conditions have to be met for citizens to be able to deliberate effectively. Deliberative democracy is contrasted with the standard representative variant, in which voters are invited only to record their personal preferences as between parties and/or policies, and these decisions aggregated by the electoral system to provide a winner. In such a world, the voter consults their preferences and decides on their priorities in light of the choices on offer.

Deliberative democracy makes different demands of citizens. Deliberation requires a degree of empathy with fellow human beings; it requires the ability to put yourself in the position of others; it requires the capacity to consider what 'we' want, rather than just what I want. Rather than registering personal preferences, the citizen is asked to reflect upon the interests of all and see how competing expectation and desires might be reconciled. Voting assumes a lower status and importance.

Goodin argues (2003: 169) that most advocates of deliberative democracy concentrate on the 'external-collective' dimension. Their assumption, he suggests, is that in an effective deliberative democracy there will be collectively agreed decisions as to what should be done. However, as Goodin notes (as have others), such a procedure is not practical in anything but small-scale societies. Goodin's solution (2003: 170–1) is to propose that we shift from the 'external–collective' to the 'internal–reflective' mode in order to achieve consensus. This means making other people 'imaginatively present' (2003: 171). He does not propose that the internal process should entirely replace the public form. There will still be a need for this, but he is sceptical of attempts to adapt external collective deliberation to the demands of large scale societies (by the use of new media). In the end, 'deliberation within' is a necessary component of deliberative democracy, whatever the technological order.

How, he asks, does internally reflective deliberation work? How do we come to understand the predicament of others if they are not, as he puts it (2003: 179), 'communicatively present'? The answer, according to Goodin (2003: 180ff), lies in the arts – in particular, film and fiction. Art allows us to experience and understand the lives of others. (This argument leads to a further one: that subsidizing the arts is necessary to a democratic society (2003: 189–92)).

Goodin proposes that the arts not only give us knowledge of other worlds, but also engage us emotionally in them (2003: 181). Cultural experience gives us access to others and to their feelings. These feelings do not substitute public, political knowledge: 'However well-informed our imaginings, we will always need to cross-check the views we attribute to others against those views they actually profess themselves to hold' (Goodin, 2003: 1983). But with this important qualification, Goodin continues to press for the importance of cultural experience in democratic deliberation.

In making his case, Goodin produces little in the way of evidence, save to cite an essay by Elaine Scarry (1996) on how fiction enables us to imagine 'the other'. But the absence of evidence, and the omission of music from the argument, should not lead to us discounting the argument altogether. There are many testimonies to the ways in which the arts have contributed to a capacity for empathy. The film critic Mark Cousins writes persuasively about how film changed his understanding of life in sectarian Northern Ireland. In more mundane fashion, I still recall the first time I heard 'Shoppin' for Clothes', a song recorded by the Coasters in 1960. It was played in the early 1970s on Charlie Gillett's BBC Radio London show. Its loping beat, reminiscent in some ways of Lou Reed's 'Walk on the Wild Side', has a witty spoken narrative, with a bitter pay-off. A cool young man talks of a trip to buy clothes. In the store, he finds the perfect suit. He asks to buy it on credit, to which the salesman replies: 'I've got to do some checking on you.' Moments later, he returns, to say 'I'm sorry, my man, but your credit didn't go through.' Neither race nor poverty are formally mentioned in the song, but they are clearly its subject matter. And in the three short minutes that it lasts, it allowed me – a white, middle-class English boy – to imagine an existence very different to my own and to feel the sense of injustice to which it appealed.

Such anecdotes receive more formal support from a recent study by George McKay, in which he talked to British jazz followers about life in the 1950s. McKay (2003: 267) quotes one suburban jazz fan as saying:

> 'When I went to university in 1959, I just gravitated towards CND. It kind of went with what I wanted to be, and though there had never been any formal "politics" in the jazz scene in [my home town of] Ilford, and there were no black people around our area in that period, it was taken for granted that we all wished we could hear black American jazz musicians. I read in the newspaper about the early civil rights movement in the States, and automatically identified with it without ever thinking why.'

What I take from McKay's example is the idea that music can, and has, produced understandings of experiences that might otherwise be overlooked and ignored. Music enables internal deliberation, but does it do more than that? Does it make us feel differently in politically significant ways?

Music and compassion

Martha Nussbaum is unusual among contemporary political philosophers in a number of ways. I will focus on three. First, she insists on the importance of emotion to ethics. Secondly, she treats music as one important way in which those emotions are 'tapped'; indeed, she concedes that music may have a special claim above the other arts in its capacity to do this (2001: 254; 265). And thirdly, and in extension of the previous point, she suggests that not all forms of music – or literature – are equally capable of tapping emotions.

Her argument begins with the claim that: 'Music has deep connections to our emotional life' (ibid.: 249). She derives this in part from her own experiences, as she puts it, 'as an amateur music lover whose musical life is profoundly influenced by musical experiences' (ibid.), and partly through the work of philosophers like Roger Scruton (1999), who share her view of music's link to the emotions. Her concern is both with the impact of music on the listener and with those 'expressive properties' (Nussbaum, 2001: 250) that inhere in the music itself. For Nussbaum, music is a form of 'symbolic representation', akin to language, but not identical to it, and that it has 'an intimate connection with our emotional depths' by which 'emotional material is embodied in peculiarly musical forms' (ibid.: 264–5).

Music provides access to emotions in ways that language, however dexterously and imaginative used, cannot, because, says Nussbaum (ibid.: 268), 'it remains difficult for language to bypass the intellectual defenses we have developed as we cope with the world.' 'Music', by contrast, 'can bypass habit, use, and intellectualizing' (ibid.: 269). But at the same time she does not consider music to represent, as Rousseau tends to, a universal human language. She contends that its capacity 'to pierce like a painful ray of light directly into the most vulnerable parts of the personality' (ibid.) depends on our appreciation of specific cultural traditions and skills (ibid.: 270–1). But from within these traditions and with these skills, music can 'embody the idea of our urgent need for and attachment to things outside ourselves that we do not control' (ibid.: 272).

Her view of music is linked to a larger set of claims about the role of compassion in personal and communal relations, and in liberal democracy more generally. She takes her inspiration from Walt Whitman's suggestion that there needs to be a 'public poetry' which 'can be made the basis for the public culture of pluralistic democracy' (ibid.: 402–3). In locating music within this public poetry, she writes about Gustav Mahler, in whom she finds an evocation of a love that can supply the 'democratic reciprocity' that, in turn, can 'overcome hatred, exclusion, and resentment' (ibid.: 643). Embedded in this argument is a deeply Romantic account of music and its place in human lives, which depends upon a very literal reading of Mahler's work. Nonetheless, her argument represents a sustained attempt to connect music to politics by way of emotion and ethics. If Goodin's insight is that art allows us to *see* the lives of others, Nussbaum's is about how art allows us to *feel* those lives. But politics is not, of course, just about deliberation and empathy. It is also about imagining and evaluating political orders.

Music and the political imagination

Just as music can allow us to imagine other people, so it may conjure up other worlds – both utopian future ones and real, alternate past ones. Simon Reynolds (2010) argues that music – or at least some music – has always looked forward, has summoned up the future, and that it has done so more effectively and plausibly than other cultural forms. The utopian power of music is evoked by Jacques Attali (1985: 133) in the notion of 'composing': 'Music was, and still is, a tremendously privileged site for the analysis and revelation of new forms in our society.' One of the examples he uses is the free jazz that emerged from the US in the late 1960s. 'Free jazz', he insists (ibid.: 138), 'was the first attempt to express in economic terms the refusal of the cultural alienation inherent in repetition, to use music to build a new culture.' It is a theme which Scott Saul (2003: 32) develops in his *Freedom Is, Freedom Ain't*, a study of the role jazz played in the civil rights movement, where a new vernacular was created, 'a new way of speaking and moving'.

George McKay (2005) detects a similarly utopian spirit within the improvisational music that emerged in the UK at roughly the same time. Figures like the drummer John Stevens and the composer Cornelius Cardew struggled to connect musical forms to ideas of political change, as did those who came after them, in the guise of bands like Henry Cow and movements like Music for Socialism. Simon Frith (1996: 274) echoes McKay's argument when he writes: 'Music-making and music listening are bodily matters; they involve what one might call *social movements*. In this respect, musical pleasure is not derived from fantasy – it is not mediated by day-dreams – but is experienced directly: music gives us real experience of what the ideal could be.'

One way by which music reveals what 'could be' is by recovering what might otherwise be lost from the past. George Lipsitz, for instance, argues that electronic mass media are unique in their capacity to enable people to recover a past that they would otherwise not have encountered. In par-ticular, it allows them to escape the heavy burden of official history, the history of their oppressors. And through these encounters with these alternative pasts, they can explore values and beliefs that are permissable in art, if not in social life. 'Popular music is', writes Lipsitz (1990: 99), 'the product of an ongoing historical conversation in which no one has the first or last word.' Taking Little Richard's 'Good Golly Miss Molly', Lipsitz (1990: 110) traces the ways in which African-American cultural history is bound up in this one song: 'the band plays a rhythmic 8/8 time featuring the "rolling bass" notes popularized by "boogie woogie" piano players in the 1930s. The drummer complements this basic rhythm with accents and afterbeats that give the song a polyrhythmic quality reminiscent of African music.' Music establishes, in this sense, an alternative cultural history, and this can then become part of an alternative political history. Echoing Marcus's 'secret histories' and Cantwell's 'memory theater', Tricia Rose (1994: 100–1) too argues that rap 'is a contemporary stage for the theater of the powerless. On this stage, rappers act out inversions of status hierarchies, tell alternative stories of contact with the police and the education process, and draw portraits of contact with dominant groups in which the hidden transcript inverts/subverts the public, dominant transcript.' In a song called 'Sound of Da Police', the rapper KRS-1 playfully elides the words 'overseer' and 'officer', connecting slavery with contemporary police harassment. Just as the powerful write history, so the powerless try to re-write it, and popular music, as the most acces-sible of mass cultural forms, becomes a crucial site in the struggle for authorship and for the memories that give meaning and legitimacy to that struggle.

Music, then, in imagining the future and restoring lost elements of the past, plays into political thought, generating the ideals and possibilities that may inspire political action. But action needs organization.

Music as political organization

Music can be seen as a product of, and producer of, forms of social organization. As McKay's (2005) portrait of the British avant-garde makes
clear, challenging musical convention also demanded new means of producing those sounds, new forms of production. Utopian possibilities were
inextricably linked to challenging the traditional, hierarchical modes of
musical production. The changes did not just involve relations between
musicians, but between them and the process of production with which
they worked.

David Hesmondhalgh (1997), in his study of Rough Trade, describes
another attempt to re-organize the production of music. He recounts how
Rough Trade, at least in its early days, was designed to operate on democratic lines. This applied to relations between the artist and the company,
and meant an end to long-term contracts and the start of equity in the
distribution of royalties. Rough Trade emulated a workers' cooperative.
While the story ends unhappily, with Rough Trade struggling to survive,
it does draw attention to the politics of music's production, and to the
relations that are established through it. The shift in power away from its
traditional locations meant that new voices could register in the making
of music.

There is a second sense in which music links to political organization,
and this entails music *creating* organization. There is a semblance of this
idea in Ron Eyerman and Andrew Jamison's description of music as a form
of 'cognitive praxis' that feeds into the mobilization of social movements.
Music becomes, they write (1998: 23–4), 'both knowledge and action, part
of the frameworks of interpretation and representation produced within
social movements'. It is not just a matter of music expressing the ideals of
the movement, or the movement providing a context for the music, but of
the music constituting 'forms of social solidarity' which serve as 'exem-
plary social action' (ibid.: 77). 'Music as experienced and performed within
social movements', they contend (ibid.: 163), 'is at once subjective and
objective, individual and collective in its form and in its effects. Through
its ritualized performance and through the memories it invokes, the music
of social movements transcends the bounds of the self and binds the individual to a collective consciousness.' This might be read as music organizing individuals into a movement by crafting a collective experience for
its audience. Keith Negus touches on this when describing what happens
when audiences sing along, and when a song becomes, in the words of
Paul Williams, an expression of 'not just personal but collective freedom'

(quoted in Negus, 2008: 153). The suggestion is that, in sharing in a song, the participants come to understand and experience a political ideal.

Music as political values: the feeling of freedom

Is it possible that we might learn the meaning of political values through music? David Widgery (1986: 90) certainly seemed to think so when he wrote of the RAR Carnival in Victoria Park in 1978: 'The punks didn't like any of the speakers, but knew exactly what the music was saying.' It is also what I understand Scott Saul to be saying when he links the practical and aesthetic ambitions of a performer like Charles Mingus. Saul (2003: 159) writes:

> Mingus understood freedom not as freedom from coercion (Isaiah Berlin's classic definition of negative liberty), but as a sphere of musical action governed by the push and pull of the Workshop dynamic. His freedom was collective action with traction: it came about when the community of the Workshop – 'these seven men set to free themselves in music' – negotiated the rules set up by Mingus the composer. The Workshop thus provided a drama of freedom enacting itself against a set of sometimes rigorous, sometimes loosely drawn, constraints.

Here, Saul suggests, the organization and the performance of the music work to create a political idea, or rather the feeling evoked by a political ideal. Mingus's music is understood to do more than describe a principle, but to live it, and to live it as part of a community.

Music as community

'Raising voices in common song', writes Theodor Gracyk (2007: 170, emphasis added), 'is a public response that *creates* rather than expresses community'. In 2002 in the UK, the Queen celebrated her Golden Jubilee – the fiftieth year of her reign. As part of the celebrations, a concert was held in the gardens of Buckingham Palace. It began with guitarist Brian May (of the other Queen) standing on the battlements playing the UK's national anthem, 'God Save the Queen'. As he postured and grimaced in the evening breeze, his efforts prompted comparison with Hendrix's rendition of the 'Star Spangled Banner' at Woodstock. While Hendrix was seen as defying the White House, May was seen as deferring to the British establishment. And in these differences, different communities and politics were summoned into existence. They were less mundane versions of what happens with each election, when parties use music to brand themselves and to forge constituencies of support (from New Labour's adoption of

D:Ream's 'Things can only get better' in 1997, to the Lighthouse Family's 'Lifted' in 2001).

These self-conscious uses of music to brand a political identity may be misguided, but their intentions are clear enough: to create an imagined community for the supporters to share. It taps into Gracyk's (2007: 167; his emphasis) description of music as 'something into which we *join*'. And in joining we become complicit in the vision it creates. 'All response to music', Gracyk says, 'is indeed a sympathetic response to a social order.'

Music as the experience of politics

What all these dimensions of music's engagement with politics have in common – whether we are talking about political values and ideals, political organization and community – is the thought that music makes it possible *to experience them*. There is now a branch of business marketing known as 'experiential marketing'. Rather than using the conventional devices of advertising and PR, where customers are told (or persuaded) of the benefits of a good, the marketing department now create an experience around their product. Sports events or concerts are used to sell a product by associating it with an experience. Events like Live 8 and Glastonbury are examples of experiential marketing in the way that causes and consumer goods – it does not matter whether it is Oxfam or O2 that is being sold – are marked with the experience of the concert or festival.

While experiential marketing may seem to be an exercise in cynical manipulation, it trades on the idea that our thoughts and actions emerge from the experiences we have, and that these experiences are the product of many things, especially the accompanying sounds.

It is even possible to see artists and events with no links to consumer capitalism engaging in experiential marketing of a kind. The raves organized by collectives like Spiral Tribe and Exodus were designed to give form to their ecological and communitarian ideals (McKay, 1996). They were not just instruments of a political cause. The raves provided a way of *living* those politics. Raves that lasted days and were attended by 25,000 people provided experience, it was claimed by one participant, of 'a world you didn't know existed. The sun goes down, the moon comes up and you see the world spinning. My record is nine days. It's a shamanic thing' (quoted in Rietveld, 1998: 248). The re-organization of time, the creation of an alternative narrative, has been used, most famously in Birmingham subcultural analysis (Willis, 1978), as a marker of resistance and subversion. The rave itself became, within this rhetoric, an alternative social world, one that broke with the codes of the protestant work ethic, that refused the rhythms of the working day, and that replaced the hierarchies of dominant order. The rave sought to create a democratic experience: there were no stars demanding attention or adulation, just dancers looking at each other (McKay, 1996; Hesmondhalgh, 1997).

The sociologist Kevin Macdonald applies this kind of argument to social movements, claiming much more than Eyerman and Jamison. He (2006: 214) argues that the global movements are 'constructed around structures of representation and delegation, and none is an expression of a process of rational deliberation. . . . [T]hese movements are involved in *doing*, where the senses are at the heart of the action.' Social movements, he suggests, are to be understood as 'experience movements'. The prime agent is rhythm. Talking about the rise of rap, the jazz musician Max Roach said that 'the politics was in the drums'. As he explained: 'The rhythm was very militant to me because it was like marching, the sound of an army on the move. We lost Malcolm, we lost King and they thought they had blotted out everybody. But all of a sudden this new art form arises and the militancy is there in the music' (quoted in Lipsitz, 1994: 38). 'To grasp the "rhythm" of a piece of music (which is in the end to listen to it)', Frith argues (1996: 153), 'means participating actively in its unfolding and trusting that this unfolding has been (or is being) shaped – that it will lead somewhere. It is at once a physical and mental process; it involves aesthetic and ethical judgements.'

In highlighting the power of rhythm, McDonald argues that 'we can think of movements as closer to music [than to texts or messages]'. Music is no longer to be understood as instrument of, or accompaniment to, politics; it is politics.

Coda

Music has the capacity to makes us do and feel things that we would not otherwise, and it does so with immediacy and directness. It has the capacity, in Keith Negus's words (2008: 152), to make the 'ordinary special'. This capacity is what is used to create the forms of *political* experience that I have traced in this book, and especially in this chapter. The various links sketched here form elements of this experience, and together they provide an answer to the question of what – politically – music *does*. As we have seen, there are many parts to the answer. Music can help constitute identities and communities; it can create organization and institutions; it can embody ideals and values.

Conclusion: repeat and fade

This book originated in a combination of professional frustration and a personal passion. The passion is obvious, and need not detain us. It is with music of all kinds, and with its ability to move and animate listeners and performers. For many years, as a reviewer of live music for *The Times*, I witnessed this on a regular basis, and then more recently when I was asked to help compile a list of the best political music to celebrate the sixtieth anniversary of the Political Studies Association. We solicited members' views on what should be included, and we were peppered with suggestions and arguments (about how everyone else's selection was misguided or just plain wrong). Music, and music that dealt with politics, matters to many people. And this, in a sense, is where the professional frustration emerges. There has been a tendency within traditional political science to overlook culture generally, and music in particular. Neither are overlooked entirely, and there are brilliant exceptions to the rule, but they remain some way distant from the mainstream, perhaps further than in other social sciences, like sociology or human geography. Economics has produced a detailed study, 'Rockonomics' (Connolly and Kreuger, n.d.), which, despite its doubtful title, is a serious examination of the incentives that operate in the music industry. Political science has, for the most part, stayed quiet on sound. But, as I hope I have shown, there is a tradition of political thought which gives sound a prominent place, and one of the aims of this book has been to draw attention to it.

But this book has not just been a work of propaganda for the need to take music seriously. It has been about what such a commitment entails, about *how* we might take it seriously. It was in trying to address this issue that I began by looking at the most obvious point of engagement between music and politics, the activities of the state (and its agents). The censorship of music represents the most blatant form of political involvement. And while many of the examples of the excesses of the over-mighty may reveal more about their delusions and paranoia than about the power of music itself, they did open up the thought that music was a source of political expression, worthy of the protection of the First Amendment.

This same thought, that music was implicated in the higher political principles, provided the theme for the subsequent discussion of music policy, and the way in which states invest music with the powers to realize and embody some notion of the 'good life'. From there it was a relatively short step to examining the use of music in political movements. Once again, though, my argument was that music's involvement constituted more than simply acting as a soundtrack ('the sound of marching, charging feet', as Mick Jagger sang on 'Street Fighting Man'). My suggestion was that music might, in the case of Rock Against Racism and Live 8, mobilize political action, and that musicians might represent causes and peoples. This does not, and cannot, happen at any time. It depends on a multiplicity of related factors – to do with the legitimation of musicians, and the distribution of a variety of forms of capital – but, under specific conditions, music does animate political action.

From this point onwards, having tried to establish the case for taking music seriously in the study of politics, my attention has been upon how music embodies or conveys politics, how it 'performs politics'. It was this concern that led to discussion of music's capacity to capture historical experience, experience that fuels the passion behind political action. It also led to examination of how argument about music's value invested it with morality and ideology. My suggestion was that in arguing about music, in evaluating it, we think through our political commitments and values, and we gain a sense of how others feel. It is for this reason that we need also to be sensitive to the mechanisms by which evaluations are made and mediated. We need to be watchful of those who are entrusted with judging music; they are playing at politics too.

So, in the end, I have tried to persuade those of you who have got this far that music does not just accompany our political thoughts and actions, and that it is not simply the object of state intervention and state policy, or the instrument of social movements, but rather that it is deeply implicated in the ideas and institutions that organize politics. My hope, as I said at the very beginning, is that I have indicated how we can and should think of music as politics, and politics as music.

References

Adorno, T. W. (2002) *Essays on Music*, edited by R. Leppert, Berkeley: University of California Press.

Adorno, T. and M. Horkheimer (1944/79) 'The culture industry: enlightenment as mass deception', in *Dialectic of Enlightenment,* London: Verso, pp. 120–67.

Ali, T. (1987) *Street Fighting Years: An Autobiography of the Sixties*, London: Collins.

Allan, S. (2003) 'Mediating citizenship: on-line journalism and the public sphere new voices', *Development*, 46(1), 30–40.

Anderson, B. (1983) *Imagined Communities: Reflections on the Origins and Spread of Nationalism*, London: Verso.

Anderson, C. (2004) 'The long tail', *Wired*, 12(10), available at: http://www.wired.com/wired/archive/12.10/tail.html.

Ankersmit, F. R. (1996) *Aesthetic Politics*, Stanford: Stanford University Press.

Ankersmit, F. R. (2002) *Political Representation,* Stanford, CA: Stanford University Press.

Arblaster, A. (1992) *Viva la Liberta! Politics in Opera*, London, Verso, 1992.

Aristotle (1962) *Politics*, Harmondsworth: Penguin.

Arrow, K. (1951) *Social Choice and Individual Values*, New Haven: Yale University Press.

Attali, J. (1985) *Noise: The Political Economy of Music*, Minneapolis: University of Minnesota Press.

Atton, C. (2002) 'New cultures and new social movements: radical journalism and the mainstream media', *Journalism Studies*, 3(2), 491–505.

Baily, J. (2001) 'The censorship of music in Afghanistan', *Freemuse*, 24 April, available at: http://www.freemuse.org/sw1106.asp.

Baily, J. (2004) 'Music censorship in Afghanistan before and after the Taliban', in M. Korpe (ed.) *Shoot the Singer: Music Censorship Today*, London: Zed Books, pp.19–28.

Barry, B. (2001) *Culture and Equality: An Egalitarian Critique of Multiculturalism*, Cambridge: Polity.

Bastian, V. and Laing, D. (2003) 'Twenty years of music censorship around the world' in M. Cloonan and R. Garofalo (eds) *Policing Pop*, Philadelphia: Temple University Press, pp. 46–64.

Bennett, J. (2001) *The Enchantment of Modern Life: Attachments, Crossings, and Ethics*, Princeton: Princeton University Press.

Bennett, T. (1990) 'Really useless "knowledge": a political critique of aesthetics', in *Outside Literature*, London: Routledge, pp. 133–66.

Birch, A. H. (1964) *Representative and Responsible Government*, London: George Allen and Unwin.

Blair, T. (2010) *A Journey*, London: Hutchinson.

Blanning, T. (2002) *The Culture of Power and the Power of Culture: Old Regime Europe 1660–1789*, Oxford: Oxford University Press.

Blanning, T. (2008) *The Triumph of Music: Composers, musicians and their audiences, 1700 to the present*, London: Allen Lane.

Bloom, A. (1987) *The Closing of the American Mind*, New York: Simon and Schuster.

Bourdieu, P. (1986) *Distinction: A Social Critique of Taste*, London: Routledge.

Bourdieu, P. (1993) *The Field of Cultural Production: Essays on Art and Literature*, Cambridge: Polity.

Bragg, B. (2007) *The Progressive Patriot: A Search for Belonging*, London: Bantam Press.

Breen, M. (2008) 'Popular music, policy making and the instrumental policy behaviour process', *Popular Music*, 27(2), 193–208.

Buckingham, D. (2000) *The Making of Citizens: Young People, News and Politics*, London: Routledge.

Buckley, D. (2000) *Strange Fascination. David Bowie: The Definitive Story*, London: Virgin.

Burchill, J. and T. Parsons (1978) *The Boy Looked at Johnny*, London: Pluto Press.

Campbell, A. (2007) *The Blair Years*, London: Hutchinson.

Cantwell, R. (1991) 'Smith's memory theater: the folkways anthology of American folk music', *New England Review*, Spring/Summer, 364–97.

Cantwell, R. (1996) *When We Were Good: the Folk Revival*, Cambridge, Mass.: Harvard University Press.

Castells, M. (2009) *Communication Power*, Oxford: Oxford University Press.

Caves, R. E. (2000) *Creative Industries: Contracts Between Art and Commerce*, Cambridge, Mass.: Harvard University Press.

Cavicchi, D. (1998) *Tramps Like Us: Music and Meaning Among Springsteen Fans*, New York: Oxford University Press.

Chambers, C. (2006) *Here We Stand: Politics, Performers and Performance*, London: Nick Hern Books.

Chastagner, C. (1999) 'The parents' music resource center: from information to censorship', *Popular Music*, 18(2), 179–92.

Cheles, L. and L. Sponza (eds) (2001) *The Art of Persuasion: Political Communication in Italy from 1945 to the 1990s*, Manchester: Manchester University Press.

Chevigny, P. (1991) *Gigs: Jazz and the Cabaret Laws in New York City*, New York: Routledge.

Christgau, R. (1982) *Christgau's Guide: Rock Albums of the 70's*, London: Vermilion.

Christgau, R. (1990) *Christgau's Record Guide: The 80's*, New York: Pantheon Books.

Christgau, R. (2000) *Christgau's Consumer Guide: Albums of the 90's*, New York: St Martin's.

Clarke, D. (1998) *The Penguin Encyclopaedia of Popular Music*, 2nd edn, London: Penguin.

Clarke, M. (1982) *The Politics of Pop Festivals*, London: Junction.

Cloonan, M. (1996) *Banned! Censorship of Popular Music in Britain, 1967–1992*, Aldershot: Ashgate.

Cloonan, M. (1999) 'Pop and the nation state: towards a theorisation', *Popular Music*, 18(2), 193–208.

Cloonan, M. (2003) 'Call that censorship? Problem of definition', in M. Cloonan and R. Garofalo (eds), *Policing Pop*, Philadelphia: Temple University Press, pp. 13–29.

Cloonan, M. (2004) 'What is music censorship? Towards a better understanding of the term', in M. Korpe (ed.) *Shoot the Singer: Music Censorship Today*, London: Zed Books, pp. 3–5.

Cloonan, M. (2007) *Popular Music and the State in the UK: Culture, Trade or Industry?*, Aldershot: Ashgate.

Cloonan, M. and S. Frith (eds) (2008) *Special Issue on Popular Music Policy*, Popular Music, 27(2).

Cloonan, M. and S. Frith (2011) *A Music Manifesto for Scotland*, Edinburgh: Royal Society of Edinburgh.

Clover, J. (2009) *1989: Bob Dylan Didn't Have this to Sing About*, Berkeley: University of California Press.

Cluely, R. (2009) 'Chained to the grassroots: the music industries and DCMS', *Cultural Trends*, 18(3), 213–25.

Cohen, R. (2000) 'Broadside magazine and records, 1962–1988', in Jeff Place and Ronald Cohen, *The Best of Broadside 1962–1988*, Washington: Smithsonian Folkways, pp. 11–16.

Cole, Richard (1971) 'Top songs in the sixties', *American Behavioral Scientist*, 14, 389–400.

Coleman, S. (2007) *Beyond the West(Minister) Wing: The Depiction of Politicians and Politics in British Soaps*, Research Report, Institute of Communications Studies, University of Leeds.

Colley, L. (1992) *Britons: Forging the Nation 1707–1837*, London: Pimlico.

Competion Commission (2010) *Ticketmaster/Live Nation: Final Report*, available at: http://www.competition-commission.org.uk/rep_pub/reports/2010/556ticket.htm.

Connolly, M. and A. Kreuger (n.d.) 'Rockonomics: the economics of popular music', available at: http://www.irs.princeton.edu/pubs/pdfs/499.pdf.

Connolly, W. E. (2002) *Neuropolitics: Thinking, Culture, Speed*, Minneapolis: University of Minnesota Press.

Corner, J. and D. Pels (eds) (2003) *Media and the Restyling of Politics*, London: Sage.

Couldry, N. (2010) *Why Voice Matters: Culture and Politics after Neoliberalism*, London: Sage.

Couldry, N., S. Livingstone and T. Markham (2007) *Media Consumption and Public Engagement: Beyond the Presumption of Attention*, Houndmills: Palgrave Macmillan.

Crossley, N. (2008) 'Pretty connected: the social network of the early UK punk movement', *Theory, Culture and Society*, 25(6), 89–116.

Crouch, C. (2004) *Post-Democracy*, Cambridge: Polity.

Cushman, T. (1995) *Notes From Underground: Rock Music Counterculture in Russia*, Albany: State University of New York Press.

Dabydeen, D., J. Gilmore, and C. Jones (eds) (2007) *The Oxford Companion to Black British History*, Oxford: Oxford University Press.

Dahl, R. (1956) *A Preface to Democratic Theory*, Chicago: University of Chicago Press.

Dawson, A. (2005) ' "Love music, hate racism": the cultural politics of rock against racism campaigns, 1976–1981', *Postmodern Culture*, 16(1), available at: http://muse.jhu.edu/journals/pmc/toc/pmc16.1.html.

Deleuze, G. and Guattari, F. (1987) *A Thousand Plateaus: Capitalism and Schizophrenia*, London: Continuum.

Denisoff, R. S. (1971) *Great Day Coming: Folk Music and the American Left*, Urbana: University of Illinois Press.

Denisoff, R. S. (1972) 'The evolution of the American protest song', in R. Serge Denisoff and Richard A. Peterson (eds), *The Sounds of Social Change*, Chicago: Rand McNally, pp. 15–25.

Denisoff, R. S. (1975) *Solid Gold: The Popular Record Industry*, New Brunswick: Transaction.

Denning, M. (1997) *The Cultural Front*, London: Verso.

DeNora, T. (2000) *Music in Everyday Life*, Cambridge: Cambridge University Press.

Denselow, R. (1989) *When the Music's Over: The Story of Political Pop*, London: Faber and Faber.

Doggett, P. (2007) *There's a Riot Going On: Revolutionaries, Rock Stars and the Rise and Fall Of '60s Counter-Culture*, Edinburgh: Canongate.

Dugan, C. N. and T. Strong (2001) 'Music, politics, theater, and representation in Rousseau', in P. Riley (ed.) *The Cambridge Companion to Rousseau*, Cambridge: Cambridge University Press, pp. 329–64.

Dworkin, R. (1985) 'Can a liberal state support art?', in *A Matter of Principle*, Cambridge, Mass.: Harvard University Press, pp. 221–31.

Ehrenreich, B. (2007) *Dancing in the Streets: A History of Collective Joy*, London: Granta.

Eliot, T. S. (1975) *Selected Prose of T. S. Eliot*, ed. with an introduction by F. Kermode, London: Faber and Faber.

Ellison, Mary (1989) *Lyrical Protest*, New York: Praeger.

EMO (European Music Office) (1996) *Music in Europe*, available at: http://www.emo.org/emo_documents.php.

English, J. (2005) *The Economy of Prestige: Prizes, Awards, and the Circulation of Cultural Value*, Cambridge, Mass.: Harvard University Press.

Everett, P. (1986) *You'll Never be 16 Again*, London: BBC Publications.

Eyerman, R. and A. Jamison (1998) *Music and Social Movements: Mobilizing Traditions in the Twentieth Century*, Cambridge: Cambridge University Press.

Falasca-Zamponi, S. (1997) *Fascist Spectacle: the Aesthetics of Power in Mussolini's Italy*, Berkeley: University of California Press.

Farrar, M. (2004) 'Social movements and the struggle over "race"', in M. Todd and G. Taylor (eds), *Democracy and Participation: Popular protest and new social movements*, London: Merlin Press.

Fishkin, J. (1991) *Democracy and Deliberation*, New Haven: Yale University Press.

Fountain, N. (1988) *Underground Press*, London: Comedia.

Fraser, N. (1992) 'Rethinking the public sphere: a contribution to the critique of actually existing democracy', in C. Calhoun (ed.) *Habermas and the Public Sphere*, Cambridge, Mass.: MIT Press, pp.109–42.

Freedman, D. (2008) *The Politics of Media Policy*, Cambridge: Polity.

Friedlander, P. (1996) *Rock and Roll: A Social History*, Boulder, Col: Westview Press.

Frith, S. (1988) *Music for Pleasure: Essays in the Sociology of Pop*, Cambridge: Polity.

Frith, S. (1993) 'Popular music and the local state', in T. Bennett, S. Frith, L. Grossberg, J. Shepherd and G. Turner (eds), *Rock and Popular Culture*, London: Routledge, pp. 14–24.

Frith, S. (1996) *Performing Rites: On the Value of Popular Music*, Oxford: Oxford University Press.

Frith, S. (2003) 'Music and everyday life', *Critical Quarterly*, 44(1), 35–48.

Frith, S. (2004) 'Does British music still matter? A reflection on the changing status of British popular music in the global music market', *European Journal of Cultural Studies*, 7(1), 43–58.

Frith, S. and L. Marshall (eds) (2004) *Music and Copyright*, 2nd edn, Edinburgh: University of Edinburgh Press.

Gamble, A. (2004) 'The drifter's escape', in Boucher, D. and Browning, G. (eds), *The Political Art of Bob Dylan*, Houndsmills: Palgrave, pp. 12–34.

Garofalo, R. (1997) *Rockin' Out: Popular Music in the USA*, Boston: Allyn and Bacon.

Garofalo, R. (1992) 'Understanding mega-events: if we are the world, then how do we change it?' in R. Garofalo (ed.) *Rockin' the Boat: Mass Music and Mass Movements*, Boston: South End Press, pp. 15–36.

Gerbner, G. and L. Gross (1976) 'Living with television: the violence profile', *Journal of Communication*, 26(2), 172–199.

Geuss, R. (2005) *Outside Ethics*, New Jersey: Princeton University Press.

Geuss, R. and R. Speirs (1999) 'Introduction' to F. Nietzsche, *The Birth of Tragedy And Other Writings*, Cambridge: Cambridge University Press, pp. vii–xxx.

Gill, J. (1995) *Queer Noise*, London: Cassell.

Gillett, C. (1983) *The Sound of the City*, revd edn, London: Souvenir Press.

Gilroy, P. (1992) *There ain't no black in the Union Jack*, London: Routledge.

Ginsburgh, V. (2003) 'Awards, success and aesthetic quality in the arts', *Journal of Economic Perspectives*, 17(2), 99–111.

Githens-Mazer, J. (2008) 'Locating agency in collective political behaviour: nationalism, social movements and individual mobilisation', *Politics*, 28(1), 41–49.

Goodin, R. E. (2003) *Reflective Democracy*, Oxford: Oxford University Press.

Goodyer, I. (2009) *Crisis Politics: The Cultural Politics of Rock Against Racism*, Manchester: Manchester University Press.

Gorman, P. (2001) *In Their Own Write: Adventures in the Music Press*, London: Sanctuary.

Gracyk, T. (2007) *Listening to Popular Music: Or, How I Learned to Stop Worrying and Love Led Zeppelin*, Ann Arbor: University of Michigan Press.

Graf, M. (1947) *Composer and Critic: Two Hundred Years of Musical Criticism*, London: Chapman and Hall.

Green, J. (1998) *All Dressed Up: The Sixties and the Counterculture*, London: Jonathan Cape.

Griffin, M. (2001) *Reaping the Whirlwind*, London: Pluto Press.

Grossberg, L. (1992) *We've Gotta Get Out of this Place*, London: Routledge.

Habermas, J. (1992) *The Structural Transformation of the Public Sphere*, Cambridge: Polity.

Hague, S., J. Street and H. Savigny (2008) 'The voice of the people? musicians as political actors', *Cultural Politics*, 4(1), 5–23.

Hallam, S. (2001) *The Power of Music: A Study Commissioned by the Performing Right Society*, London: PMRS.

Haralambos, M. (1974) *Right on: From Blues to Soul in Black America*, London: Edison Press.

Harewood, S. (2008) 'Policy and performance in the Caribbean', *Popular Music*, 27(2), 209–224.

Harker, D. (1980) *One for the Money: Politics and popular song*, London: Hutchinson.

Harker, D. (1992) 'Still crazy after after all these years' in B. Moore-Gilbert and J. Seed (eds), *Cultural Revolution? The Challenge of the Arts in the 1960s*, London: Routledge, pp. 236–54.

Harrington, A. (2004) *Art and Social Theory*, Cambridge: Polity.

Harris, J. (2003) *The Last Party: Britpop, Blair and the Demise of English Rock*, London: Fourth Estate.

Hay, C. (2007) *Why We Hate Politics*, Cambridge: Polity.

Hebdige, D. (1988) *Hiding in the Light: On Images and Things*, London: Routledge.

Hesmondhalgh, D. (1997) 'Post-punk's attempt to democratise the music industry: the success and failure of rough trade', *Popular Music*, 16(3), 255–274.

Hesmondghalgh, D. (1999) 'Indie: the aesthetics and the institutional politics of a popular music genre', *Cultural Studies*, 13(1), 34–61.

Hesmondhalgh, D. (2007) *The Culture Industries*, 2nd edn, London: Sage.

Hewison, R. (1988) *Too Much: Art and Society in the Sixties 1960–75*, London: Methuen.

Hindman, M. (2009) *The Myth of Digital Democracy*, Princeton: Princeton University Press.

Hoberman, J. (1998) 'Franklin D, listen to me', *London Review of Books*, 17 September.

Hobsbawm, E. (1995) *Age of Extremes: The Short Twentieth Century 1914–1991*, London: Abacus.

Hoffman, A. (1969) *Woodstock Nation: A Talk-Rock Book*, New York: Random House.

Homan, S. (2003) *The Mayor's A Square: Live Music and Law and Order in Sydney*, Newtown, NSW: Local Consumption Publications.

Homan, S. (2008) 'A portrait of the politician as a young pub rocker: live music reform in Australia', *Popular Music*, 27(2), 243–256.

Hornby, N. (2000) *Fever Pitch*, London: Penguin.

IFPI (International Federal Phonographic Industry) (2010) *Recording Industry in Numbers*, available at: http://www.ifpi.org/content/section_news/20100428.html.

Index on Censorship (2010) *Smashed Hits 2.0*, 39(3).

Index on Censorship (1998) *Smashed Hits: The Book of Banned Music*, 27(6).

Jackson, D. (2007) 'Star power? Celebrity and politics among Anglophone Canadian youth', *British Journal of Canadian Studies*, 20(1), 75–98.

Jackson, D. and T. Darrow (2005) 'The influence of celebrity endorsements on young adults' political opinions', *Press/Politics*, 10(3), 80–98.

Jara, J. (1983) *Victor: An Unfinished Song*, London: Jonathan Cape.

Johnson, B. (2003) 'Two Paulines, two nations: an Australian case study in the intersection of popular music and politics', *Popular Music and Society*, 26(1), 53–72.

Johnson, B. and M. Cloonan (2009) *Dark Side of the Tune: Popular Music and Violence*, Farnham: Ashgate.

Jones, S. (1988) *Black Culture, White Youth: The Reggae Tradition from JA to UK*, Basingstoke: Macmillan.

Jonze, T. (2010) 'Rapper Giggs's tour cancelled after police warning', *Guardian Unlimited*, 23 February.

Jowell, T. (2004) *Government and the Value of Culture*, London: Department of Culture, Media and Sport.

Kahn-Harris, K. (2007) *Extreme Metal: Music and Culture on the Edge*, Oxford: Berg.

Kane, J. (2001) *The Politics of Moral Capital*, Cambridge: Cambridge University Press.

Kater, M. (1997) *The Twisted Muse: Musicians and their Music in the Third Reich*, Oxford: Oxford University Press.

KEA (2006/9) *Market Research and Policy Reports for the Music Business on Key EU Markets*, available at: http://www.keanet.eu/report/rep_musc1.html.

Keane, J. (2002) *Whatever happened to Democracy?*, London: IPPR.

Kelley, R. G. (1997) *Yo' mama's disfunktional! Fighting the Culture Wars in Urban America*, Boston: Beacon Press.

Kelly, P. (ed.) (2002) *Multiculturalism Reconsidered*, Cambridge: Polity.

Krause, T. (2008) ' "Amerrrika ist wunderrrbarrr": promotion of Germany through *Radio Goethe*'s cultural export of German popular music to North America', *Popular Music*, 27(2), 225–242.

Kureishi, H. and J. Savage (eds) (1995) *The Faber Book of Pop*, London: Faber and Faber.

Lahusen, C. (1996) *The Rhetoric of Moral Protest: Public Campaigns, Celebrity Endorsement and Political Mobilization*, Berlin: Walter de Gruyter.

Laing, D. (1985) *One Chord Wonders*, Milton Keynes: Open University Press.

Laing, D. (1986) 'The music industry and the "cultural imperialism" thesis', *Media, Culture and Society*, 8(3), 331–341.

Laing, D. (1999) 'The European music industry and European music policy', *Cultural Trends*, 9(34), 31–56.

Laing, D. (2003) 'Resistance and protest', in J. Shepherd, D. Horn, D. Laing, P. Oliver and P. Wicke (eds), *Continuum Encyclopedia of Popular Music of the World*, London: Continuum, pp. 345–6.

Larkin, C. (1993) *The Guinness Encyclopaedia of Popular Music* (Concise Edition), London: Guinness Publishing.

Leppert, R. (2002) Commentary, in T. Adorno, *Essays on Music*, Berkeley: University of California Press.

Levitin, D. (2008) *This is Your Brain on Music: Understanding a Human Obsession*, London: Atlantic Books.

Li, L. (2011) 'Whispering: the murmur of power in a lo-fi world', *Media, Culture and Society*, 33(1), 19–34.

Lieberson, S. (2000) *A Matter of Taste: How Names, Fashions, and Culture Change*, New Haven: Yale University Press.

Lipsitz, G. (1990) *Time Passages: Collective Memory and American Popular Culture*, Minneapolis: University of Minnesota Press.

Lipsitz, G. (1994) *Dangerous Crossroads: Popular Music, Postmodernism and the Poetics of Place*, London: Verso.

Liu, D. and Y. Shih (2005) 'Integrating AHP and data mining for product recommendation based on customer lifetime value', *Information Management*, 42(3), 387–400.

Lynskey, D. (2011) *33 Revolutions Per Minute: A History of Protest Music*, London: Faber and Faber.

McClary, S. (1991) *Feminine Endings: Music, Gender, and Sexuality*, Minnesota: University of Minnesota Press.

McDonald, K. (2006) *Global Movements: Action and Culture*, Oxford: Blackwell.

McDonnell, E. and A. Powers (eds) (1995) *Rock She Wrote: Women Write about Rock, Pop, and Rap*, London: Plexus.

McGuigan, J. (1996) *Culture and the Public Sphere*, London: Routledge.

McKay, G. (1996) *Senseless Acts of Beauty: Cultures of Resistance since the Sixties*, London: Verso.

McKay, G. (2003) 'Just a closer walk with thee: New Orleans-style jazz and the campaign for nuclear disarmament in 1950s Britain', *Popular Music*, 22(3), 261–282.

McKay, G. (2005) *Circular Breathing: The Cultural Politics of Jazz in Britain*, Durham: Duke University Press.

McLean, I. (1987) *Public Choice: An Introduction*, Oxford: Blackwell.

McLeod, K. (2001) '*1/2: a critique of rock criticism in North America', *Popular Music*, 20(1), 47–60.

McMaster, B. (2008) *Supporting Excellence in the Arts: From Measurement to Judgement*, London: Department of Culture, Media and Sport.

Majrooh, N. (1998) 'The Taliban have banned all music in Afghanistan', 1st World Conference on Music and Censorship, Copenhagen: Danish Center for Human Rights, pp. 49–56.

Mäkelä, J. (2008) 'The state of rock: a history of Finland's cultural policy and music export', *Popular Music*, 27(2), 257–270.

Mancini, P. and D. Swanson, (1996) 'Politics, media, and modern democracy: introduction', in D. Swanson and P. Mancini (eds), *Politics, Media, and Modern Democracy*, Westport: Praeger.

Marcus, G. (1975) *Mystery Train: Images of America in Rock'n'Roll Music*, New York: E. P. Dutton.

Marcus, G. (1989) *Lipstick Traces: A Secret History of the 20th Century*, Cambridge, Mass.: Harvard University Press.

Marcus, G. (1992) *Dead Elvis: A Chronicle of a Cultural Obsession*, London: Viking.

Marcus, G. (1993) *In the Fascist Bathroom*, London: Penguin.

Marcus, G. (1997) *Invisible Republic: Bob Dylan's Basement Tapes*, London: Macmillan.

Marcus, G. (2000) *Double Trouble: Bill Clinton and Elvis Presley in a Land of No Alternatives*, London: Faber and Faber.

Marsh, D. (1987) *Glory Days: A Biography of Bruce Springsteen*, London: Sidgwick and Jackson.

Marsh, D. (1983) *Before I Get Old: The Story of the Who*, London: Plexus.

Mason, P. (2003) 'Assessing the Impact of Australian music requirements for radio', accessed at http://www.mca.org.au/research/research-reports/research-reports/637-assessing-the-impact-of-australian-music-requirements-for-radio.

Mattern, M. (1998) *Acting in Concert: Music, Community, and Political Action*, New Brunswick: Rutgers University Press.

Mayo, M. (2005) *Global Citizens: Social Movements and the Challenge of Globalization*, London: Zed Books.

Meyer, G. (2002) 'Frank Sinatra: the popular front and an American icon', *Science and Society*, 66(3), 311–335.

Meyer, M. (1991) *The Politics of Music in the Third Reich*, New York: Peter Lang.

Meyer, T. (2002) *Media Democracy: How the Media Colonize Politics*, Cambridge: Polity.

Meyrowitz, J. (1985) *No Sense of Place*, Oxford: Oxford University Press.

Mill, J. S. (1989) *'On Liberty' and other Writings*, Cambridge: Cambridge University Press.

Mill, J. S. (1972) *'On Liberty', 'Considerations on Representative Government', 'Utilitarianism'*, London: Everyman Edition.

Miller, D. (1992) 'Deliberative democracy and social choice', *Political Studies*, Vol. XL, Special Issue, 54–67.

Murray, C. S. (1989) *Crosstown Traffic: Jimi Hendrix and Post-War Pop*, London: Faber and Faber.

Nash, K. (2000) *Contemporary Political Sociology: Globalization, Politics and Power*, Oxford: Blackwell.

Neal, M. A. (1999) *What the Music Said*, London: Routledge.

Negus, K. (1996) *Popular Music in Theory: An Introduction*, Cambridge: Polity.

Negus, K. (1999) *Music Genres and Corporate Cultures*, London: Routledge.

Negus, K. (2008) *Bob Dylan*, London: Equinox.

Negus, K. and M. Pickering (2004) *Creativity, Communication and Cultural Value*, London: Sage.

Nietzsche, F. (1999) *The Birth of Tragedy and Other Writings*, edited by R. Geuss and R. Speirs, Cambridge: Cambridge University Press.

Nussbaum, M. (2001) *Upheavals of Thought: The Intelligence of Emotions*, Cambridge: Cambridge University Press.

Oakeshott, M. (1962) *Rationalism in Politics and Other Essays*, London: Methuen.

O'Brien, G. (2004) *Sonata for Jukebox: Pop Music, Memory, and the Imagined Life*, New York: Counterpoint.

O'Dea, M. (1995) *Jean-Jacques Rousseau: Music, Illusion and Desire*, Basingstoke: Macmillan.

Odell, M. (2005) Interview with Bob Geldof, *Q*, April, 106–109.

Olson, M. (1965) *The Logic of Collective Action: Public Goods and the theory of Groups*, Cambridge, Mass.: Harvard University Press.

O'Neill, O. (1990) 'Practice of toleration', in J. Lichtenberg (ed.), *Democracy and the Mass Media*, Cambridge: Cambridge University Press, pp. 155–185.

Osgerby, B. (1998) *Youth in Britain Since 1945*, Oxford: Blackwell.

O'Sullivan, N. (1987) 'Conservatism', in D. Miller (ed.) *The Blackwell Encyclopaedia of Political Thought*, Oxford: Blackwell, pp. 97–101.

Palmer, R. (1988) *The Sound of History: Songs and Social Comment*, Oxford: Oxford University Press.

Parekh, B. (2000) *Rethinking Multiculturalism*, Cambridge, Mass.: Harvard University Press.

Parry, G., Moyser, G., and Day, N. (1992) *Political Participation and Democracy in Britain*, Cambridge: Cambridge University Press.

Peddie, I. (ed.) (2006) *The Resisting Music: Popular Music and Social Protest*, Aldershot: Ashgate.

Pekacz, J. (1994) 'Did rock smash the wall? The role of rock in political transition', *Popular Music*, 13(1), 41–49.

Pels, D. (2003) 'Aesthetic representation and political style: re-balancing identity and difference in media democracy', in J. Corner and D. Pels (eds) *Media and the Resyling of Politics*, London: Sage, pp. 41–66.

Pitkin, H. (1967) *The Concept of Representation*, Berkeley, Calif.: University of California Press.

Plato (1961) *The Collected Dialogues of Plato Including the Letters*, Edith Hamilton and Huntington Cairns (eds), New York: Pantheon Books.

Power, M. (1997) *The Audit Society: Rituals of Verification*, Oxford: Oxford University Press.

Prashad, V. (2001) *Everybody was Kung Fu Fighting: Afro-Asian Connections and the Myth of Cultural Purity*, Boston: Beacon Press.

Putnam, R. (2000) *Bowling Alone: The Collapse and Revival of American Community*, New York: Simon and Schuster.

Putnam, R. (1993) *Making Democracy Work: Civic Traditions in Modern Italy*, Princeton, NJ: Princeton University Press.

Qureshi, R. B. (2002) *Music and Marx: Ideas, Practice, Politics*, New York: Routledge.

Ramet, S. P. (ed.) (1994) *Rocking the State: Rock Music and Politics in Eastern Europe and Russia*, Boulder: Westview Press.

Redhead, S. and J. Street (1989) 'Have I the right? Legitimacy, authenticity and community in folk's politics', *Popular Music*, 8(2), 177–184.

Renton, D. (2006) *When We Touched the Sky: The Anti-Nazi League 1977–1981*, Cheltenham: New Clarion Press.

Reynolds, S. (1998) *Energy Flash: Journey through Rave Music and Dance Culture*, London: Picador.

Reynolds, S. (2009) 'Sonic fiction', *Loops*, Issue 01, 204–222.

Reynolds, S. (2010) 'Sound Envisioned: Science Fiction and Future Music', Loops 02, London: Faber and Faber, pp. 107–127.

Rietveld, H. (1998) 'Repetitive beats: free parties and the politics of contemporary DiY dance culture in Britain', in G. McKay (ed.) DiY Culture: Party and Protest in Nineties Britain, London: Verso, pp. 243–68.

Rijven, S., G. Marcus and W. Straw (1985) Rock for Ethiopia, IASPM Working Paper 7.

Riker, W. (1982) Liberalism Against Populism: A Confrontation between the Theory of Democracy and the Theory of Social Choice, San Francisco: W. H. Freeman.

Ritter, J. and J. M. Daughtry (eds) (2007) Music in the Post-9/11 World, London: Routledge.

Roberts, M. (2010) 'A working-class hero is something to be: the American Musicians' Union's attempt to ban the Beatles, 1964', Popular Music, 29(1), 1–16.

Robertson, M. (1985) The Penguin Dictionary of Politics, Harmondsworth: Penguin.

Robinson, L. (2007) Gay Men and the Left in Post-War Britain, Manchester: Manchester University Press.

Rose, J. (2010) The Intellectual Life of the British Working Class, New Haven: Yale University Press.

Rose, T. (1994) Black Noise: Rap Music and Black Culture in Contemporary America, London: Weslyan University Press.

Rosen, C. (2002) Piano Notes: The Hidden World of the Pianist, London: Allen Lane.

Ross, A. (2007) The Rest is Noise: Listening to the Twentieth Century, New York: Farrar, Straus and Giroux.

Rousseau, J-J. (1997) The Discourses and other Early Political Writings, edited by V. Gourevitch, Cambridge: Cambridge University Press.

Rousseau, J-J. (1998) Essay on the Origin of Languages and Writings Related to Music, translated and edited by J. T. Scott, Hanover and London: University Press of New England.

Russell, D. (1987) Popular Music in England, 1840–1914: A Social History, Kingston and Montreal: McGill-Queen's University Press.

Sandel, M. (1996) Democracy's Discontent: America in Search of a Public Philosophy, Cambridge, Mass.: Harvard University Press.

Sardar, Z. and Davies, M. W. (2004) The No-Nonsense Guide to Islam, London: Verso.

Saul, S. (2003) Freedom Is, Freedom Ain't: Jazz and the Making of the Sixties, Cambridge, Mass.: Harvard University Press.

Saunders, F. S. (2000) Who Paid the Piper? The CIA and the Cultural Cold War, London: Granta.

Savage, J. (1991) England's Dreaming: Sex Pistols and Punk Rock, London: Faber and Faber.

Saward, M. (2006) 'The representative claim', *Contemporary Political Theory*, 5(3), 297–318.

Scarry, E. (1996) 'The difficulty of imagining other people', in J. Cohen (ed.), *For Love of Country: Debating the Limits of Patriotism*, Boston: Beacon Press, pp. 98–110.

Schafer, R. M. (1994) *The Soundscape: Our Sonic Environment and the Tuning of the World*, Rochester, Vermont: Destiny Books.

Scott, J. C. (1990) *Domination and the Arts of Resistance: Hidden Transcripts*, New Haven: Yale University Press.

Scott, J. T. (1997) 'Rousseau and the melodious language of freedom', *The Journal of Politics*, 59(3), 803–829.

Scruton, R. (1974) *Art and Imagination: A Study in the Philosophy of Mind*, London: Methuen.

Scruton, R. (1980) *The Meaning of Conservatism*, Harmondsworth: Penguin.

Scruton, R. (1982) *A Dictionary of Political Thought*, London: Macmillan.

Scruton, R. (1998) *An Intelligent Person's Guide to Modern Culture*, London: Duckworth.

Scruton, R. (1999) *The Aesthetics of Music*, Oxford: Oxford University Press.

Sebag Montefiore, S. (1996) 'Spice Girls back sceptics on Europe', *The Spectator*, 14 December.

Shammont, B. (1998) 'The situation of musicians in the Arab world', 1st World Conference on Music and Censorship, Copenhagen: Danish Center for Human Rights, pp. 45–49.

Shapiro, M. (2006) *Deforming American Political Thought: Ethnicity, Facticity, and Genre*, Lexington, Ken.: University of Kentucky Press.

Sheeran, Paul (2001) *Cultural Politics in International Relations*, Aldershot: Ashgate.

Shepsle, K. and M. Bonchek (1997) *Analyzing Politics: Rationality, Behaviour, and Institutions*, New York: W. W. Norton.

Shields, C. (1997) *Larry's Party*, London: Fourth Estate.

Shuker, R. (2008) 'New Zealand popular music, government policy, and cultural identity', *Popular Music*, 27(2), 271–287.

Sim, S. (2007) *Manifesto for Silence: Confronting the Politics and Culture of Noise*, Edinburgh: Edinburgh University Press.

Sinclair, D. (2004) *Wannabe: How the Spice Girls Reinvented Pop Fame*, London: Omnibus Press.

Skinner, K. (2006) ' "Must be born again": resurrecting the Anthology of American Folk Music', *Popular Music*, 25(1), 57–76.

Slobin, M. (ed.) (1996) *Retuning Culture: Musical Changes in Central and Eastern Europe*, Durham: Duke University Press.

Smith, S. (1999) *Dancing in the Street: Motown and the Cultural Politics of Detroit*, Cambridge, Mass.: Harvard University Press.

Snow, D., E. B. Rochford, S. K. Worden and R. D. Benford (1986) 'Frame alignment processes, micromobilization, and movement participation', *American Sociological Review*, 51, 464–481.

Spitz, R. S. (1979) *Barefoot in Babylon: The Creation of the Woodstock Music Festival, 1969*, New York: Viking.

Starr, F. (1983) *Red and Hot: The Fate of Jazz in the Soviet Union*, Oxford: Oxford University Press.

Staffordshire Music Partnership (2008–9) *Annual Report*, available at: http://education.staffordshire.gov.uk/Curriculum/Services/Staffordshire PerformingArts/Music/smp/.

Steinberg, M. W. (2004) 'When politics goes pop: on the intersections of popular and political culture and the case of Serbian student protests', *Social Movement Studies*, 3(1), 3–27.

Strauss, N. (2003) 'The pop life: online music business, neither quick nor sure', *New York Times*, 29 October.

Street, J. (1986) *Rebel Rock: The Politics of Popular Music*, Oxford: Blackwell.

Street, J., S. Hague and H. Savigny (2008) 'Playing to the crowd: the role of music and musicians in political participation', *British Journal of Politics and International Relations*, 10(2), 269–285.

Surowiecki, J. (2004) *The Wisdom of Crowds: Why the Many Are Smarter than the Few*, London: Abacus.

Swindler, A. (1986) 'Culture in action: symbols and strategies', *American Sociological Review*, 51, 273–286.

Symes, C. (2004) *Setting the Record Straight: A Material History of Classical Recording*, Middletown, Conn.: Wesleyan University Press.

Symon, P. (2001) 'IASPM UK 2000', *Popular Music*, 20(2), 265–267.

Szemere, A. (2001) *Up from the Underground: The Culture of Rock Music In Postsocialist Hungary*, Pennsylvania: Pennsylvania State University Press.

Taylor, C. (1992) *Sources of the Self: The Making of the Modern Identity*, Cambridge: Cambridge University Press.

Thompson, B. (1998) *Seven Years of Plenty*, London: Gollanz.

Thompson, E. P. (1963) *The Making of the English Working Class*, London: Victor Gollancz.

Thompson, J. (1995) *The Media and Modernity: A Social Theory of the Media*, Cambridge: Polity.

Tocqueville, A. de (1988) *Democracy in America*, New York: HarperPerennial.

Topic Records (2009) *Three Score and Ten: A Voice of the People*, London: Topic Records.

Toynbee, J. (1993) 'Policing Bohemia, pinning up the grunge: the music press and generic changes in British pop and rock', *Popular Music*, 12(3), 289–300.

Toynbee, J. (2000) *Making Popular Music: Musicians, Creativity and Institutions*, London: Arnold.

Treasure, J. (2007) *Sound Business*, Cirencester: Management Books.

Turino, T. (2008) *Music as Social Life: The Politics of Participation*, Chicago: University of Chicago Press.

UK Music (2010) *Liberating Creativity*, available at: http://www.ukmusic.org/assets/media/Liberating%20Creativity.pdf.

Urban, M. (2004) *Russia Gets the Blues: Mass, Culture, and Community in Unsettled Times*, London: Cornell University Press.

Van Zoonen, L. (2004) 'Imagining the fan democracy', *European Journal of Communication*, 19(1), 39–52.

Van Zoonen, L. (2005) *Entertaining the Citizen: When Politics and Popular Culture Converge*, New York: Rowman and Littlefield.

Verney, P. (1998) 'Does Allah like music?', *Index on Censorship*, 27(6), 75–78.

Walker, M. (1977) *The National Front*, London: Fontana.

Wallis, R. and K. Malm (1984) *Big Sounds from Small Peoples: The Music Industry in Small Countries*, London: Constable.

Wanner, C. (1996) 'Nationalism on stage: music and change in Soviet Ukraine', in M. Slobin (ed.) *Retuning Culture: Musical Changes in Central and Eastern Europe*, London: Duke University Press, pp. 136–155.

Ward, B. (1998) *Just my Soul Responding: Rhythm and Blues, Black Consciousness and Race Relations*, London: UCL Press.

Ward, E., G. Stokes and K. Tucker (1987) *Rock of Ages: The Rolling Stone History of Rock and Roll*, London: Penguin.

Watson, B. and E. Leslie (2001) 'The punk paper: a dialogue', available at: www.militantesthetic.co.uk/Punk/Punkcomb.html<http://www.militantesthetic.co.uk/Punk/Punkcomb.html>.

Weinstein, D. (2006) 'Rock protest songs: so many and so few', in I. Peddie (ed.), *Resisting Music: Popular Music and Social Protest*, Aldershot: Ashgate, pp. 3–17.

Whiteley, S. (ed.) (1997) *Sexing the Groove: Popular Music and Gender*, London: Routledge.

Whitney, J. (2003) 'Infernal noise: the soundtrack to insurrection', in Notes from Nowhere (eds), *We are Everywhere: The Irresistible Rise of Global anticapitalism*, London: Verso, 216–227.

Wicke, P. (1992) ' "The times they are a-changin" ': rock music and political change in Eastern Germany, in Reebee Garofalo (ed.), *Rockin' the Boat: Mass Music and Mass Movements*, Boston: South End Press, pp. 81–93.

Widgery, D. (1986) *Beating Time: Riot'n'Race'n'Rock'n'Roll*, London: Chatto and Windus.

Wiener, J. (1984) *Come Together: John Lennon in his Time*, New York: Random House.

Wikstrom, P. (2009) *The Music Industry: Music in the Cloud*, Cambridge: Polity.

Wilentz, S. (1998) 'Dylan's old weird America', *Dissent*, Spring, pp. 100–106.

Williams, P. (2005) 'Blair's commission for Africa: problems and prospects for UK policy', *Political Quarterly*, 76(4), 529–539.

Willis, P. (1978) *Profane Culture*, London: Routledge and Kegan Paul.

Wokler, R. (2001) *Rousseau: A Very Short Introduction*, Oxford: Oxford University Press.

Wolff, J. (1983) *Aesthetics and the Sociology of Art*, London: Allen and Unwin.

Wu, C-T. (1998) 'Embracing the enterprise culture: art institution in the 1980s', *New Left Review*, 1/230, 28–57.

Yonwin, J. (2004) *Electoral Performance of Far-Right Parties in the UK*, available at: ttp://www.parliament.uk/documents/commons/lib/research/notes/snsg-01982.pdf.

Yusufzai, R. (1998) 'All quiet in Kabul', *Index on Censorship*, 27(6), 135–138.

Index